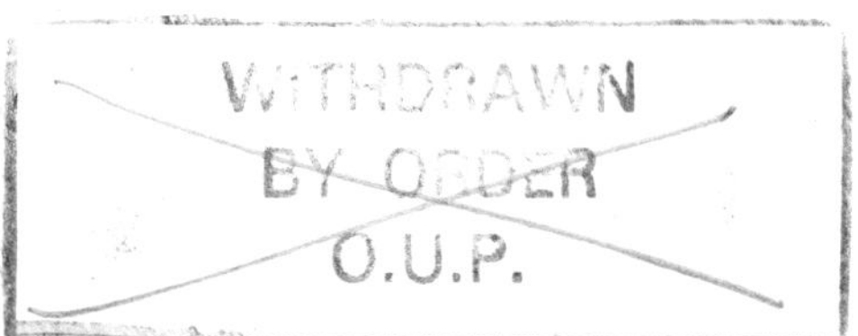
WITHDRAWN
BY ORDER
O.U.P.

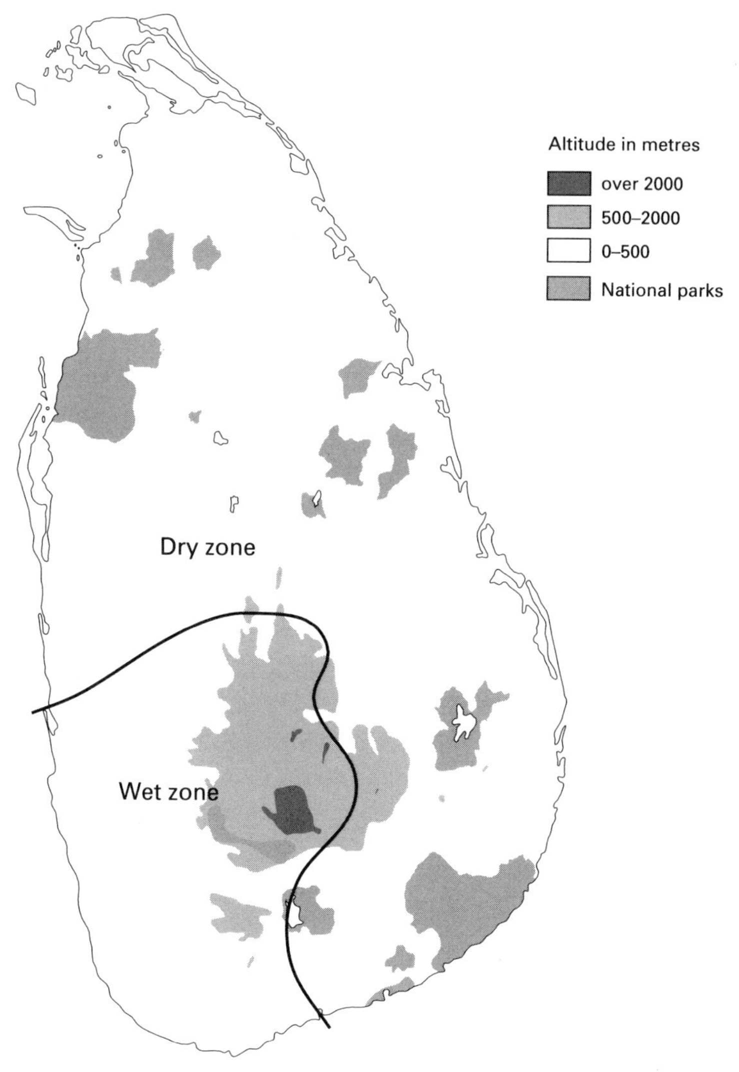

Altitude in metres
over 2000
500–2000
0–500
National parks
Dry zone
Wet zone

A Field Guide to the Birds of Sri Lanka

A FIELD GUIDE TO

The Birds of Sri Lanka

JOHN HARRISON

Illustrations by

TIM WORFOLK

UNIVERSITY PRESS

OXFORD
UNIVERSITY PRESS

Great Clarendon Street, Oxford OX2 6DP

Oxford New York
Athens Auckland Bangkok Bogotá Bombay Buenos Aires Calcutta
Cape Town Dar es Salaam Delhi Florence Hong Kong Istanbul
Karachi Kuala Lumpur Madras Madrid Melbourne Mexico City Mumbai
Nairobi Paris São Paulo Singapore Taipei Tokyo Toronto Warsaw

and associated companies in Berlin Ibadan

Oxford is a trade mark of Oxford University Press

Published in the United States
by Oxford University Press Inc., New York

A catalogue record for this book is available from the British Library

Library of Congress Cataloging in Publication Data
(Data avalable)

ISBN 0 19 854961 X (Hbk)
0 19 854960 1 (Pbk)

Typeset by EXPO Holdings, Malaysia

Printed in China

Preface

SRI LANKA is a delightful country with friendly people, beautiful countryside, rich wildlife, and an enviably long tradition of conservation. The predominantly Buddhist tradition has instilled in the people a respect for animals which respond by being generally more confident of people and thus more approachable than elsewhere. Because of this, birdwatching is a joy in Sri Lanka. It is also different because the island has its own avian specialities—more than twenty endemic species and over seventy races found only in Sri Lanka. Add to these the species shared with nearby India and beyond, the migrants, plus eighty or so vagrants and you have an official checklist of some 426 species, all of which are covered in this guide.

As science progresses, some currently recognized as races could be given full species status and, no doubt, field observers will add extra species to the list. During the preparation of this guide the Rufous-necked Stint *Calidris ruficollis* and the Fork-tailed Swift *Apus pacificus* have been added. The stint has previously probably been unrecognized, being very difficult to distinguish in the field from the Little Stint in non-breeding plumage. Others will certainly follow.

I have also included a number of species of which there have been unconfirmed sightings, some of these may one day be confirmed as being present in Sri Lanka. Races that can be readily distinguished in the field are also covered.

Paradoxically Sri Lanka's ornithology has suffered from being too successful too soon. W. V. Legge's *A History of the Birds of Ceylon*, in four volumes written in 1880, was meticulously detailed and illustrated but not intended for use in the field. It is also long out of print. W. E. Wait wrote a comprehensive *Manual of the Birds of Ceylon* in 1925 and G. M. Henry's *A Guide to the Birds of Ceylon*, which first fired my enthusiasm for the subject, was first published in 1955. Henry included many of his own field observations and illustrated the book himself. It is a fine work, elegantly written in the style of his day, illustrated by this description of the call of the Greater Racket-tailed Drongo in a flock of forest birds:

> Often, the first sign of the approach of one of these mixed troops of small birds is a sudden, explosive medley of whistles, bell-like notes, and harsh scoldings, emanating from a pair of these drongos, where, a minute before, the solemn, mysterious silence of the jungle prevailed.

The version revised by T. Hoffmann, D. Warakagoda, and U. Ekanayake with footnotes and an increased species list takes account of the many changes since Henry's day. Despite all this wealth of literature there is not a fully illustrated field guide in the modern style. Following in the footsteps of such ornithological giants is a daunting prospect but Sri Lanka urgently needs a comprehensive modern field guide to its birds. This work is offered, in deference to Legge, Wait, Henry *et al.*, to fill the gap.

Acknowledgements

A WORK of this nature is inevitably based on the knowledge gathered over the years by an enormous number of people to whom I am deeply indebted.

More specifically, I would like to thank my illustrator, Tim Worfolk, for continuing unstinting support throughout the gestation period, not simply in the painstaking attention to detail in his beautiful artwork but also in much very constructive advice on the text; Upali Ekanayake, of the University of Peradeniya, for patient field guidance in Sri Lanka and commenting on the text; Paul Dukes, John Martin, and Martin Elliott also for commenting on text; Thilo Hoffmann, Chairman of the Ceylon Bird Club, for use of CBC records and literature; D. P. Wijesinghe, of the American Museum of Natural History, for allowing me to use the distribution data from his *Checklist of the Birds of Sri Lanka*.

Thanks are also due to Dr Robert Prys-Jones, of the Bird Group of the Natural History Museum; Alan Baker and Rob Collis of the BBC Natural History Unit Film Library; Helen Wharam of the BBC Natural History Unit Sound Library; Jeffery Boswell; Robert Gillmor and Stacey Redway. Also: the Oriental Bird Club; Colombo Museum; Faculty of Agriculture, University of Peradeniya; Biological Sciences Library, Bristol University; Royal Society for the Protection of Birds Library; Royal Geographical Society.

Last but not least, I thank the staff at OUP for their patient support. Despite all these names any errors are mine.

Bristol 1998 JH

Tim Worfolk adds:

I would like to thank—in no particular order—John Archer and Graeme Spinks for their help and company during fieldwork in Sri Lanka. Upali Ekanayake and our driver/guide Wajira for their generous help, advice, and field skills. Sunil at Sinharaja for finding us Spurfowl and Scaly Thrush. Clive Byers for field testing many of the plates. Paul Dukes and Dave Holman for giving me the benefit of their extensive experience of Sri

Lankan birds. Martin Elliott for help with the gulls. Finally, I would like to thank my wife Carolyn for her support and understanding, and our children, Jack and Sally, for still recognizing me when I 'came back from the jungle'.

Bristol 1998 TW

Contents

The plates are to be found between pp. 00 and 00.

LIST OF PLATES

BACKGROUND

Introduction to the country

THIS guide covers Sri Lanka, including the offshore waters visible from the coast, and Adam's Bridge.

Geography

Sri Lanka is a tropical island about 430 km long and 230 km across at its widest point lying approximately between 6° and 9° north of the equator. It is almost joined to the coast of south-east India by a series of islands, sand-banks, and shoals less than 100 km long called Adam's Bridge,

The coastal areas are mainly low lying, with many lagoons and wetland areas. The northern half of the island is mostly flat, intersected by rivers with a number of reservoirs known locally as tanks. The centre of the island is mountainous with the highest point, Mount Pidurutalagala (commonly known as 'Pedro') reaching 2524 m. The hill country also has a number of tanks, some very large.

Climate

There are two seasons in Sri Lanka. Normally from about May to September the south-west monsoon brings rain to the south-west and to the hills facing the wind (the wet zone) leaving the rest of the country fairly dry. During the other months the north-east monsoon blows bringing rain to the north and, less so, to the east and south-east (the dry zone), also to the hills and the south-west, with most of the rain falling between November and February.

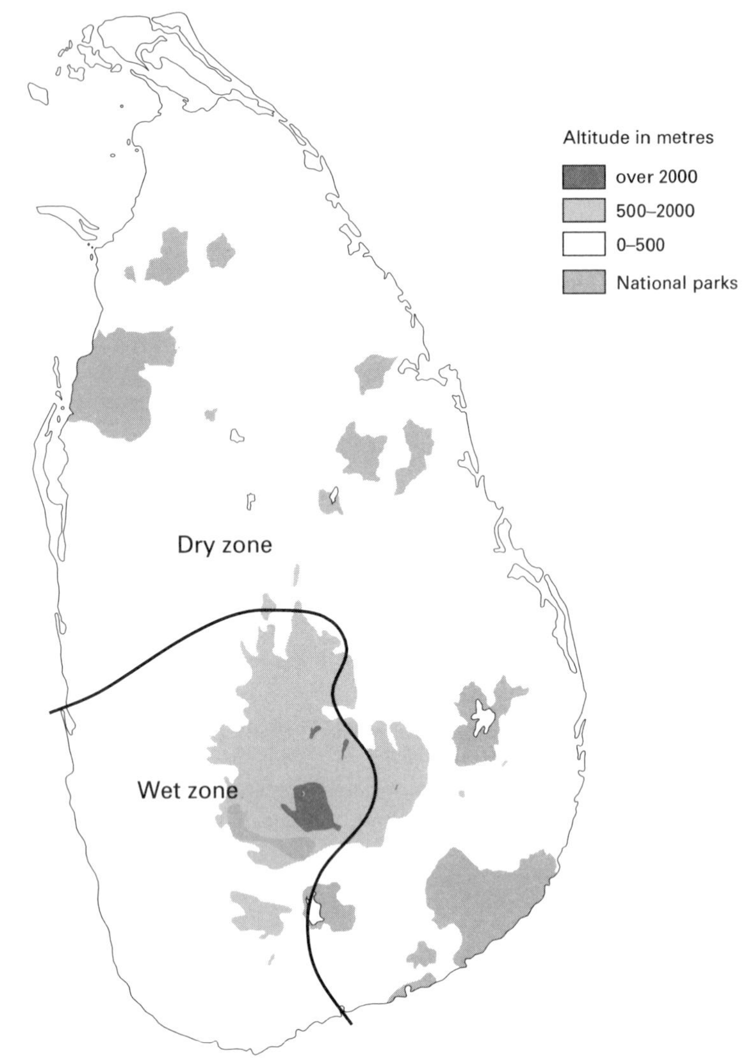
Altitude in metres
over 2000
500–2000
0–500
National parks
Dry zone
Wet zone

Fig. 1

The annual rainfall in the wet zone ranges between about 5000 mm and 2000 mm. In the dry zone it is around 1875 mm in the north falling to 625 mm in the south-east.

Midday temperatures at sea level average 27°C and in the higher hills a cool and often damp 16°C.

Vegetation

As one would expect from the rainfall pattern the vegetation in the wet zone is lush while that in the dry is sparse. The needs of agriculture and forestry have modified the original cover over much of the land but some virgin rainforest survives in the wet zone, mainly in protected areas, the largest of which is the Sinharaja Forest Reserve near Ratnapura. The forests of the dry zone have also suffered centuries of shifting agriculture and much of what remains is secondary forest and scrub.

Areas of wildlife interest

These areas are listed in alphabetical order, giving their location, type of habitat, whether a fee is payable, and a list of birds of particular interest likely to be seen. (Note: A very rough rule of pronunciation in place names is that the first syllable is stressed. SL = Sri Lankan.)

Bodinigala/Ingiriya

A lowland secondary forest reserve by a monastery near Ingiriya, 20 km south-west of Colombo.
Green-billed Coucal, SL Junglefowl, SL Spurfowl, SL Hanging Parrot, Layard's Parakeet, SL Grey Hornbill, barbets, Malabar Trogon.

Bundala National Park

Scrub jungle with lagoons, saltpans, and shore on south coast, 10 km east of Hambantota. Fee.
Egrets, Asian Openbill, Eurasian Spoonbill, SL Junglefowl, Brown-capped Babbler. Winter waders.

*Gal Oya National Park**

Large dry zone reserve surrounding a reservoir, 50 km east of Badulla. Fee. White-bellied Fish Eagle, Grey-headed Fish Eagle, Painted Francolin, Jungle Bush Quail, SL Spurfowl, SL Junglefowl, Layard's Parakeet.

*Giant's Tank**

Very large reservoir in the north-west near Mannar.
Spot-billed Pelican, Eurasian Spoonbill, Water Rail. Many winter migrant waders and duck.

Gilimale Forest Man and Biosphere Reserve

A wet zone forest adjoining the Peak Wilderness Sanctuary, 10 km north-east of Ratnapura. Similar birds as at Peak Wilderness.

Hakagala Gardens

Botanical Gardens and adjacent forest high in hills, 10 km south of Nuwara Eliya. Fee.
SL Woodpigeon, Bar-winged Flycatcher-shrike, Black Bulbul, SL Whistling Thrush, SL Bush Warbler, Dull-blue Flycatcher, SL White-eye.

Horton Plains National Park

A remote, high (2000 m) plateau with forest and grassland adjoining the Peak Wilderness Sanctuary, 15 km south of Nuwara Eliya. Fee.
SL Whistling Thrush, SL Magpie, Dull-blue Flycatcher, Orange-billed Babbler, Black-throated Munia.

Kalametiya

A coastal wetland about half way between Tangalle and Hambantota on the south coast. Lagoons, mangroves, and scrub.
Asian Openbill, Eurasian Spoonbill, egrets, Purple Swamphen, Black-winged Stilt. Many winter migrants.

Kitulgala

Forest reserve adjoining Peak Wilderness Sanctuary, 40 km east of Colombo. Similar birds as at Peak Wilderness Sanctuary.

Knuckles/Corbett's Gap

A pass, with a public road, through the eastern edge of the hills, 25 km east of Kandy.
SL Junglefowl, Black Eagle, SL Woodpigeon, SL Hanging Parrot, Indian Swiflet, Lesser Yellownape, Yellow-eared Bulbul, White-browed Bulbul, Black-headed Yellow Bulbul, Grey-headed Canary Flycatcher, Yellow-fronted Barbet, Dull-blue Flycatcher.

*Lahugala National Park**

Two dry zone reservoirs and surrounding land near Pottuvil on the east coast.
White-bellied Fish Eagle, Grey-headed Fish Eagle, Malabar Trogon, White-rumped Shama, Greater Racket-tailed Drongo, nightjars.

Peak Wilderness Sanctuary (Adam's Peak)

Long strip of wet zone forest including the pilgrimage mountain of Adam's Peak, 45 km east of Colombo.
SL Junglefowl, SL Woodpigeon, White-faced Starling, Black-throated Munia, Dollarbird, Blue Magpie, Chestnut-backed Owlet, Ashy-headed Laughingthrush, Yellow-fronted Barbet, SL Hanging Parrot.

Ritigala

A forested ridge in the dry zone about half way between Anuradhapura and Polonnoruwa. Fee for the archaelogical site.
SL Spurfowl, SL Junglefowl, SL Grey and Malabar Hornbills, Spot-winged Thrush.

Sinharaja Man and Biosphere Reserve (World Heritage Site)

Large area of rain forest 20 km south of Ratnapura. It is advisable to contact the Forest Department (see below) in advance.

SL Spurfowl, SL Junglefowl, Green-billed Coucal, Red-faced Malkoha, Blue Magpie, Spot-winged Thrush, Scaly Thrush, White-faced Starling, Chestnut-backed Owlet, Black-throated Munia, SL Myna, Greater Racket-tailed Drongo.

Uda Walawe National Park

A large area of scrub, grass, and old plantation around a large reservoir, 50 km south-east of Ratnapura.
Woolly-necked Stork, Black-headed Ibis, SL Junglefowl, White-bellied Fish Eagle, Crested Serpent Eagle, Changeable Hawk Eagle.

Udawattakele

Forest sanctuary on the northern edge of Kandy. Fee.
Layard's Parakeet, SL Hanging Parrot; Yellow-fronted, Crimson-fronted, and Brown-headed Barbets; Golden-fronted and Jerdon's Leafbirds; Stork-billed, Common, and Oriental Dwarf Kingfishers.

Victoria Park

A park in the centre of Nuwara Eliya, the highest town in Sri Lanka. Small fee.
Yellow-eared Bulbul, Blackbird, in winter Pied Thrush and Kashmir Flycatcher.

Wasgomuwa National Park

A large dry zone reserve bounded on the east by the Mahaweli Ganga river, 60 km north-west of Kandy. Fee.
Lesser Adjutant, Oriental Darter, Red-faced and Blue-faced Malkoha, Stork-billed Kingfisher and Ashy-crowned Sparrow Lark, Black-headed Ibis, Oriental Darter, Changeable Hawk Eagle, Grey-headed Fish Eagle, White-bellied Fish Eagle, Streaked Weaver.

*Wilpattu National Park**

Very large area of dry forest, scrub, open ground, pools, rivers and shore line, 40 km west of Anuradhapura. Fee.

Painted Stork, Oriental Darter, Purple Swamphen, SL Junglefowl, SL Grey and Malabar Pied Hornbills, White-rumped Shama and, in winter, many migrant waders and ducks.

Yala/Ruhunu National Park

A very large reserve with rivers, lagoons, salt pans, rocky outcrops, shoreline and forest in the south-east, 40 km east of Hambantota. Fee.
SL Junglefowl, White-bellied Fish Eagle, Grey-headed Fish Eagle, Painted Stork, Black-necked Stork, Lesser Adjutant, Pompadour Green Pigeon, Orange-breasted Green Pigeon, Brown Fish Owl, Red-faced Malkoha, three species of bee-eaters, large numbers of waders including three species of pratincole and two thick-knees, and large flocks of flamingoes.

*Note: Some of these sites (marked *) may be inaccessible because of the political situation. It is advisable to contact your Foreign Office (or equivalent) and travel agent for up to date information before making any travel arrangements. Check again with the Wildlife Conservation Department (see below) on arriving in Sri Lanka.
One hopes that soon the problems will be solved and once again it will be possible to travel freely about the whole country.

Useful addresses

Wildlife Conservation Department, 18 Gregory's Road, Colombo 7. Tel: (0)1 694241.
Forest Department, 82 Rajalmalwatta Road, Battaramulla, Colombo, Tel: (0)1 866631.
Ceylon Bird Club, 39 Chatham St., Colombo 1. Tel: (0)1 328625. E-mail: birdclub@usa.net.
Oriental Bird Club, c/o The Lodge, Sandy, Bedfordshire, SG19 2DL, UK.
Wildlife and Nature Protection Service, Chatiya Road, Colombo 1. Tel: (0)1 325248.

A recommended specialist bird tour operator is: A. Baur & Co. Ltd, Wildlife and Birdwatching Service, PO Box 11, Colombo 1. Tel: (0)1 320551. Fax: (0)1 448493.

Notes on the guide

Order of species and naming policy

The order, scientific names, and taxonomy largely follow those of Howard and Moore's *Complete checklist of the birds of the world*, Second Edition, with a few exceptions where I have been influenced by the more recent Oriental Bird Club's *Annotated checklist of the birds of the oriental region* and the Ceylon Bird Club's *Checklist of the birds of Sri Lanka*, by D. P. Wijesinghe. The English names are based on Sibley and Munroe's *A world checklist of birds*, again with a few exceptions where distinct races have widely accepted names not included in their list.

The scientific name is normally given as a binomial but the trinomial is used where the third tag is relevant because a race is unique to Sri Lanka, or because it helps to clarify the identity of a species where there has been a change in the taxonomy, or to emphasize a particular race. To save space names are sometimes abbreviated, for example *Oriolus oriolus oriolus* becomes *O. o. oriolus.*

Synonyms

Synonyms are given in brackets below both scientific and common names, again to help clarify identity. In some cases 'lumping' or 'splitting' species can mean a synonym may also apply to a different species, for example *Anthus novaeseelandiae richardi* and *A. n. rufulus* are now split into *A. richardi,* Richard's Pipit, and *A. rufulus,* Paddyfield Pipit; both entries are given the synonym *A. novaeseelandiae.* English names present a real problem with many duplications and potential ambiguities. The Rufous-tailed Scrub Robin, *Cercotrichas galactotes* is known in different part of the world as the Greyish Scrub Robin, Rufous Bush Chat, Rufous Warbler, African Scrub Robin, Grey-backed Warbler, and various other permutations of those names. Many people are now travelling widely to look at birds, so below the preferred English name I have included some synonyms in brackets which again might help clarification.

General

The brief introductory notes at the beginning of each family refer to the representatives of that family found in Sri Lanka and do not necessarily apply globally.

The measurement starting the identification section is the length in centimetres from tip of bill to end of tail. Where the length differs between the sexes, male and female are abbreviated to M and F. Care is needed in interpreting these figures—the Blue-faced Malkoha is 39 cm long but much of this is its long tail.

Lying in the tropics, Sri Lanka has no spring, summer, autumn, or winter in the temperate sense, nevertheless visiting migrant birds are affected mainly by the northern seasons and so 'winter visitor', for example, is used for a species that migrates south to Sri Lanka during the northern winter. Similarly, 'spring', 'summer', and 'autumn' refer to the northern seasons.

The terms used to describe abundance are difficult to define. Birds of prey normally have a low population density and the term 'common' when applied to them would mean something quite different from when used for seed-eating flocking birds, such as the Baya Weaver. Similarly, irregular winter visitors, such as the Rosy Starling, can occur in flocks of a thousand or so, perhaps not to be seen at all the following winter. A vagrant seabird can be unreported for many years and then a small flock may be seen. So, please keep a broad mind when interpreting the terms used to indicate the abundance of a species.

Inclusion of a species in the guide implies presence or possible presence in Sri Lanka, so, to avoid unnecessary repetition, 'Sri Lanka' is omitted from the '**Range**' sections except for endemic species. For simplicity, '**Range**' includes both summer and winter grounds. Myanmar is used in preference to Burma.

Abbreviations used in the '**Range**' sections are the conventional **N, S, E,** and **W** representing north, south, east, and west, and their combinations. In addition, **C** is used to represent Central.

Lastly, I would like this guide to be accessible to as many people as possible. Too many bird books use language that seems designed to frighten off the uninitiated or those not over-familiar with English. Why refer to a 'gular pouch' when 'throat pouch' is more likely to be understood? So, 'nuchal' becomes the noun-adjective 'nape', 'axilla' becomes 'armpit', 'supercilium' becomes 'eyebrow', and so on. I have to give in on 'lore' and a few other more technical words, 'the area between the eye and the bill' is too wasteful of valuable space. A definition of 'lore' and other words that may need an explanation can be found in the glossary.

Glossary

arboreal: living in trees.
armpit: *see* axillary.
axillary: of the base of the underwing, the 'armpit' of the wing.
bund: an earth bank, especially at the margin of a paddy-field.
carpal joint: the joint at the bend of the wing which rests on the side of the breast when the wing is folded; the wrist.
casque: a structure on the upper mandible, as in the Malabar Pied Hornbill.
cere: bare skin at the base of the upper mandible of some birds containing the nostrils, well developed in the parrots and many birds of prey.
chena: land used for slash and burn shifting cultivation.
crepuscular: active in the half light of dawn and dusk.
decurved: curving downwards.
diurnal: active during the day.
eclipse: a period, usually after the breeding season, when the male of a species assumes a plumage similar to that of the female.
endemic race: a race or subspecies restricted to Sri Lanka.
endemic species: a species restricted to Sri Lanka.
erectile: capable of being erected.
Eurasian: of both Europe and Asia.
eyebrow: a stripe of distinctly coloured feathers over the eye; a supercilium.
feral: returned to the wild from domestication.
fingers: primary flight feathers when clearly separated in flight.
frontal shield: a rearward extension of the upper mandible over the forehead, as in some members of the rail family.
fulvous: a reddish-yellow colour.
gape: the junction between the upper and lower mandibles. The 'corners' of the 'mouth'.
goliath: giant; from the biblical character of the same name.
gorget: a coloured patch curving from the gape across the throat.
gular: of the throat.
hand: the primaries and their coverts; the wing beyond the wrist.
hepatic: of the liver; in this context, liver coloured.
lanceolated: having lance or spear-shaped markings.
lantana: a prickly shrub with orange-pink flowers and black berries that forms dense patches on waste land and chenas.
loiterer: a bird, often immature, that resists the urge to migrate staying in the wintering areas.

loranthus: a genus of plants parasitic on trees, a common representative of which bears greeny-red berries attractive to some fruit-eating birds.
loreal or loral: of the lores.
lore, lores: the area between the bill and the eye.
malar: of the cheek.
mana: lemon grass growing in large tussocks in the patana.
mandible: the upper or lower part of the bill.
morph: a colour form of a species; *see also* phase.
orbit: the area around the eye.
orbital: of the orbit.
nocturnal: active during the night.
nuchal: of the nape.
patana: open areas of grassland in hills, especially on the eastern slopes of the hills.
paddy, paddy-field: land flooded for part of the season for growing rice.
pelagic: ocean-living.
phase: a colour form of a species. *see also* morph.
pirating: a method of feeding used by skuas and some other seabirds where other birds are chased until they disgorge their catch. The pirate then steals the food.
polymorphism: occurring in different forms, usually in plumage or in size.
primaries: outer flight feathers attached to the 'hand' of the wing.
raptor: a bird of prey.
salterns: evaporation pools of sea water for salt production.
secondaries: flight feathers on the 'forearm' of the wing.
sexual dimorphism: a difference between the sexes, usually in plumage or size.
shola: woodland, usually in a valley, surrounded by farm or grassland.
speculum: coloured patch on secondary wing feathers important in the identification of some ducks.
striated: marked with fine streaks.
supercilium: *see* eyebrow.
tank: in Sri Lanka, a reservoir.
tarsus: the section of a bird's leg above the foot.
taxonomy: the science of classifying organisms.
tertials: the inner four or five secondary flight feathers.
tibia, plural tibiae: in this context, the section of a bird's leg above the tarsus but also the bone within.
vernacular name: the English or common name of a species.
wattle: lobe of bare skin, usually on head.
wrist: the joint at the bend of the wing which rests on the side of the breast when the wing is folded; the carpal joint.

Caption Pages

Identification features are summarized against each species.
Endemic species are labelled simply as 'Endemic'. Endangered species are also labelled.

Distribution maps

Distribution maps are included on the caption pages of resident and common visiting species. Where insufficient information is available, as in vagrants and rare visitors, no map is shown, the status being printed in place of the map. Care should be exercised in interpreting these maps. Each species is only likely to be present in the appropriate habitats in the shaded areas. Also, such maps reflect to some degree the abundance of observers as much as that of the birds. Access to parts of the country has been difficult because of political problems and birds in these areas have sometimes not been well recorded. Remember, too, that bad weather or injury can bring birds to the most unlikely places: the maps only reflect their normal distribution.

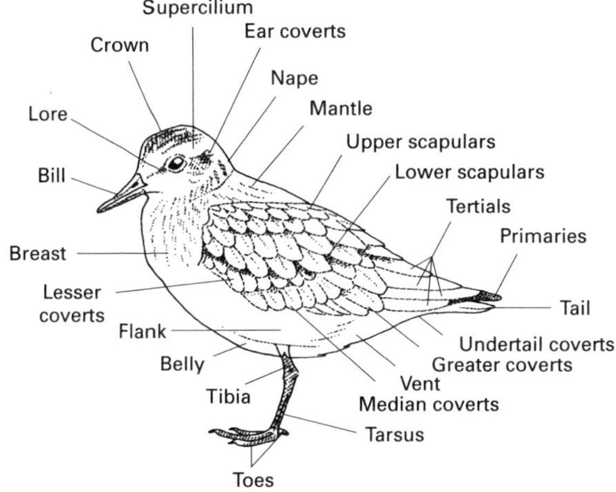
Supercilium
Ear coverts
Crown
Nape
Mantle
Lore
Upper scapulars
Bill
Lower scapulars
Tertials
Primaries
Breast
Lesser coverts
Tail
Flank
Undertail coverts
Belly
Greater coverts
Vent
Tibia
Median coverts
Tarsus
Toes

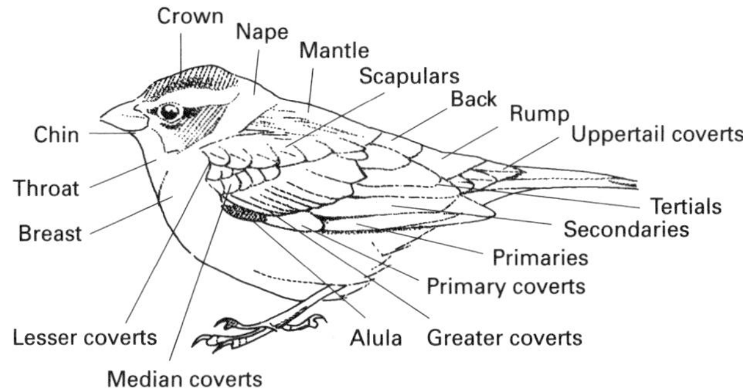
Crown
Nape
Mantle
Scapulars
Back
Rump
Chin
Uppertail coverts
Throat
Tertials
Breast
Secondaries
Primaries
Primary coverts
Lesser coverts
Alula
Greater coverts
Median coverts

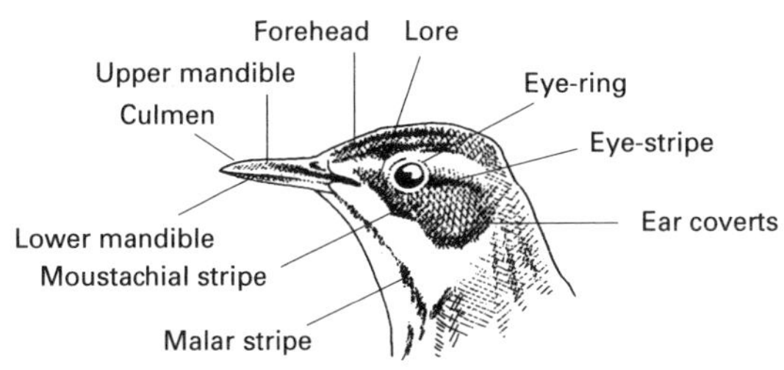
Forehead
Lore
Upper mandible
Eye-ring
Culmen
Eye-stripe
Ear coverts
Lower mandible
Moustachial stripe
Malar stripe

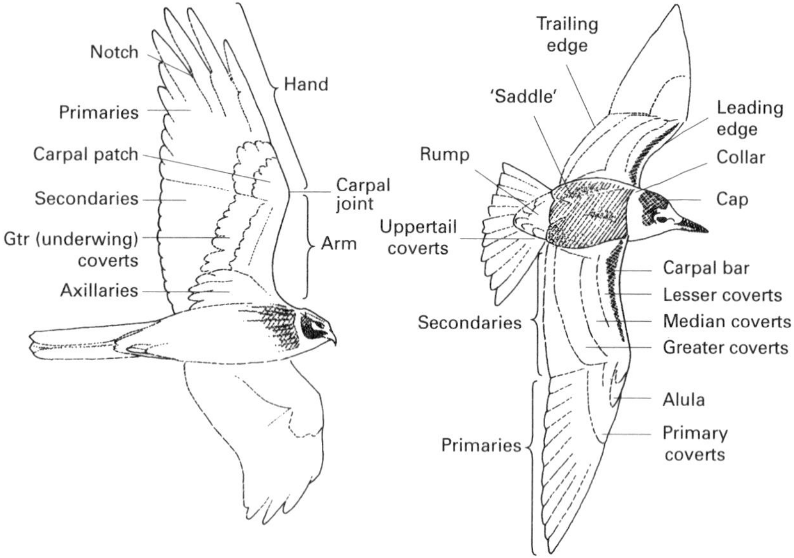

Notch
Primaries
Carpal patch
Secondaries
Gtr (underwing) coverts
Axillaries
Hand
Carpal joint
Arm
Trailing edge
'Saddle'
Rump
Uppertail coverts
Leading edge
Collar
Cap
Carpal bar
Lesser coverts
Median coverts
Greater coverts
Secondaries
Alula
Primaries
Primary coverts

Fig. 2

Plates

Illustrations are of adults except where indicated.
Legend: ♂ = Male. ♀ = Female. Juv. = Juvenile. Imm. = Immature.

Map Key

- Present all year
- Rare but possible all year
- Winter visitor
- Rare but possible in winter

Plate 1. Petrels, Shearwaters and Storm-petrels

Vagrant	1.	**White-headed Petrel** *Pterodroma lessonii* White head, dark underwing, and whitish tail. **p. 16**
Vagrant	2.	**Barau's Petrel** *Pterodroma baraui* Sturdy with stubby neck, short stout bill, and distinctive underwing pattern. **p. 16**
Vagrant	3.	**Soft-plumaged Petrel** *Pterodroma mollis* White underparts, grey breast band, and grey pattern on dark underwing. **p. 16**
Vagrant	4.	**Streaked Shearwater** *Calonectris leucomelas* Large, grey brown above with whitish face, black streaked crown, mostly white underwing. **p. 17**
Vagrant	5.	**Jouanin's Petrel** *Bulweria fallax* All dark. Larger than Bulwer's with relatively large head and little or no wing bar. **p. 17**
Vagrant	6.	**Bulwer's Petrel** *Bulweria bulwerii* All sooty brown with pale diagonal upperwing bar. **p. 17**
Passage Migrant	7.	**Flesh-footed Shearwater** *Puffinus carneipes* Distinctive bill, dark underwing, pink feet. Shorter tail than Wedge-tailed. **p. 18**
Vagrant	8.	**Short-tailed Shearwater** *Puffinus tenuirostris* Relatively short bill, grey underwing pattern, and legs extend beyond short tail. **p. 18**
Vagrant	9.	**Sooty Shearwater** *Puffinus griseus* Whitish underwing pattern, longer tail than Short-tailed. **p. 18**
Vagrant	10.	**Audubon's Shearwater** *Puffinus lherminieri* Small and sturdy. White underparts with pink feet against dark undertail coverts. **p. 19**
Visitor to coastal waters	11.	**Wedge-tailed Shearwater** *Puffinus pacificus* Long wedge tail only seen when turning, normally pointed. (i) Dark morph. (ii) Pale morph (rarer). **p. 18**
Visitor to coastal waters	12.	**Wilson's Storm-petrel** *Oceanites oceanicus* Conspicuous white rump, straight trailing edge on broad wings, legs trail behind square tail. **p. 19**
Vagrant	13.	**Swinhoe's Storm-petrel** *Oceanodroma monorhis* Dark rump. Wings (longer than Wilson's) have bend on trailing edge at wrist. Forked tail. **p. 20**

1
1
2
3
3
2
5
6
4
4
13
10
12
10
7
8
9
11(i)
11(ii)

Plate 2. **Tropicbirds, Boobies, and Frigatebirds**

Summer visitor to SW coastal waters

1. **Red-billed Tropicbird** *Phaethon aethereus*
Red bill, barred upperparts and long white tail-streamers. Juvenile has dark line across nape and black on outer wing extending onto primary coverts. **p. 20**

Uncommon visitor to coastal waters

2. **White-tailed Tropicbird** *Phaethon lepturus*
Yellow bill and obvious diagonal black patches across secondaries and their coverts, white wing tips on upperwings. Long, white tail streamers. Juvenile lacks dark nape line and has short black patch on primaries. **p. 21**

Vagrant

3. **Masked Booby** *Sula dactylatra*
White head with dark face mask and black tail. Juvenile has white collar and a thin black stripe behind leading edge of underwing. **p. 22**

Vagrant

4. **Red-footed Booby** *Sula sula*
Occurs in various different morphs, all with red feet and a pale blue bill with a pinkish base. (i) Adult white morph. White tail (Masked has black on tail). (ii) Adult white-tailed and white-headed morph. (iii) Adult white-tailed brown morph. (iv) Adult brown morph. Uniform pale brown. **p. 23**

Vagrant

5. **Brown Booby** *Sula leucogaster*
Adult similar to immature Masked but lacks the white collar and has different underwing pattern. Juvenile has buff-brown underparts. **p. 23**

Vagrant

6. **Christmas Island Frigatebird** *Fregata andrewsi*
Brown upperwing bar. Male has white belly patch, female has white 'star' on belly and axillaries. Immatures all have pale bellies. **p. 26**

Vagrant

7. **Great Frigatebird** *Fregata minor*
No axillary spurs. Male: all black with red feet. Female: white throat and upper breast. Juv: pale head and belly. Immature: white belly shades to black with maturity. **p. 26**

Vagrant

8. **Lesser Frigatebird** *Fregata ariel*
Smaller than **6** and **7** above, with white axillary spurs. Male: white only on axillaries. Female: black throat, white breast and spurs. Juv: rusty head, white belly, and spurs. Immature: belly darkens with maturity. **p. 26**

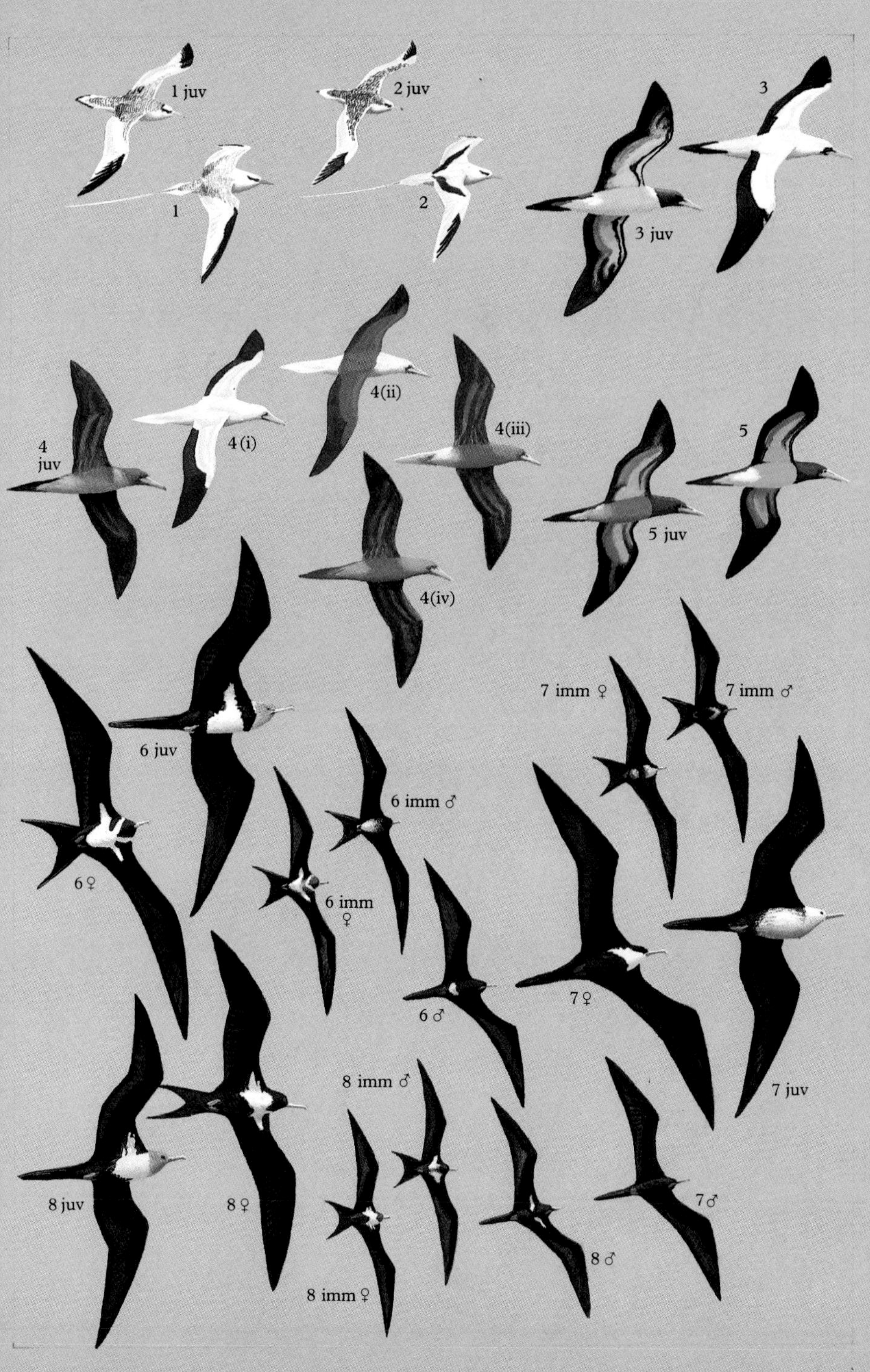
1 juv
2 juv
3
1
2
3 juv
4 juv
4(i)
4(ii)
4(iii)
5
5 juv
4(iv)
7 imm ♀
7 imm ♂
6 juv
6 imm ♂
6 ♀
6 imm ♀
6 ♂
7 ♀
7 juv
8 imm ♂
8 juv
8 ♀
7 ♂
8 ♂
8 imm ♀

Plate 3. Pelicans, Cormorants, Darter, and Flamingoes

1. **Spot-billed Pelican** *Pelecanus philippensis*
Smaller than Great White and with grey-brown flight feathers. **p. 22**

Vagrant 2. **Great White Pelican** *Pelecanus onocrotalus*
Very large with black flight feathers. **p. 21**

3. **Great Cormorant** *Phalacrocorax carbo*
Large with white on cheek and throat, yellow or orange facial skin, grey bill with yellow pouch. Juv. white underparts. (i) Breeding: white on neck and white thigh patch. (ii) Non-breeding. **p. 24**

4. **Little Cormorant** *Phalacrocorax niger*
Small. Relatively short, deep-based bill making an almost conical head. Long tail. Juv: off-white throat and breast. (i) Breeding. (ii) Non-breeding: off-white throat. **p. 24**

5. **Indian Cormorant** *Phalacrocorax fuscicollis*
Medium size, long thin bill. Lacks the white on cheeks of Great, has speckled throat and scaly pattern on wings. (i) Breeding: small tuft of white behind the ear coverts. (ii) Non-breeding. **p. 24**

6. **Oriental Darter** *Anhinga melanogaster*
Large with very thin, kinked neck. Sits very low in water. **p. 25**

Vagrant 7. **Lesser Flamingo** *Phoeniconaias minor*
Normally darker pink than Greater, dark red bill with smaller black patch on tip. **p. 38**

8. **Greater Flamingo** *Phoenicopterus ruber*
Very large with extensive black tip to bill. **p. 38**

1 juv
1
1
2
3(ii)
3(i)
3(ii)
3(i)
3 juv
4(ii)
4(i)
4 juv
4(i)
5(ii)
5(i)
5 juv
5(i)
8
7
8
7
6 juv
6
6
6
7 juv
8 juv

PLATE 4. Larger Herons, Eurasian Bittern and White Egrets

1. **Goliath Heron** *Ardea goliath*
Vagrant — Very large. Slate bill and dark grey legs. Plain grey upperwing, dark chestnut underwing. **p. 27**

2. **Purple Heron** *Ardea purpurea*
Generally dark with thin angular neck. Smaller than Grey. Little contrast between brown and grey flight feathers and dark coverts, grey tinged green-brown above and chestnut below. **p. 28**

3. **Grey Heron** *Ardea cinerea*
Appears pale with grey above and white neck. Black flight feathers contrasting with pale grey coverts. **p. 27**

4. **Eurasian Bittern** *Botaurus stellaris*
Vagrant — Large and stocky. Streaked brown with dark crown and moustache. **p. 33**

5. **Intermediate Egret** *Mesophoyx intermedia*
Bill shorter and less pointed than Great's, gape line not behind eye. Black legs and feet. (i) Breeding: black bill with yellow base. (ii) Non-breeding: yellow bill with dusky tip. **p. 28**

6. **Great Egret** *Casmerodius albus*
Much larger than other white egrets. Long bill, gape line extends behind eye. (i) Breeding. (ii) Non-breeding. **p. 28**

7. **Little Egret** *Egretta garzetta*
Black bill all seasons. Black legs with yellow feet. (i) Breeding. (ii) Non-breeding. **p. 29**

8. **Western Reef Egret** *Egretta gularis*
Sturdier, has more square head and stouter, less pointed bill than Little. (i) Pale morph: dark legs (tarsi usually paler than Little) with yellow or yellow-green feet. (ii) Dark morph: feet as in pale morph. Intermediates also occur. **p. 29**

9. **Cattle Egret** *Bubulcus ibis*
Small and sturdy with stout bill and deep 'jowl'. (i) Breeding: golden-buff head, neck and dorsal plumes. (ii) Non-breeding: off-white. **p. 30**

1
2
3
1
2
3
4
4
5(i)
5(ii)
6(ii)
6(i)
6
5
9(ii)
7
8(i)
8(ii)
7(i)
9(i)
7(ii)
8(i)
8(ii)
9(ii)

PLATE 5. Smaller Herons and Bitterns

1. **Indian Pond Heron** *Ardeola grayii*
Well camouflaged when standing, obvious white wings and tail in flight. (i) Non-breeding/juvenile: streaked head and breast. (ii) Breeding. **p. 30**

Vagrant

2. **Chinese Pond Heron** *Ardeola bacchus*
Breeding: chestnut head, neck, and breast and grey back. Non-breeding: similar to Indian Pond female but slightly larger and browner. **p. 31**

3. **Striated Heron** *Butorides striatus*
Generally dark with black crown and long crest. Juvenile smaller than juvenile Black-crowned and has darker crown. **p. 31**

4. **Black-crowned Night Heron** *Nycticorax nycticorax*
Stocky. Black above, grey on sides and white below. Juvenile has paler crown than juvenile Striated and heavy spotting on mantle. **p. 31**

5. **Malayan Night Heron** *Gorsachius melanolophus*
Short, stout bill. Mainly juveniles are seen in Sri Lanka: black crown and nape crest with white tips, fine buff barring on dark wings and scapulars, more than on juvenile Black-crowned and lacking its whitish spots. Adult: black crown and crest, chestnut above; white below with black streaked sandy breast and black and rufous spots on belly. **p. 32**

6. **Yellow Bittern** *Ixobrychus sinensis*
Paler than the Cinnamon and with slaty-black flight-feathers and tail. Male and juvenile have dark crowns. Juvenile paler than Cinnamon juvenile and wing coverts less heavily marked. **p. 32**

7. **Cinnamon Bittern** *Ixobrychus cinnamomeus*
Darker and sturdier than Yellow with white 'moustache'. Male: uniform chestnut above. Female: some spotting on wing and dark crown. Both appear all cinnamon in flight, no black on wings or tail. Juvenile: streaked brown with dark crown and pale fringes above. **p. 32**

8. **Black Bittern** *Ixobrychus flavicollis*
Long dagger bill. Dark with characteristic buff shading to white patch on sides of neck. Heavily streaked breast. **p. 33**

1(i)
1(ii)
2
1(ii)
3 juv
3
4
3
4
4 juv
6 ♀
6 ♂
5
6 juv
6 ♂
5
7 ♂
7 ♀
5 juv
7 juv
7
8 ♂
8 ♀
8 juv
8 ♂

Plate 6. Storks, Ibises, and Spoonbill

1. **Painted Stork** *Mycteria leucocephala*
Long, slightly down-curved, sturdy bill and bare orange-pink skin on face. **p. 34**

2. **Asian Openbill** *Anastomus oscitans*
Smallest local stork with characteristic gap between mandibles when bill is closed. **p. 34**

Vagrant 3. **White Stork** *Ciconia ciconia*
Red bill, black rear scapulars, flight feathers, and greater coverts. White tail. **p. 35**

4. **Woolly-necked Stork** *Ciconia episcopus*
Bill appears black. Black crown, white neck, rest black except white undertail coverts. **p. 35**

Vagrant 5. **Black Stork** *Ciconia nigra*
Black with white belly and under tail coverts, red bill and legs. **p. 34**

6. **Black-necked Stork** *Ephippiorhynchus asiaticus*
Black neck and bill, characteristic black and white wing pattern. Endangered. **p. 35**

7. **Lesser Adjutant** *Leptoptilos javanicus*
Very large with big, strong yellow bill, naked yellow head and neck with thin grey down. Endangered. **p. 36**

8. **Glossy Ibis** *Plegadis falcinellus*
All dark with sturdy down-curved bill. Breeding illustrated. Non-breeding: duller with white streaks on head and neck. **p. 37**

9. **Black-headed Ibis** *Threskiornis melanocephalus*
Naked black head, neck and down-curved bill, red strip on underwing. **p. 36**

10. **Eurasian Spoonbill** *Platalea leucorodia*
Very distinctive bill shape. (i) Breeding: yellow-orange crest and flush on breast. (ii) Non-breeding: all white. **p. 37**

1
1
2
2
2 juv
3
3
4
4
5
5
6
6
7
7
8
8
8 juv
9
9
10(ii)
10(i)

PLATE 7. Grebes, Goose, and Ducks

1. **Little Grebe** *Tachybaptus ruficollis*
Small, dumpy, appearing tail-less. Short, pointed bill with yellow-white spot at base. (i) Breeding. (ii) Non-breeding. **p. 15**

Vagrant

2. **Fulvous Whistling-duck** *Dendrocygna bicolor*
Larger than Lesser with black line down back of neck, white streaks on flanks, off-white uppertail coverts. **p. 39**

3. **Lesser Whistling-duck** *Dendrocygna javanica*
Smaller than Fulvous. Maroon wing coverts contrast with black on wings. Chestnut uppertail coverts. **p. 39**

4. **Cotton Pygmy-goose** *Nettapus coromandelianus*
Smallest local duck. Breeding male: glossy black collar, bold white wing bar. Female: dark eye stripe, dingier below, white bar on tips of secondaries. Non-breeding male like female but keeps white wing bar. **p. 40**

Vagrant

5. **Ruddy Shelduck** *Tadorna ferruginea*
Rather goose-like but orange-brown with white patch on upper forewing and white underwing with black flight-feathers. (i) Breeding male has thin black collar. **p. 40**

Vagrant

6. **Greylag Goose** *Anser anser rubrirostris*
Only true goose likely in Sri Lanka. Large. Orange or pink bill. **p. 39**

Extinct in Sri Lanka

7. **Comb Duck** *Sarkidiornis melanotos*
Large. Speckled head and neck. Black wings with blue-green sheen, bronze speculum, grey flanks; white below. Male has comb on bill. **p. 40**

Vagrant

8. **Red-crested Pochard** *Netta rufina*
Stocky. Male: orange-chestnut head and crest. Red bill, black neck, breast, and belly with white flank patches. Female: brown crown contrasts with pale grey face. **p. 44**

Vagrant

9. **Common Pochard** *Aythya ferina*
Male: chestnut head with high crown and no crest. Female: pale eye-stripe and throat. No white on wing in flight. **p. 44**

Vagrant

10. **Tufted Duck** *Aythya fuligula*
Stocky with obvious white wing bar. Male: bold black and white. Female: brown with small crest. White wing bar in flight. **p. 45**

1(ii)
1(i)
1(ii)
2 juv
2
2
4 ♂
4 ♀
3 juv
3
3
4 ♂
4 ♀
5 ♀
5
6
7 ♂
5(i)
7 juv
7 ♀
7 ♂
8 ♀
9 ♀
10 ♀
8 ♂
9 ♂
10 ♂
10 ♂
10 ♀
8 ♂
8 ♀
9 ♀
9 ♂

Plate 8. **Ducks**

1. **Eurasian Wigeon** *Anas penelope*
Stocky. Round head with slight peak on steep forehead. White (pale grey in female) inner wing, white belly and dark pointed tail in flight. **p. 41**

Vagrant

2. **Gadwall** *Anas strepera*
White speculum, squarish head. Female has dark grey upper mandible with sharply defined orange sides. **p. 41**

3. **Northern Shoveller** *Anas clypeata*
Long, broad spoon-like black bill. Blue-grey inner wing and green speculum on upperwing. White underwing coverts contrasting against chestnut belly in male and dark belly in female. **p. 43**

Vagrant

4. **Mallard** *Anas platyrhynchos*
Purple-blue speculum with white borders. Male: dark green head and yellow bill. Female and eclipse male: obvious purple-blue speculum. **p. 42**

5. **Spot-billed Duck** *Anas poecilorhyncha*
Black bill with bright yellow tip and two red spots at base (less obvious in female). In flight shows white bordered green speculum and white underwing coverts. **p. 42**

6. **Northern Pintail** *Anas acuta*
Slim, thin necked, and pointed tail. Male: white stripe down neck and long, pointed tail. Female: indistinct brown speculum with white trailing edge. **p. 42**

7. **Common Teal** *Anas crecca*
Very small. Male: distinctive head pattern and buff triangle on under tail. Female by size, from Garganey by face pattern, shorter bill, and less contrast on underwing. **p. 41**

8. **Garganey** *Anas querquedula*
Small. Male: brown head with obvious pale eyebrow. Female: distinctive face pattern and white throat. Grey-green speculum. **p. 43**

Vagrant

9. **Marbled Teal** *Marmaronetta angustirostris*
Generally pale with dark brown eye-patch continuing down neck. **p. 44**

1♂
1♂
2♂
3♂
3♂
1♀
1♀
2♂
2♀
2♀
3♀
3♀
1♀
2♂
3♀
1♂
2♀
3♂
4♂
4♂
5
6♂
6♀
4♀
4♀
5
6♂
6♀
4♀
5♂
5♀
6♀
4♂
6♂
7♂
7♂
8♀
8♂
8♂
9
7♀
7♀
8♀
8 juv
8♂
9
7♀
7♂
8♀
9

PLATE 9. **Birds of Prey**

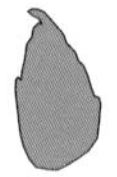

1. **Oriental Honey-buzzard** *Pernis ptilorhynchus*
Small head. (i) Typical adult male: grey face, pale throat, dark gorget. Broad dark trailing edge, two narrow inner bars, no contrast on carpals on underwing. Broad dark-pale-dark bars on under tail. (ii) Typical adult female: brown face, weaker gorget, three even spaced dark bars and narrow trailing edge on underwing; two narrow dark bars separated by broad pale bar under tail. (iii) Dark morph adult male. (iv) Pale morph adult female. (v) Typical juvenile faint bar on trailing edge; 4–5 weak bars on tail. **p. 47**

2. **Long-legged Buzzard** *Buteo rufinus*
Vagrant
Heavily built. (i) Typical adult: pale head, unmarked under tail, pale patches on upperwing primaries. (ii) Adult rufous morph. (iii) Juvenile dark morph. (iv) Typical juvenile pale morph. **p. 53**

3. **Common Buzzard** *Buteo buteo*
Dark tips to flight feathers, dark carpal patches on underwing but very variable. (i) Typical adult. (ii) Adult pale morph. (iii) Adult dark morph. Usually has dark tip to tail. (iv) Typical juvenile: faint trailing edge to underwing secondaries. **p. 53**

4. **Brahminy Kite** *Haliastur indus*
Adult: distinctive chestnut with white head and breast. Black tips to primaries. Juvenile: pale tail, dark underwing coverts. **p. 48**

5. **Black Kite** *Milvus migrans*
Dark with pale area on upperwing and forked tail but tail, constantly moving in flight, can appear square. Juvenile: paler, more streaked. From juvenile **4** by non-contrasting underwing coverts and dark tip to longer tail. **p. 47**

6. **Osprey** *Pandion haliaetus*
Whitish underparts, dark line through eye, variable dark breast band, usually more obvious in female. Dark carpal underwing patch. **p. 45**

7. **Rufous-bellied Eagle** *Hieraatus kienerii*
Broad winged and relatively short tailed. Adult: dark cap, white throat and breast. Rufous underparts often appear dark unless close. Underwing primaries paler than secondaries. Juvenile: brownish above, pale below; no underwing dark carpal patches. Immature (2nd year) rufous patches on belly and underwing. Endangered. **p. 55**

1(i)
1(i)
1(i)
1(iv)
1(ii)
1(iii)
1(v)
2(i)
2(iii)
3(iii)
3(ii)
2(ii)
2(iv)
3(iv)
3(i)
3(i)
2(i)
2(i)
5
4
4
4
4 juv
5
5 juv
5
7 imm
7 juv
6 juv
6♀
7
7 juv
7
6♂
7

PLATE 10. **Birds of Prey**

1. **Jerdon's Baza** *Aviceda jerdoni*
Female: rufous breast, rufous barred belly. Thin dark centre line on throat. White-tipped black crest normally erect when perched. Narrowly based wings with black trailing edge. Barred under tail with white-tip, rufous markings below. Male: rufous-brown markings below. **p. 46**

Rare winter visitor

2. **Black Baza** *Aviceda leuphotes*
Black crest normally erect when perched. Bold black and white with chestnut barring on breast. Unbarred under tail. **p. 46**

3. **Crested Goshawk** *Accipiter trivirgatus*
Adult: black line on throat, sharp border between cheek and throat, heavily streaked breast. Crest not always visible. Broad narrow-based wings, three dark bands under tail. Juvenile: plain buff underparts with a few darker spots. **p. 52**

4. **Besra** *Accipiter virgatus*
Slimmer, longer legged and generally darker and more strongly barred than Shikra but with streaks on breast. Black throat stripe, sharp border between dark cheek and white throat. Underwing boldly barred. Tail barred above and below. Juvenile: strongly barred flanks, flight, and outer tail feathers; dark rump and upper tail. **p. 52**

5. **Shikra** *Accipiter badius*
Paler and more finely barred than Besra. Dark cheeks shade into white throat. Central uppertail feathers unbarred in adult. Underparts only faintly marked. Very pale below with darker wing tips. Juvenile: white on rump and uppertail coverts, five narrow bands on tail. **p. 52**

6. **Black-winged Kite** *Elanus caeruleus*
Falcon-like. Black tip on underwing, black shoulder patch. Juvenile: browner with obvious pale fringes. **p. 47**

1♀
1♂
1♀
2
2
2
3
3 juv
4♂
3
4♀
3 juv ♂
4♀
4♀
3♀
4 juv ♀
4♂
5♀
4 juv ♀
4 juv ♂
5♀
5 juv ♀
6
6
5♂
5♀
5 juv ♀
6
5 juv ♂
6 juv
5♂
6 juv

PLATE 11. **Harriers**

1. **Western Marsh Harrier** *Circus aeruginosus*
Large with broad wings. (i) Male: silver-grey on wings and tail. (ii) Female: dark brown, with variable buff patches on crown, throat and leading edge. (iii) Second year male: variable grey in wing, pale head. (iv) Juvenile: usually all dark. (v) Adult male dark morph (rare variant). **p. 51**

2. **Montagu's Harrier** *Circus pygargus*
Long, narrow-based wings with pointed 'hand' of four 'fingers'.(i) Male: black wing-tips and bar on secondaries. Black and chestnut barred underwing. (ii) Female: paler face than Pallid, hindmost pale bar on underwing continues broad to body, central dark bar darker than trailing edge, chestnut chequering on axillaries, dark trailing edge to inner primaries. (iii) Typical juvenile: rusty below, dark cheek mark only to gape. Faint pale collar. Bases of outer primaries faintly barred. (iv) Juvenile: copper-brown morph. (v) Second year female: breast and underwing markings appearing. (vi) Second year male: adult axillary marking appears. (vii) Adult male dark morph: dark secondaries and barred tail. **p. 51**

3. **Pallid Harrier** *Circus macrourus*
Four-fingered primaries. (i) Male: pale grey with narrow wedge of black at wing-tip. (ii) Female: broader wings than in female Montagu's, dark 'moustache' above pale collar. Underwing primaries: paler tips, more barred in centre and lack a dark trailing edge. Secondaries darker than primaries, central pale bar darkens and tapers away towards body. Underwing coverts heavily marked. (iii) Juvenile: pale collar usually with darker area behind, dark cheek mark extends under bill. Underwing primaries like adult female. (iv) Second year female. (v) Second year male. **p. 50**

4. **Pied Harrier** *Circus melanoleucos*
Broader wings than on Pallid and Montagu's with five primary 'fingers'. (i) Male: black head, white below. (ii) Female: pale head, obviously barred pale upperwing with pale leading edge. (iii) Juvenile: streaked dark below. (iv) Second year female. **p. 50**

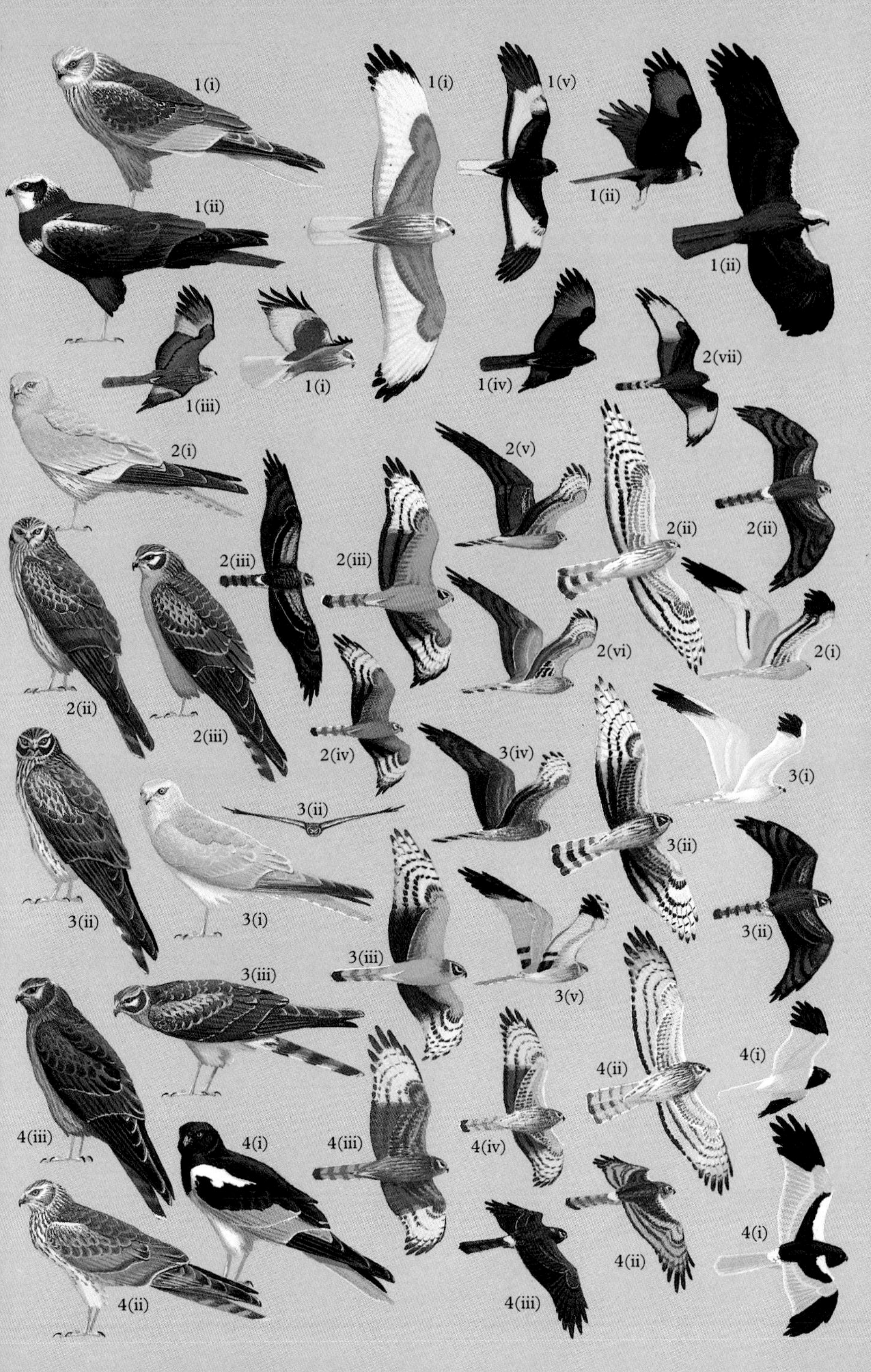
1(i)
1(i)
1(v)
1(ii)
1(ii)
1(ii)
1(iii)
1(i)
1(iv)
2(vii)
2(i)
2(v)
2(iii)
2(iii)
2(ii)
2(ii)
2(vi)
2(i)
2(ii)
2(iii)
2(iv)
3(iv)
3(i)
3(ii)
3(ii)
3(ii)
3(i)
3(iii)
3(v)
3(ii)
3(iii)
4(ii)
4(i)
4(iii)
4(i)
4(iii)
4(iv)
4(i)
4(ii)
4(ii)
4(iii)

PLATE 12 Eagles and Vulture

1. **Crested Serpent Eagle** *Spilornis cheela*
Dark body and underwing coverts. Broad rounded wings with bold black and white pattern from below, double band on carpals. Juvenile: white underwing with dark trailing edge. **p. 49**

2. **Black Eagle** *Ictinaetus malayensis*
All dark with broad narrow-rooted wings and separated up-curved' fingers'; and long tail. Juvenile: pale streaked head, underparts and underwing coverts. (i) Second year. **p. 54**

3. **Mountain Hawk Eagle** *Spizaetus nipalensis*
Very broad short wings, narrower at bases. Dark brown hood with thin black crest. Rufous barring on belly and flanks. Juvenile: very pale below with almost unmarked buff underwing coverts. Endangered. **p. 55**

4. **Changeable Hawk Eagle** *Spizaetus cirrhatus*
Slimmer than **3** with less broad wings and long tail. Slender with a few streaks on off-white breast and belly. White tipped crest. Juvenile: off-white head and very pale underparts. **p. 55**

5. **White-bellied Fish Eagle** *Haliaeetus leucogaster*
White with black flight feathers. Long winged with narrow 'hand' and separated 'fingers'. Black base to white under tail. Juvenile: dark underwing secondaries contrast with pale coverts.(i) Second year. **p. 48**

6. **Grey-headed Fish Eagle** *Ichthyophaga ichthyaetus*
Grey head, white lower belly, thighs and base of tail with broad black terminal band. Much shorter, more square wings than **5**. Juvenile: secondaries normally paler than underwing coverts. (i) Second year. **p. 49**

7. **Booted Eagle** *Hieraaetus pennatus*
Broad wings and plain square tail. (i) Pale morph: dark underwing with pale coverts. (ii) Dark morph: paler inner primaries, pale base to tail. **p. 54**

8. **Bonelli's Eagle** *Hieraaetus fasciatus*
Vagrant
Slender with a long, square black-tipped tail. Pale patch on upper back. Broad black band across underwing coverts, pale inner leading edge and grey patch at bend of wing. Juvenile: rufous-buff body. **p. 54**

9. **Egyptian Vulture** *Neophron percnopterus*
Vagrant
Yellow head and slender bill. All white wedge-shaped tail. Juvenile: pale head and underwing coverts. **p. 49**

1
1 juv
1
1 juv
2
2(i)
2 juv
2
2 juv
3
3 juv
3
3 juv
4
4 juv
4
4 juv
5
5 juv
7(i)
7(i)
8
5
8 juv
7(ii)
5 juv
5(i)
9
6 juv
6
9
9 juv
6
6 juv
6(i)

PLATE 13. **Falcons**

1. **Peregrine Falcon** *Falco peregrinus calidus*
Heavy bodied, broad-based pointed wings, relatively short tail. Blackish hood, white cheeks, and dark moustache stripe, finely barred below. Male much smaller than female. Juvenile: browner above and streaked below. **p. 58**

2. **Shaheen** *Falco peregrinus peregrinator*
Dark race of the peregrine. Smaller, darker above, rufous below with weak barring on body. Plumage variable. Juvenile: streaked below. **p. 58**

3. **Oriental Hobby** *Falco severus*
Black hood. Throat and cheek-patch white. Like small Shaheen but with unmarked rufous underwing coverts. Juvenile: streaked below with barring on underwing coverts. **p. 57**

4. **Red-necked Falcon** *Falco chicquera*
Vagrant
Only local falcon with a chestnut head. Dark outer upperwing, all pale below. Barred tail with dark sub-terminal tip. **p. 57**

5. **Amur Falcon** *Falco amurensis*
Vagrant
Reddish cere, orange-yellow eye ring. Orange legs and feet. Male: slaty grey with white underwing coverts, deep chestnut lower belly and thighs. Female: whitish below with streaks and arrows, pale orange thighs and undertail coverts, barred underwing. Juvenile: no orange on thighs, heavily barred underwing, especially lesser coverts. **p. 57**

6. **Lesser Kestrel** *Falco naumanni*
Vagrant
Smaller than Common. Wing-tip reaches sub-terminal tail band when perched. Male: no spots on mantle, faintly spotted below, blue-grey upperwing greater coverts, buff-white underwing, no moustachial stripe. Female: pale underwing contrasts with darker coverts, and pale claws. (i) Second year male: no grey on inner upperwing. **p. 56**

7. **Common Kestrel** *Falco tinnunculus*
Wing-tip does not reach sub-terminal tail band when perched. Male: grey head, dark 'moustache', spotted mantle, spotted breast and belly. Female and juvenile: more heavily barred and spotted on underwing than Lesser. Black claws. **p. 56**

1 juv ♂
1♀
2♀
2♀
1♀
2 juv ♂
4
1 juv ♂
2 juv ♂
3
3
4
3 juv
3
4
5♂
5♀
5♀
5♀
5♂
6♀
5 juv
5 juv
6♀
6♂
7♀
6(i)
7♀
7♂
6♂
7♂
6♂
6♀
7♂
7♀

Plate 14. **Game-birds and Buttonquails**

1. **Painted Francolin** *Francolinus pictus watsoni*
Chestnut face. Black (brown-black in female and young) outer tail feathers and rufous on the wings in flight. Male spotted below, female finely barred. Endangered. **p. 59**

2. **Grey Francolin** *Francolinus pondicerianus ceylonensis*
Brown head with broad pale eyebrow and obvious black-edged rufous throat patch. Broadly barred with pale shaft streaks above, finely barred below. Shows chestnut on tail in flight. **p. 59**

3. **Rain Quail** *Coturnix coromandelica*
Characterisitic face pattern in male and breast with heavy black streaking. Female has buff eyebrow and brown streaking on breast below a buff throat. **p. 60**

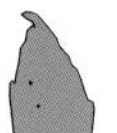

4. **Blue-breasted Quail** *Coturnix chinensis*
Very small with bright yellow legs. Male: black and white throat pattern, blue-grey breast, chestnut belly. Female: buff throat, finely barred breast. **p. 60**

5. **Jungle Bush Quail** *Perdicula asiatica*
Characteristic facial pattern and brick-red throat. Male: barred below. Female: rufous below. **p. 60**

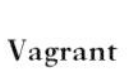

6. **Small Buttonquail** *Turnix sylvatica*
Vagrant
Note: Buttonquails have dark flight feathers contrasting with pale coverts. Tiny with sharply pointed tail. Brown crown with white central stripe, spotted buffish breast. **p. 62**

7. **Barred Buttonquail** *Turnix suscitator leggei*
Indistinct pale central line on crown. Wing coverts boldly spotted buff and black. Female more colourful than male with black throat, barred breast and flanks, rufous belly. Male: buff throat, barred breast, tawny belly. **p. 62**

8. **Sri Lanka Spurfowl** *Galloperdix bicalcarata*
Bright red legs and feet. Red bill and orbital skin, duller in female. White spots above and below on male. Female: reddish brown with white chin. Endemic. **p. 61**

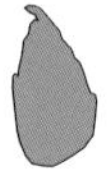

9. **Sri Lanka Junglefowl** *Gallus lafayettii*
Male like a small domestic rooster. Female: bare faced, spotted and streaked below, heavily barred on wing. Endemic. **p. 61**

10. **Indian Peafowl** *Pavo cristatus*
Crest of bare-shafted feathers. Male has distinctive train. **p. 61**

1♂
1♀
2
3♂
3♀
4♂
4♀
5♀
5♂
6
7♀
7♂
8♀
8♂
9♂
9♀
10♂
10♀

Plate 15. **Rails, Crakes, Coot, and Jacana**

1. **Slaty-breasted Rail** *Rallus striatus*
Chestnut crown and nape, slate breast, brown and white banded upperparts. Juvenile: brown breast and duller with barring less distinct. **p. 63**

Vagrant

2. **Water Rail** *Rallus aquaticus*
Long, thin bill with red lower mandible, pinkish legs and feet. Olive streaked black upperparts, slate-grey face, eyebrow, and breast, broad barring on flanks. **p. 63**

3. **Slaty-legged Crake** *Rallina eurizonoides*
Chestnut head, neck, and breast, unmarked brown back, black and white barred belly and flanks. Slate legs. Juvenile: duller, lacks chestnut. **p. 64**

Vagrant

4. **Corncrake** *Crex crex*
Blue-grey eyebrow, face, and breast. Brown and buff banded belly. Short thick bill. Shows chestnut wings if flushed. **p. 64**

5. **Baillon's Crake** *Porzana pusilla*
Small with white spots on mantle. Short bill, dull pink legs. **p. 64**

6. **Ruddy-breasted Crake** *Porzana fusca*
Orange legs. Chestnut head and breast, plain brown neck and upperparts. Weakly barred belly and rear flanks. Juvenile: lacks chestnut and is duller with pale eyebrow. **p. 65**

7. **White-breasted Waterhen** *Amaurornis phoenicurus*
White face, throat, and breast, dark grey back. Juvenile: brown-grey above, off-white face and below. **p. 65**

8. **Watercock** *Gallicrex cinerea*
Large with very long toes. (i) Breeding male. (ii) Non-breeding: large, brownish, streaked above, faintly barred below. Appears dark and nondescript. **p. 65**

9. **Common Moorhen** *Gallinula chloropus*
Sooty-black with white stripe on flank. White under tail. Red shield on bill. Juvenile: brown with white as in adult. No shield. **p. 66**

10. **Purple Swamphen** *Porphyrio porphyrio*
Large. Green-blue with pale head, greenish wings, and white under tail. Shield smaller in female. Juvenile: grey with smaller shield. **p. 66**

11. **Common Coot** *Fulica atra*
Slaty-black with white shield on bill. No white on flanks or under tail. **p. 67**

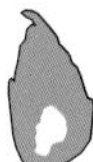

12. **Pheasant-tailed Jacana** *Hydrophasianus chirurgus*
Distinctive. White, brown and yellow head pattern. Very long thin toes. (i) Breeding female. (ii) Non-breeding. **p. 67**

1 juv
1
2
3 juv
3
4
4
5
6
6 juv
7
7 juv
8(i)
8(ii)
9 juv
9
10
10 juv
11 juv
11
12 juv
12(i)
12(ii)

Plate 16. Crab-plover, Oystercatcher, Stilt, Avocet, and Thick-knees

1. **Crab-plover** *Dromas ardeola*
Distinctive. Large black bill and sturdy, blue-grey legs. Juvenile: greyer upperparts, speckled crown. **p. 69**

2. **Eurasian Oystercatcher** *Haemotopus ostralegus*
Distinctive. Non-breeding: long, sturdy, orange-red bill. Juvenile: browner upperparts, narrower dusky tip to bill. **p. 69**

3. **Black-winged Stilt** *Himantopus himantopus*
Very long red legs and black needle-like bill. Head pattern variable.
(i) Breeding male: glossy black upperparts, variable blackish crown. (ii) Breeding female: browner, duller upperparts. (iii) Non-breeding female, grey on crown. Juvenile: brown upperparts with pale fringes and white trailing edge to wings. **p. 70**

4. **Pied Avocet** *Recurvirostra avosetta*
Long, thin, tapering, upturned black bill and striking black and white wing pattern. **p. 70**

5. **Eurasian Thick-knee** *Burhinus oedicnemus*
Staring yellow eye, chunky head, short neck and distinctive pattern on closed wing. Juvenile: less obvious face pattern, duller wing markings, warm brown upperparts. **p. 71**

6. **Great Thick-knee** *Esacus recurvirostris*
Long, slightly upturned, yellow-based black bill, large squarish head, big yellow eye with bold black and white face pattern. **p. 71**

1
2
2 juv
1 juv
1
2
3(i)
3(iii)
3(i)
3(ii)
3 juv
3(i)
3 juv
4 juv
4
4
5
6
6
5 juv
5

PLATE 17. Courser, Pratincoles, Lapwings, and *Pluvialis* Plovers

1. **Indian Courser** *Cursorius coromandelicus*
Chestnut crown, white eyebrow, black eye-stripe. Short, decurved bill. Chestnut breast, dark fore belly contrasts with white lower belly. White legs. Juvenile: dark brown crown with cream spots, pale lores, barred brown and buff upperparts, slightly spotted pale belly. **p. 72**

2. **Collared Pratincole** *Glareola pratincola*
Very similar to 3. Deeply forked tail, longer than in Oriental. Grey-brown upperwing coverts. Thin white trailing edge on secondaries. **p. 72**

3. **Oriental Pratincole** *Glareola maldivarum*
Forked tail, shorter than in Collared. Dark upperwing. No white on trailing edge of secondaries. Breeding adult illustrated, non-breeding is briefly duller and the necklace is replaced by streaks. **p. 73**

4. **Small Pratincole** *Glareola lactea*
Black line from eye to bill (often absent in winter). Slightly forked tail. White wing bar on upper- and underwing. Black underwing coverts and most of primaries, often with a white primary patch. **p. 73**

5. **Yellow-wattled Lapwing** *Vanellus malabaricus*
Yellow wattles, black crown, white line from eye to nape. Diagonal white wing bar. White underwing with black tips to flight feathers. **p. 74**

6. **Sociable Lapwing** *Vanellus gregarius*
No wattles. Obvious eyebrows from forehead to nape. White secondaries. (i) Non-breeding: pale buff forehead and eyebrow, grey-brown crown. (ii) Breeding: white forehead and eyebrow, black crown. Black belly. **p. 75**

7. **Red-wattled Lapwing** *Vanellus indicus*
Red wattles and eye-ring. Black-tipped red bill. Black crown, throat and bib, white ear patch. Broad diagonal white wing bar. More black on underwing than 5. **p. 75**

8. **Pacific Golden Plover** *Pluvialis fulva*
Appears brown above with yellow-buff eyebrow. Grey-brown underwing. (i) Non-breeding. (ii) Breeding: black belly and under tail, brighter yellow fringes above, white eyebrow continues to flank. Juvenile: like non-breeding but more clearly spotted yellow above. **p. 75**

9. **Grey Plover** *Pluvialis squatarola*
Large head, sturdy black bill. White underwing with black 'armpit'. White rump and broad white wing bar. (i) Non-breeding. (ii) Breeding. Juvenile: like non-breeding but more clearly spotted (often yellowish) above. **p. 76**

1 juv
1
1
3 juv
3
3
2
4
4
6(ii)
6(i)
7
7
5
5
6(i)
9(ii)
8 juv
8(ii)
8(i)
9 juv
9(i)
9(i)
8(i)

Plate 18. *Charadrius* Plovers

1. **Common Ringed Plover** *Charadrius hiaticula*
Black-tipped orange bill. Drab eye-ring. White wing bar. Orange to orange-yellow legs. (i) Non-breeding. (ii) Breeding. **p. 76**

2. **Long-billed Plover** *Charadrius placidus*
Vagrant
Longish thin bill. Browner head pattern with no black on ear coverts. Faint narrow wing bar. Pale yellow legs. Tail projects well beyond folded wings. **p. 77**

3. **Little Ringed Plover** *Charadrius dubius*
Smaller and slimmer than 1. Obvious yellow eye-ring. Very narrow wing bar. Dusky yellow legs. Juvenile: pale head and pale fringed scapulars. (i) Breeding *jerdoni* race. (ii) Non-breeding *curonicus* race. **p. 77**

4. **Kentish Plover** *Charadrius alexandrinus*
Dumpy with large head. Dark spurs on sides of breast, no full breast band. Broad white wing bar. Juvenile: pale fringes on scapulars. (i) Race *seebohmi*, breeding and non-breeding: grey-brown crown. (ii) Race *alexandrinus*, breeding male: rufous tinge on crown. **p. 78**

5. **Mongolian Plover** *Charadrius mongolus*
Shorter, slimmer and less pointed bill than Greater Sand and more rounded head. Usually dark grey legs. White eyebrow. White wing bar even width across primaries. Feet do not project beyond tail. (i) Non-breeding: white or buff forehead and eyebrow. (ii) Breeding male: often all black forehead. **p. 78**

6. **Greater Sand Plover** *Charadrius leschenaultii*
Longer, more pointed bill and flatter head than Mongolian, and usually paler legs. Faint eyebrow. White wing bar broadens across primaries. Feet project beyond tail. (i) Non-breeding. (ii) Breeding male: variable white patch on forehead (never black). **p. 79**

7. **Caspian Plover** *Charadrius asiaticus*
Thin bill, obvious whitish eyebrow. Long wings with narrow wing bar. White underwing coverts. (i) Non-breeding: complete grey-brown breast-band. (ii) Breeding male. **p. 79**

8 **Oriental Plover** *Charadrius veredus*
Vagrant
Long pointed wings. Larger than 7. with all dark underwing. Very faint wing bar. Longer yellow-pink legs, projecting well beyond tail in flight. (i) Non-breeding. (ii) Breeding male. **p. 80**

1(ii)
2
2 juv
1(i)
2
1(i)
3(ii)
4(ii)
4(i)
3(i)
3(i)
4(i)
3 juv
5(ii)
5 juv
4 juv
5(i)
7(ii)
5
7(i)
6 juv
6
7
6(i)
8(i)
8 juv
6(ii)
8(ii)

Plate 19. Dowitcher, Godwits, and Curlews

Vagrant

1. **Asian Dowitcher** *Limnodromus semipalmatus*
Blunt-tipped, nearly parallel, mainly black bill. Chevrons on flanks. No clear wing bar. Paler underwing and smaller bodied than 3. Juvenile: neatly fringed scapulars and mantle, buff on breast. (i) Non-breeding. (ii) Breeding. **p. 90**

2. **Black-tailed Godwit** *Limosa limosa*
Tall and slim. Straight tapering two-toned bill. Black tail band. Bold broad white wing bar. Black-edged white underwing. Legs project well beyond tail in flight. Juvenile: usually warmer toned than juvenile 3. (i) Non-breeding: poorly marked above. (ii) Breeding: orange-rufous only to breast. **p. 80**

3. **Bar-tailed Godwit** *Limosa lapponica*
Slightly upcurved two-toned bill. No wing bar. Narrow bars on white tail. Shorter legs than Black-tailed, projecting only a little beyond tail in flight. (i) Non-breeding: pale fringes and dark shaft streaks above. (ii) Breeding: orange-rufous extends to belly. **p. 81**

4. **Eurasian Curlew** *Numenius arquata*
Large with very long down-curved bill. Whitish wedge on back with variably brown barred lower rump and tail. Usually has white underwing coverts. **p. 82**

5. **Whimbrel** *Numenius phaeopus phaeopus*
Long bill, down-curved at tip. Dark crown with pale central stripe. White underwing coverts. (i) Race *variegatus*, brown and white barred underwing coverts, back, and rump. **p. 81**

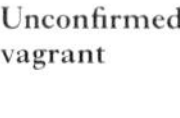

Unconfirmed vagrant

6. **Slender-billed Curlew** *Numenius tenuirostris*
Smaller and paler than 4 and 5 with shorter fine-tipped all dark bill, generally colder tones, dark crown, and faint eyebrow. White underwing coverts, back, and rump: dark spots (not streaks or barbs) on flanks and finely barred tail. Highly endangered. **p. 82**

1(i)
1(ii)
3(ii)
2(ii)
1 juv
2 juv
1(i)
2(i)
2(i)
3(i)
3 juv
3(i)
4
5
5(i)
4
5
6
6

Plate 20. **Redshanks, Greenshanks, and Marsh Sandpiper**

1. **Common Redshank** *Tringa totanus*
Orange-red legs. White secondaries continuing onto inner primaries. Orange bill with dark tip. Juvenile: often yellowish bill and legs, more clearly spotted above. (i) Non-breeding. (ii) Breeding. **p. 83**

2. **Spotted Redshank** *Tringa erythropus*
Red legs. Long, fine bill with red at base of lower mandible. Short white eyebrow, dark lores, and white cheeks. No white on upperwing, white underwing becoming grey on primaries. Juvenile: dark, variably barred below. (i) Non-breeding: pale lores. (ii) Breeding. **p. 82**

3. **Marsh Sandpiper** *Tringa stagnatilis*
Long, fine, straight bill. White eyebrow. Longish, thin neck. Long legs projecting well beyond tail in flight. (i) Non-breeding. (ii) Breeding. **p. 83**

4. **Common Greenshank** *Tringa nebularia*
Larger than 3. Relatively sturdy slightly up-curved bill with grey-green base. Long, grey-green legs. (i) Non-breeding. (ii) Breeding. **p. 84**

5. **Nordmann's Greenshank** *Tringa guttifer*
Slightly up-curved bill with yellow-green base and black-tip. Yellow to brownish legs, shorter and sturdier than in 4, just reaching tip of tail in flight. Paler underwing than **4**.
Vagrant — Juvenile: browner above with more pronounced cap. (i) Non-breeding: generally paler than **4**, especially the head. (ii) Breeding: white spots on scapulars, larger and fewer than on **4**. **p. 84**

1 juv
1(ii)
2 juv
2(ii)
1(i)
2(i)
2(i)
1(i)
3(i)
3 juv
5(i)
4(i)
4(i)
3(i)
5(ii)
4(ii)
3(ii)
4 juv
5 juv
4(i)
5(i)

Plate 21. Smaller *Tringa* Sandpipers; Common, Terek, and Buff-breasted Sandpipers, Ruff, Turnstone, and Phalarope

1. **Green Sandpiper** *Tringa ochropus*
Non-breeding: White eyebrow only from bill to eye. Dark olive-brown above with faint white spots, white rump contrasts with dark back, white tail with black bars. Green-brown legs. Dark underwing, white belly. **p. 85**

2. **Wood Sandpiper** *Tringa glareola*
Non-breeding: paler than **1**. Obvious white eyebrow extends behind eye. Usually more spotted on upperparts than **1**. Yellow-green legs, longer than on **1**. Pale underwing. **p. 85**

3. **Terek Sandpiper** *Xenus cinereus*
Non-breeding: long, slightly up-curved bill. Even brown above with short pale eyebrow. Shortish orange-yellow legs. Broad white trailing edge to secondaries. Pale grey rump. Breeding and juvenile often have dark line on upper scapulars. Very busy feeders. **p. 86**

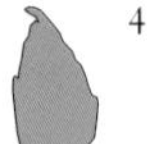

4. **Common Sandpiper** *Actitis hypoleucos*
Non-breeding: white on belly extends up to form line on side of breast. Broad white wing bar. White on outer tail feathers. Bobbing stance. **p. 86**

5. **Ruff** *Philomachus pugnax*
Small head, long neck, and plump bodied. Long legs. Shortish slightly down-curved bill. Narrow white wing bar. Two white oval patches at sides of rump. Feet project behind tail. Much variation, often white-faced in winter. (i) Non-breeding male. (ii) Female moulting to breeding. **p. 97**

6. **Ruddy Turnstone** *Arenaria interpres*
Dumpy, short-legged and short-billed. Black and white wing, rump and tail pattern obvious in flight. (i) Non-breeding: distinctive dark breast band, off-white chin. (ii) Breeding. **p. 87**

7. **Red-necked Phalarope** *Phalaropus lobatus*
Small. Very thin black bill. White wing bar and patches on sides of rump. Swims. (i) Non-breeding: prominent black eye-patch. (ii) Breeding female. The male is duller. **p. 87**

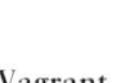

Vagrant

8 **Buff-breasted Sandpiper** *Tryngites subruficollis*
Smaller than **5**. Buff face and breast. Short, black bill. Yellow legs. Dark outer wing, brown and buff inner wing. No white wing bar. No white patches on sides of rump. Dark edged white underwing with dark bar on primary coverts. Feet do not project behind tail. **p. 96**

1
1
2
2 juv
3 juv
3
2
3
4
8 juv
5 juv ♀
5(ii)
4
5 juv ♀
8 juv
5(i)
7(i)
7(ii)
6(ii)
6(i)
6(i)
7 juv
7(i)

Plate 22. Woodcock and Snipe

1. **Greater Painted-snipe** *Rostratula benghalensis*
White eye-ring merging into short stripe towards nape, white 'harness', white belly and long straight bill curving down slightly and thickening at tip. Long legs trail in flight. Male: smaller, much less boldly marked and greyer about the head and breast, more spotted and barred on scapulars and wings than female. **p. 68**

2. **Eurasian Woodcock** *Scolopax rusticola*
Large and stocky. Crown barred brown and buff, not striped. Bars below continue onto breast. **p. 87**

Doubtful winter visitor

3. **Wood Snipe** *Gallinago nemoricola*
Note: All local snipe have striped head pattern and pale parallel lines on mantle. Big, stocky and dark with dark upperparts and underwing. Barred belly (no white). Very little white on corners of tail. **p. 88**

4. **Pintail Snipe** *Gallinago stenura*
Relatively shorter bill than in other similar sized snipe. Buff eyebrow broader than eye-stripe. Central crown stripe usually reaches bill. Scapulars evenly fringed. Lacks the Common's white trailing edge. Inner wing contrastingly pale. Plain dark underwing. **p. 88**

Vagrant

5. **Swinhoe's Snipe** *Gallinago megala*
Very similar to Pintail but with longer bill, noticeably larger in flight with toes projecting less beyond longer tail. Central crown stripe usually not reaching bill. **p. 89**

6. **Common Snipe** *Gallinago gallinago*
Broad dark eye-stripe in front of eye. Cheek usually paler than eyebrow. Fringes on scapulars much broader on outer webs than inner. Extensive white belly. Dark upperwing with white trailing edge on secondaries, broad white bars on underwing. **p. 90**

Vagrant

7. **Great Snipe** *Gallinago media*
Stout. More extensively barred below than **4.** and **6.** Prominent white wing bars. Extensive white patch on outer tail feathers. Narrow white trailing edge on wings (less so in juvenile). **p. 89**

8. **Jack Snipe** *Lymnocryptes minima*
Small and relatively short-billed. No buff central crown stripe but has a double buff eyebrow. No white on tail. **p. 90**

1 ♂
1 ♂
2
2
1 ♀
3
3
4
4
4
5
5
6
6
6
7
7
8

Plate 23. **Knots, Sanderling, Sharp-tailed and Curlew Sandpipers, Dunlin**

1. **Red Knot** *Calidris canutus*
Stocky and rounded in appearance. Straight bill as long as the head. Faint pale eyebrow. Short grey-green legs. White wing bar, rump appears pale grey in flight. Juvenile: pale fringed above with buff wash above and on breast and flanks. (i) Non-breeding. (ii) Breeding, spring. **p. 91**

2. **Great Knot** *Calidris tenuirostris*
Larger, sturdier, with longer bill and more streaked above than **1**. Wings project beyond tail when folded (equal in **1**). Narrow wing bar, white rump. Juvenile (and breeding): shows plain, often dark face and dark breast. (i) Non-breeding: plainer face, paler usually with darker shaft streaks above. (ii) Breeding, spring. **p. 91**

3. **Sanderling** *Calidris alba*
Black bill and legs. Broadest white wing bar of small waders. Lacks hind toe. Very busy when feeding. Juvenile: black, buff, and white above, buff streaks on sides of breast and flanks. (i) Non-breeding: appears very pale with dark patch at bend of wing. (ii) Breeding, spring. **p. 92**

4. **Sharp-tailed Sandpiper** *Calidris acuminata*
Vagrant
Rufous tinged brown cap, long white eyebrow and prominent eye-ring. Pale legs. Juvenile: orangey, buff, and white fringes above; rich buff breast with brown streaks on sides. (i) Non-breeding. (ii) Breeding, spring: orangey throat and breast with dark spots, white below with dark chevrons on upper belly and flanks. **p. 94**

5. **Dunlin** *Calidris alpina*
Rare winter visitor
Shorter and straighter bill than **6**. but with slightly down-curved tip. Black legs. (i) Non-breeding: fine grey streaks on throat and breast. (ii) Breeding, spring; only small black bellied wader. **p. 95**

6. **Curlew Sandpiper** *Calidris ferruginea*
Long down-curved bill. Longish black legs. Clear white eyebrow. White rump. Juvenile: scaly dark grey-brown upperparts with buff fringes, and buff wash on neck and breast. (i) Non-breeding: grey-brown patches on sides of breast, usually less streaked than 5. (ii) Breeding, spring. **p. 95**

1(ii)
1 juv
1(i)
2(i)
2(ii)
1(i)
2 juv
3(ii)
2(i)
3 juv
3(i)
3(i)
4 juv
4(ii)
4(i)
5(ii)
4(i)
6(ii)
5 juv
6(i)
6(i)
5(i)
5(i)
6 juv

Plate 24. **Stints; White-rumped, Spoonbill, and Broad-billed Sandpipers**

Unconfirmed vagrant

1. **White-rumped Sandpiper** *Calidris fuscicollis*
Non-breeding: short bill, slightly down-curved at tip with some yellow at base. White eyebrow. White band across upper tail. Long wings usually extend beyond tail. Dark legs. Juvenile: chestnut cap, buff ear coverts, dark scapulars with chestnut fringes, finely streaked grey breast. **p. 94**

2. **Temminck's Stint** *Calidris temminckii*
Very faint pale eyebrow. Tail projects beyond wings. White on sides of rump and outer tail feathers. Narrow wing bar. Pale legs. Juvenile: brownish upperparts with neat thin buff fringes, buff breast band. (i) Non-breeding: uniform grey-brown above like a miniature Common Sandpiper. (ii) Breeding. **p. 93**

3. **Little Stint** *Calidris minuta*
Dark legs. Juvenile: dark centres to rear lower scapulars and tertials. (i) Non-breeding: paler above and on head than non-breeding **2**. Usually darker centres on scapulars than non-breeding **4**. (ii) Breeding: rufous on head and breast, streaking on breast and throat, throat always white. **p. 92**

Vagrant

4. **Rufous-necked Stint** *Calidris ruficollis*
Bill slightly thicker at tip than on **3**. Dark legs. Juvenile: lower scapulars and tertials less extensively black centred and contrast with upper scapulars. (i) Non-breeding: slightly paler centres on scapulars than **3**. but almost identical in non-breeding. (ii) Breeding: usually more extensively reddish on face and breast (and often throat); streaks always below the reddish breast band. **p. 92**

5. **Long-toed Stint** *Calidris subminuta*
Longish neck. Grey-brown above with dark centres on scapulars and mantle. Longish yellowish legs with central toe longer than bill. Short faint white inner wing bar. Juvenile: black centres and chestnut fringes on mantle, scapulars, and tertials, white lines on mantle. (i) Non-breeding. (ii) Breeding. **p. 93**

Vagrant

6. **Spoonbill Sandpiper** *Eurynorhynchus pygmeus*
Non-breeding: Distinctive bill. Double white eyebrow. White throat and breast. Dark legs. Narrow wing bar, white sides to rump. **p. 95**

7. **Broad-billed Sandpiper** *Limicola falcinellus*
Non-breeding: long bill, down-curved near tip. Double white eyebrow but upper rather indistinct. Short legs. Black leading edge and narrow white wing bar. Juvenile: eyebrow pattern more obvious, dark centres with pale buff and white fringes above, faint streaking on breast. **p. 96**

1 juv
1 juv
2(i)
1
2(ii)
3(i)
2 juv
3 juv
2(i)
3(ii)
4 juv
3(i)
4(ii)
5(ii)
4(i)
5(i)
7 juv
5 juv
6 juv
7
6

PLATE 25. **Skuas and larger Gulls**

Rare summer visitor

1. **South Polar Skua** *Catharacta maccormicki*
(i) Pale morph: contrast between grey-buff underbody and blackish underwing.
(ii) Dark morph: usually shows paler nape and forehead. Intermediate morphs occur.
p. 98

Regular summer visitor

2. **Antarctic Skua** *Catharacta antarctica*
Large and sturdy. No pale collar. Yellow streaks on nape. No obvious contrast between dark underwing and belly. **p. 98**

Regular summer visitor

3. **Pomarine Jaeger** *Stercorarius pomarinus*
Larger, bulkier, and deeper billed than Parasitic with rounded elongated tail feathers. Juvenile: rump always paler than nape and often with double pale patch on underwing. (i) Breeding, pale morph: black hood extends below bill. Flanks and breast darker than Parasitic; blacker brown than Parasitic. (ii) Non-breeding: pale morph: (iii) Non-breeding, dark morph. **p. 98**

Vagrant

4. **Parasitic Jaeger** *Stercorarius parasiticus*
Slimmer and thinner billed than Pomarine with narrower wings and longer tail ignoring the pointed (not rounded) elongated central feathers. Juvenile: nape always paler than rump. (i) Non-breeding: dark morph: warmer brown than Pomarine. (ii) Non-breeding, pale morph. **p. 99**

5. **Heuglin's Gull** *Larus heuglini*
Large. Dark upperparts and upperwing with white trailing edge. (i) Non-breeding: white head with grey streaking on nape. (ii) First winter: all dark primaries, secondaries, and greater coverts; extensive dark barred tail and dark underwing coverts. (iii) Second winter. **p. 100**

Rare winter visitor

6. **Yellow-legged Gull** *Larus cachinnans*
Large. Grey upperparts. Distinctive wing-tip pattern. (i) Non-breeding: white head, pale grey streaking on nape. (ii) First winter. (iii) Second winter. **p. 100**

7. **Great Black-headed Gull** *Larus ichthyaetus*
Very large with heavy bill and long sloping forehead. Long thin wings. Pale grey upperwing with white outer primaries and distinctive wing-tip pattern. Black and red band near bill tip. (i) Non-breeding: grey ear coverts and brown streaks on lower hind neck. Pale upperparts with faint white fringes. (ii) First winter. (iii) Second winter. (iv) Breeding: black hood. **p. 101**

1(i)
2
3(iii)
3(i)
4(i)
4(ii)
3 juv
3(ii)
1(ii)
4 juv
5(iii)
5(ii)
5 (i)
5(i)
5(i)
5(ii)
6(iii)
6(ii)
6(i)
6(ii)
6(i)
6(i)
7(i)
7(iv)
7(i)
7(ii)
7(iv)
7(iii)
7(ii)

PLATE 26. **Smaller Gulls and Noddies**

1\. **Sooty Gull** *Larus hemprichii*
Vagrant
Brown on head extends to bib. White hind collar and belly. Long, strong yellowish bill with black band and then red at the tip. (i) Juvenile/First winter. **p. 100**

2\. **Brown-headed Gull** *Larus brunnicephalus*
White mirrors on black wing-tips in adult. Obvious white eye-ring, yellow iris. (i) Non-breeding: thick red bill with dark tip. (ii) Breeding: brown hood, dark red bill. (iii) First winter: largely dark flight feathers and tail band. **p. 102**

3\. **Common Black-headed Gull** *Larus ridibundus*
White wedge on outer wing, black tips on outer primaries. Dark iris. (i) Non-breeding. (ii) Breeding. (iii) First winter. **p. 102**

4\. **Slender-billed Gull** *Larus genei*
Vagrant
Flat forehead. Relatively long bill and legs. Faint to absent ear spot. Pale iris. (i) Non-breeding. (ii) First winter. **p. 102**

5\. **Brown Noddy** *Anous stolidus*
Vagrant
Large with heavy bill. White cap shades to grey on nape. Sharp division on lores between white forehead and brown cheek. Inner underwing appears pale brown in flight. **p. 110**

6\. **Lesser Noddy** *Anous tenuirostris*
Vagrant
Long, slim bill. White cap shades to brown on lores and neck. Dark grey-brown body. **p. 110**

7\. **Black Noddy** *Anous minutus*
Vagrant
Very dark. Long, slim bill. Sharp division at margin of white cap. Appears uniformly dark in flight. **p. 110**

1
1(i)
1
1(i)
2(i)
2(ii)
2(i)
2(iii)
2(ii)
2(iii)
3(iii)
3(i)
3(ii)
3(i)
3(iii)
4(ii)
4(i)
4(ii)
4(i)
6
7
6
5
7
5

Plate 27. Larger Terns

1. **Caspian Tern** *Hydroprogne caspia*
Very large. Red bill darkening towards tip with paler end. Extensive dark tip on underwing. (i) Breeding. (ii) Non-breeding. (iii) First year, non-breeding. **p. 105**

2. **Great Crested Tern** *Thalasseus bergii velox*
Large and stocky with long wings and grey rump. Large slightly down-curved green-yellow bill. Race *velox* has dark grey upperparts. (i) Breeding. (ii) First year, non-breeding. (iii) Non-breeding, race *thalassinus*. Paler upperwing. **p. 108**

3. **Lesser Crested Tern** *Thalasseus bengalensis*
Smaller and slimmer than **2** with orange bill and grey rump. (i) Breeding. (ii) Non-breeding. (iii) First year, non-breeding: obvious carpal bars. **p. 109**

4. **Sandwich Tern** *Thalasseus sandvicensis*
Vagrant
Small crest. Yellow-tipped black bill in adult. White rump. (i) Breeding. (ii) Non-breeding. (iii) First year, non-breeding. **p. 109**

5. **Gull-billed Tern** *Gelochelidon nilotica*
No crest. Stockier than Sandwich. All black, gull-like bill. Pale grey rump. Narrow black trailing edge on outer primaries. (i) Breeding. (ii) Non-breeding. (iii) First year, non-breeding. **p. 104**

1(i)
1(ii)
1 juv
1(iii)
2(i)
2(ii)
2(i)
2 juv
2(iii)
3(i)
3(ii)
3(ii)
3(iii)
4(ii)
4(ii)
4(i)
4(iii)
5 juv
5(ii)
5(i)
5(iii)

Plate 28. **Medium sized Terns**

1. **Common Tern** *Sterna hirundo*
Darker grey above than Roseate. Dark grey wedge on wing-tip (not always during moult). White rump and tail. (i) Breeding: usually has black tip to bill.
(ii) Non-breeding: bill sometimes has red on base. Usually has dark carpal and secondary bars on upperwing. (iii) Juvenile / First winter: strong carpal bar. **p. 105**

2. **Roseate Tern** *Sterna dougallii*
Pale grey above, with dark leading edge of wing tip. White rump and tail. (i) Breeding: long tail streamers. Variable rosy tinge below. (ii) Juvenile / First winter: dark barring on saddle, dark grey upperwing with white trailing edge. **p. 106**

3. **White-cheeked Tern** *Sterna repressa*
Vagrant
Dark grey. Darker underwing secondaries. Grey rump and tail. (i) Breeding: white cheek stripe, long tail streamers. (ii) First winter: generally dark grey above with dark outer primaries and coverts, grey rump and tail. **p. 106**

4. **Black-naped Tern** *Sterna sumatrana*
Vagrant
Appears white at distance. Black eye-stripe continues to meet on nape. Juvenile: narrow carpal bar. **p. 106**

5. **Bridled Tern** *Sterna anaethetus*
Vagrant
Dark brown above. White eyebrow continues behind eye. Juvenile: brown above with white streaks on grey crown, buff tips on scapulars and wing coverts. Pale grey below. **p. 107**

6. **Sooty Tern** *Sterna fuscata*
Vagrant
Darker than Bridled. White eyebrow does not continue behind the eye. Juvenile: brown with white tips on scapulars and wing coverts, and buff tips on lower belly; distinguish from noddies by white vent and under tail. **p. 107**

1(i)
1(ii)
1(ii)
1(iii)
2(ii)
2(ii)
2(i)
2(i)
3(ii)
3(ii)
3(i)
3(i)
4
4
4 juv
5
5
5 juv
5 juv
6
6 juv
6 juv
6

PLATE 29. Marsh Terns, Little and Saunder's Terns

1. **Whiskered Tern** *Chlidonias hybridus*
Black on head continues to nape. Pale underwing. Juvenile: saddle darker than upperwing, grey rump, no dark carpal or secondary bars. (i) Almost full summer plumage; some white fringes on crown, cheeks, and breast. (ii) Non-breeding: blackish eye stripe extends to meet on nape, does not drop behind eye. (iii) Breeding: *Sterna*-like black cap and obvious white cheek. Blue-grey below with white vent. **p. 103**

2. **White-winged Tern** *Chlidonias leucopterus*
Black eye-stripe drops behind eye in all non-breeding plumages. White collar and white rump. Short, sturdy bill. Juvenile: black ear patch drops below eye level, pale upperwing with dark carpal and secondary bars. (i) Spring moult. (ii) Non-breeding: pale grey upperwing with faint dark carpal bar and darker flight feathers. (iii) Breeding: black body and underwing coverts, pale grey flight feathers, very pale upperwing, white rump, and vent. **p. 103**

3. **Black Tern** *Chlidonias niger*
Vagrant
Non-breeding plumages show obvious dark grey patches on sides of breast at wing roots. Grey rump. Juvenile: saddle and upperwing equally dark, dark carpal and secondary bars, black ear patch drops below eye level, dark patch on side of breast. (i) Breeding: black body, dark upperwing, grey underwing, white undertail coverts. (ii) Non-breeding: dark carpal and secondary bars on upperwing. **p. 104**

4. **Saunders's Tern** *Sterna saundersi*
Very similar to **5**. White forehead, no eyebrow, broad black leading edge on upperwing outer primaries. Breeding illustrated. **p. 108**

5. **Little Tern** *Sterna albifrons*
Small with white forehead. (i) Breeding: black-tipped yellow bill, short white eyebrow. Narrow black upperwing outer primaries. (ii) Non-breeding: black bill (sometimes has yellow base), more extensive white on forehead. **p. 107**

1(i)
1 juv
1(ii)
1(ii)
1(iii)
2(i)
2(ii)
2 juv
2(iii)
2(i)
2(ii)
3(ii)
3(i)
3(ii)
3 juv
3(i)
5(i)
5(ii)
5 juv
4
5(ii)
5(i)
4
5 juv

Plate 30. **Pigeons and Doves**

1. **Rock Pigeon** *Columba livia*
Wild relative of the **Feral Pigeon**. Two black bands on inner wing show as lines on closed wing. **p. 111**

2. **Sri Lanka Woodpigeon** *Columba torringtoni*
Prominent 'chess-board' on nape, dark grey wings glossed green, dark vinous underparts and broad tail. Endemic. **p. 111**

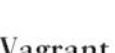

3. **Pale-capped Pigeon** *Columba punicea*
Pale grey cap. No 'chess-board'. Vinous-chestnut upperparts with slaty-grey rump and dark brown tail. **p. 112**

4. **Oriental Turtle Dove** *Streptopelia orientalis*
Much larger, stockier, and darker than Spotted. In flight the dark grey rump and white tipped blackish tail contrast with the rusty scapulars. **p. 112**

5. **Eurasian Collared Dove** *Streptopelia decaocto*
Pale sandy grey with narrow black hind collar. Under tail pattern obvious in flight. Much paler upper tail than Oriental Turtle. **p. 112**

6. **Red Collared Dove** *Streptopelia tranquebarica*
Very small and plump with short, white-cornered tail. Male: warm pinky-brown with grey head and plain mantle. Female from Eurasian Collared by smaller size, shorter differently patterned tail. **p. 113**

7. **Spotted Dove** *Streptopelia chinensis ceylonensis*
Slender, pink-grey with white spots and 'chess-boards'. Long wedge-shaped tail. Common. **p. 113**

8. **Emerald Dove** *Chalcophaps indica robinsoni*
Small and short-tailed. Glossy green mantle, black and white barred back. White eyebrow, less obvious in female. Chestnut underwing. **p. 113**

9. **Orange-breasted Green Pigeon** *Treron bicincta leggei*
Grey nape and hind neck, yellow-green face, grey upper tail. Male: purple and orange band on breast and cinnamon under tail. Female: almost plain vent and under tail. **p. 114**

10. **Pompadour Green Pigeon** *Treron pompadora pompadora*
Ashy blue rear crown and nape becoming green on hind neck. Vent and under tail strongly marked dark green. Maroon mantle in male. **p. 114**

11. **Yellow-footed Green Pigeon** *Treron phoenicoptera phillipsi*
Only local pigeon with yellow legs and feet. Yellow collar and lilac patch on shoulders. **p. 115**

12. **Green Imperial Pigeon** *Ducula aenea*
Largest local pigeon. Plain lilac-grey head, neck, and underparts. Glossy green back and tail, chestnut undertail coverts. **p. 115**

1
2
3
6♀
6
4
4
6♂
5
7
5
7
8♀
8♂
11
9♀
9♂
12
10♀
10 ♂

PLATE 31. Parrots, Koel, Malkohas, and Coucals

1. **Sri Lanka Hanging Parrot** *Loriculus beryllinus*
Much smaller than the parakeets. Crimson crown and rump; short, square tail. Female duller with little blue on throat. Juvenile: green crown and throat. Endemic. **p. 116**

2. **Alexandrine Parakeet** *Psittacula eupatria*
Largest local parakeet. Large bill. Large maroon shoulder patch. **p. 116**

3. **Rose-ringed Parakeet** *Psittacula krameri*
Smaller bill than Alexandrine with black lower mandible. No red shoulder patches. **p. 117**

4. **Plum-headed Parakeet** *Psittacula cyanocephala*
Male: plum coloured head and maroon patches on shoulders. Female: blue-grey head, yellow collar, small shoulder patch, white tip to blue and yellow tail. **p. 117**

5. **Layard's Parakeet** *Psittacula calthropae*
Blue-grey head with a green forehead and eye-patch, deep green collar, pale blue-grey back and relatively short deep blue yellow-tipped tail. Female: blackish bill. Endemic. **p. 117**

6. **Red-faced Malkoha** *Phaenicophaeus pyrrhocephalus*
Bare, crimson face, pale green bill. White below with black breast. Long, white-tipped graduated tail. Probable endemic (see text). **p. 123**

7. **Blue-faced Malkoha** *Rhopodytes viridirostris*
Pale green bill, blue bare skin around eye and white-tipped feathers on long graduated tail. **p. 122**

8. **Asian Koel** *Eudynamys scolopacea*
Male: yellow-green bill, slimmer and with longer tail than crows. Female: uniquely spotted and barred. **p. 122**

9. **Sirkeer Malkoha** *Taccocua leschenaultii*
Pale sandy with cherry red bill and broad white-tipped outer feathers on long, graduated tail. **p. 122**

10. **Green-billed Coucal** *Centropus chlororhynchus*
Smaller than Greater with pale yellowish-green or ivory bill, purple sheen on head and neck, deep chestnut wings. Endemic and endangered. **p. 123**

11. **Greater Coucal** *Centropus sinensis*
Black bill, blue sheen on head and neck, bright chestnut wings. Common. **p. 124**

Vagrant

12. **Lesser Coucal** *Centropus bengalensis*
Smallest of the local coucals. Pale streaks on mantle. **p. 124**

1 juv
1 ♂
2 ♂
2 ♀
3 ♀
3 ♂
4 ♀
4 ♂
5 ♀
5 ♂
6
7
8 ♂
8 ♀
9
10
11
12
12 juv

Plate 32. Cuckoos

1. **Chestnut-winged Cuckoo** *Clamator coromandus*
Black hood and crest, rufous-buff throat, white belly and hind collar, chestnut wings, and long tail. **p. 118**

2. **Pied Cuckoo** *Oxylophus jacobinus*
Black hood and crest, white underparts. Black wings with white patch on primaries, white tips to tail feathers. Juvenile: browner above, buffish below. **p. 118**

3. **Common Hawk Cuckoo** *Cuculus varius ciceliae*
Grey hood, streaked throat, rufous breast band, distinctive tail banding. (cf. Shikra, Plate 10(5)). Juvenile: no breast band, browner and barred above, streaks on breast. **p. 119**

4. **Indian Cuckoo** *Cuculus micropterus*
Broad black sub-terminal band on pale greyish tail. Broader barring below than Common and darker iris. Female: browner breast than Common. Juvenile: broad white tips to head, mantle and wing feathers. **p. 119**

Vagrant

5. **Common Cuckoo** *Cuculus canorus*
Pale yellowish eye. Male: dark grey tail contrasting with paler rump. Barring on underparts finer than on Indian and Lesser. Females occur in two morphs: (i) grey: (ii) hepatic. **p. 120**

6. **Lesser Cuckoo** *Cuculus poliocephalus*
Smaller than Common. Blackish tail contrasting little with dark rump. Broader barring below than on Common. (i) Female hepatic morph/Juvenile. **p. 120**

7. **Banded Bay Cuckoo** *Penthoceryx sonneratii waiti*
White finely barred brown on face, white eyebrow and prominent dark ear coverts. All white below with fine wavy brown bands. **p. 120**

8. **Plaintive Cuckoo** *Cacomantis merulinus*
Grey with white vent, white-tipped blackish tail. Juvenile: bright orange-rufous with diamond markings along tail, not bars. **p. 121**

9. **Drongo Cuckoo** *Surniculus lugubris*
White barring on undertail coverts and bases of outer tail feathers. Sometimes variable patch of white on nape. Thin bill. (cf. Black Drongo, Plate 48(1)) Juvenile: spotted white. **p. 121**

Vagrant

10. **Asian Emerald Cuckoo** *Chalcites maculatus*
Tiny. Male: green with black and white barred belly. Female: rufous barred crown; brown and white barred below. **p. 121**

1
2 juv
2
3
3 juv
4 ♀
5(i)
6 ♂
5(ii)
6(i)
4 ♂
4 juv
5 ♂
8 juv
7
9 juv
9
8
10 ♂
10 ♀

PLATE 33. **Smaller Owls, Nightjars, and Frogmouth**

1. **Oriental Scops Owl** *Otus sunia leggei*
Tiny. Yellow eyes. Whitish scapular stripe, well marked underparts. No pale collar. Ear-tufts not always erect. Two morphs: (i) grey: (ii) rufous. **p. 125**

2. **Collared Scops Owl** *Otus bakkamoena*
Ear-tufts, brown eyes, and buff collar on hind neck. Poorly marked underparts. **p. 126**

3. **Brown Hawk Owl** *Ninox scutulata*
Dark, slender, and hawk-like. Round headed with yellow eyes and a dark face. Relatively long wings and tail. **p. 128**

4. **Jungle Owlet** *Glaucidium radiatum*
No ear-tufts, white eyebrows. Barred dark brown and white upper- and underparts, barring continues on rear flanks. **p. 127**

5. **Chestnut-backed Owlet** *Glaucidium castanonotum*
Chestnut mantle faintly barred black. Rear flanks streaked, not barred. Yellow eyes, white eyebrows. Endemic. **p. 127**

6. **Sri Lanka Frogmouth** *Batrachostomus moniliger*
Wide bill with tuft of bristles at base, yellow eyes. Broken white fore collar. Long tail. **p. 128**

7. **Grey Nightjar** *Caprimulgus indicus kelaarti*
Dark. Male has two white spots on throat, white patch on primaries and small white patch on tips of outer tail feathers. Female lacks white apart from a moustache. **p. 129**

8. **Indian Nightjar** *Caprimulgus asiaticus eidos*
Small and pale. Two white spots on throat. **p. 130**

9. **Jerdon's Nightjar** *Caprimulgus atripennis*
Large. Contrastingly marked and relatively long tailed. Single white patch on throat. Appears darker than Indian. **p. 129**

1(i)
1(ii)
2
3
4
5
6♂
6♀
7♂
7♂
7♀
7♂
8
8
8
9
9
9

PLATE 34. Larger Owls, Hornbills and Crows

1. **Spot-bellied Eagle Owl** *Bubo nipalensis blighi*
Largest local owl. Strikingly spotted above and below. Brown eyes, prominent black and white 'ears'. Strong, feathered legs. **p. 126**

2. **Brown Fish Owl** *Bubo zeylonensis zeylonensis*
Large. Yellow eyes. Bare tarsi. Sandy brown upperparts with dark and white streaking. Buff below with fine streaks. **p. 126**

3. **Brown Wood Owl** *Strix leptogrammica ochrogenys*
No 'ears', brown eyes, obvious facial disc and white eyebrows. Finely barred above and below with narrow white lines on mantle. **p. 127**

4. **Oriental Bay Owl** *Phodilus badius assimilis*
Short ear-tufts, triangular facial disc with dark eyebrows. Rich chestnut upperparts, pink-buff below. Short rounded wings. Endangered. **p. 125**

5. **Barn Owl** *Tyto alba*
Slender, long-legged and long-winged. Round head, heart-shaped white facial disc. **p. 124**

6. **Short-eared Owl** *Asio flammeus*
Slender with relatively long wings. Short 'ears', yellow eyes, dark-streaked buff facial disc. Streaking on breast reduces on belly and flanks. **p. 128**

7. **Sri Lanka Grey Hornbill** *Tockus gingalensis*
White throat, no casque. Outer tail feathers become whiter with age and underparts paler. Endemic. **p. 140**

8. Malabar Pied Hornbill *Anthracoceros coronatus*
Large casque. Black neck. White trailing edge to wing. Male has black on rear of casque and red eye. **p. 140**

9. **House crow** *Corvus splendens*
Dark brown nape and neck, shading to black on breast. Very gregarious. **p. 201**

10. Large-billed Crow *Corvus macrorhynchos*
Larger than House Crow. All black. **p. 202**

1
2
3
4
6
6
7♀
5
7♂
7♂
8♂
8♀
8♂
9
10

Plate 35. Trogon, Kingfishers, Bee-Eaters, Rollers and Hoopoe

1. **Malabar Trogon** *Harpactes fasciatus*
Strikingly coloured with long, square-tipped tail. Female: brown head, orange-brown below. **p. 133**

2. **Stork-billed Kingfisher** *Halcyon capensis*
Large, stocky with huge bill. Brown head with buff collar. No white on wing. **p. 135**

3. **White-throated Kingfisher** *Halcyon smyrnensis*
Chocolate brown head and underparts, white throat and bib. In flight: white patch at base of primaries. **p. 136**

Rare winter visitor

4. **Black-capped Kingfisher** *Halcyon pileata*
Black cap, white collar and orange-buff below. In flight: white patch at base of primaries. **p. 136**

5. **Oriental Dwarf Kingfisher.** *Ceyx erithacus*
Tiny. Orange-purple head, neck, rump, and tail. Purple wings. **p. 135**

6. **Blue-eared Kingfisher** *Alcedo meninting*
Blue ear coverts. Deep blue above and dark orange below. Male: less orange on bill. **p. 135**

7. **Common Kingfisher** *Alcedo atthis*
Orange ear coverts. Brilliant blue above (paler and greener blue than **6**). Orange below. Male has black bill. **p. 134**

8 **Pied Kingfisher** *Ceryle rudis*
Only black and white local kingfisher. Female has single breast band. **p. 134**

9. **Little Green Bee-eater** *Merops orientalis ceylonicus*
Small. Pale green throat, bronze rear crown, chestnut underwing. **p. 137**

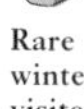

Rare winter visitor

10. **European Bee-eater** *Merops apiaster*
White forehead, chestnut and yellow upperparts, green-blue below. Pale grey brown underwing. **p. 137**

11. **Chestnut-headed Bee-eater** *Merops leschenaulti*
Chestnut crown and nape, yellow throat. Blue tinge on rump. Square tail. **p. 138**

12. **Blue-tailed Bee-eater** *Merops philippinus*
Green crown, blue cheeks, chestnut throat and blue tail. Deep chestnut underwing. **p. 137**

13. **Indian Roller** *Coracias benghalensis*
Dull brown and blue when perched, brilliant lilac and pale blue in flight. **p. 138**

14. **Dollarbird** *Eurystomus orientalis*
Dark green-blue. Broad red bill and red legs. Pale 'dollars' on open wing. Endangered. **p. 139**

15. **Eurasian Hoopoe** *Upupa epops*
Distinctive black and white wing markings and crest. Crest obvious even when closed. **p. 139**

1 ♂
1 ♀
2
3
4
3
4
5
6 ♀
7 ♀
8 ♂
9
9
9
10
10
11
11
12
12
12
12
13
13
14
14
15
15

PLATE 36. **Barbets and Woodpeckers**

1. **Coppersmith Barbet** *Megalaima haemacephala*
Darker green than 2, larger red patch on upper breast, no blue below the cheeks. Streaked breast. **p. 142**

2. **Crimson-fronted Barbet** *Megalaima rubricapilla rubricapilla*
Unstreaked green below, small red spot on breast, blue below cheeks. **p. 141**

3. **Brown-headed Barbet** *Megalaima zeylanica*
Large. Pale-streaked brown head and breast. Reddish bill and bare facial skin. **p. 141**

4. **Yellow-fronted Barbet** *Megalaima flavifrons*
Yellow forehead and crown, blue on face and throat. Pale green bill. Endemic. **p. 141**

5. **Brown-capped Woodpecker** *Picoides moluccensis gymnophthalmus*
Very small. Black and white with dark brown cap. Red flash on side of head not always visible in male and is absent in female which also has grey on forehead and crown. **p. 143**

6. **Yellow-crowned Woodpecker** *Picoides mahrattensis*
Small. Yellow forehead, red patch on belly. Pale yellow-grey face gives pale appearance. **p. 143**

7. Lesser Yellownape *Picus chlorolophus wellsi*
Bright yellow nape. Red on inner primaries and secondaries. **p. 144**

8. **Streak-throated Woodpecker** *Picus xanthopygaeus*
No yellow on nape. Whitish eyebrow and moustachial stripe on throat. Pale greenish-white underparts with scaly pattern. Yellow rump. **p. 144**

9. **Rufous Woodpecker** *Celeus brachyurus*
Female lacks red patch below eye and is paler. **p. 144**

10. **Black-rumped Flameback** *Dinopium benghalense*
(i) **Golden-backed Woodpecker** *D. b. jaffnense*
Golden back, no white on upper back. White spots on shoulders. White-speckled black throat and eye-stripe. Creamy white with dark streaks below. Red-brown eye, three toes. Replaces Red-backed in northern coastal areas.
(ii) **Red-backed Woodpecker** *D. b. psarodes*
Smaller than Greater Flameback with shorter, darker bill. White-speckled black throat and eye-stripe. White spots on shoulders. Creamy white with dark streaks below. Red-brown eye, three toes. **p. 145**

11. **Greater Flameback** *Chrysocolaptes lucidus stricklandi*
Horny brown bill paling at tip. Bill longer than head. White throat and hind neck. Narrow double black lines from bill to neck. Deep crimson mantle. Yellow eye. **p. 145**

12. **White-naped Woodpecker** *Chrysocolaptes festivus tantus*
Large. Long, dark bill. White nape continues into white triangle on upper back. Black lower back. **p. 146**

1
2
3
5♂
6♀
6♂
4
7♂
9♂
7♀
8♀
8♂
10(i) ♂
11♂
10(ii) ♂
12♂
11♀
10♀
12♀

Plate 37. **Larks, Wagtails and Pipits**

1. **Rufous-winged Lark** *Mirafra assamica*
Plump and thick-billed. Rufous patch on wing, also visible in flight. No white on tail. **p. 147**

2. **Oriental Skylark** *Alauda gulgula*
Thinner bill than 1. Buff outer tail feathers. Small crest usually held down. **p. 147**

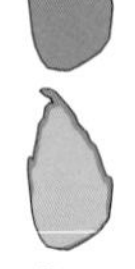

3. **Ashy-crowned Sparrow Lark** *Eremopterix grisea*
Sparrow-like but smaller. Thick, conical bill. **p. 148**

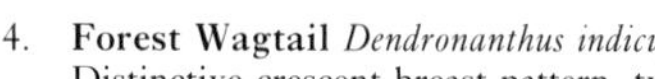

4. **Forest Wagtail** *Dendronanthus indicus*
Distinctive crescent breast pattern, two creamy bars across wing coverts. **p. 151**

5. **Yellow Wagtail.** *Motacilla flava*
Olive-green back, two whitish wing bars.
(a) Grey-headed Wagtail *M. f. thunbergi*
(i) Breeding male. (ii) Non-breeding female. (iii) First winter.
(b) Sykes' Yellow Wagtail *M. f. beema*
(iv) Adult male. (v) First winter.
(c) Yellow-headed Wagtail *M. f. lutea*
(vi) Adult. (vii) First winter.
(d) Siberian Yellow Wagtail *M. f. simillima*
(viii) Adult. (ix) First winter.
(e) White-chinned Wagtail *M. f. melanogrisea*
(x) Adult breeding male. (xi) First winter. **p. 152**

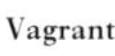

Vagrant

6. **Citrine Wagtail** *Motacilla citreola*
Grey back, yellow breast shading on belly to white under tail. Long tail. (i) Breeding male. (ii) Non-breeding female. (iii) First winter. **p. 153**

7. **Grey Wagtail** *Motacilla cinerea*
Dark grey back and greenish-yellow rump. Long tail. (i) Non-breeding adult. (ii) Breeding male. **p. 153**

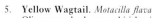

8. **White Wagtail** *Motacilla alba*
White forehead and fore crown. No yellow. (i) Non-breeding adult. (ii) Breeding adult male. (iii) First winter. **p. 153**

Rare winter visitor

9. **White-browed Wagtail** *Motacilla maderaspatensis*
Large. All black above with white eyebrow. (i) First winter: browner. **p. 153**

10. **Richard's Pipit** *Anthus richardi*
Large. Long, heavy bill, long legs, very long hind claw. Contrasting warm buff rear flanks. **p. 154**

11. **Paddyfield Pipit** *Anthus rufulus*
Medium length hind claw. **p. 154**

Probably winter visitor

12. **Blyth's Pipit** *Anthus godlewskii*
Slightly shorter and more pointed bill than Richard's, more evenly warm buff below, different pattern on median coverts. Short hind claw. **p. 154**

Vagrant

13. **Olive-backed Pipit** *Anthus hodgsoni*
Small. Olive-green back (fades when worn). Heavy streaking on breast and flanks. Distinctive ear covert pattern. White bar on wings. **p. 155**

1
2
3 ♂
3 ♀
4
5(xi)
5(viii)
5(ix)
5(x)
5(v)
5(i)
6(i)
5(iv)
5(vi)
5(ii)
6(ii)
5(vii)
5(iii)
6(iii)
7(ii)
7(i)
8(iii)
8(ii)
8(i)
9(i)
9
10
11
12
13

Plate 38. **Treeswift, Swifts, Martins, and Swallows**

1. **Grey-rumped Treeswift** *Hemiprocne longipennis*
Pale belly, long tail. Crest usually erect when perched. Female lacks chestnut cheek. **p. 133**

2. **Asian Palm Swift** *Cypsiurus balasiensis*
Small and dark. Narrow sharply pointed wings, deeply forked tail (seen when turning). **p. 131**

3. **Alpine Swift** *Tachymarptis melba*
Large. Long wings, forked tail. Brown breast band on white throat and belly. No white under tail. **p. 132**

4. **Brown-backed Needletail** *Hirundapus giganteus*
Large. Broad wings, very short square tail (usually appears pointed). White 'horseshoe' under tail extending to flanks. **p. 131**

5. **Little Swift** *Apus affinis*
Small and dark with white throat and rump. Square tail. **p. 132**

6. **Indian Swiftlet** *Aerodramus unicolor*
Small and uniformly dark, with relatively broad wings (not so pointed as in **2**) and notched tail. **p. 131**

7. **Pale Martin** *Riparia diluta*
Small. White below with brown breast band (often less complete than as illustrated). Shallow fork on tail. **p. 148**

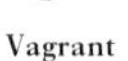

Vagrant

8. **Dusky Crag Martin** *Hirundo concolor*
Uniform dark brown with row of white spots on square tail. **p. 149**

9. **Barn Swallow** *Hirundo rustica*
Deeply forked tail with long streamers.
(i) **East Asian Swallow** *H. r. gutteralis*
Bright chestnut face, blue-black breast band usually incomplete.
(ii) **Tytler's Swallow** *H. r. tytleri*
As East Asian but with pale chestnut underparts. **p. 149**

10. **Hill Swallow** *Hirundo tahitica domicola*
Chestnut face and throat, no breast band, shallow forked tail without streamers. Rest of underparts dingy grey with white spots under tail. **p. 149**

Vagrant

11. **Wire-tailed Swallow** *Hirundo smithii filifera*
All white underparts. Long 'wire' streamers with other tail feathers more square than Eurasian Swallow. **p. 150**

12. **Red-rumped Swallow** *Hirundo daurica*
Deeply forked tail and sturdy build.
(i) **Sri Lanka Swallow** *H. d. hyperythra*
Deep chestnut underparts and rump, 'dipped-in-ink' tail.
(ii) **Nepal Red-rumped Swallow** *H. d. nipalensis*
Paler chestnut rump, coarser streaking on underparts.
(iii) **Indian Red-rumped Swallow** *H. d. erythropygia*
Chestnut rump and hind collar, rusty white underparts with fine brown streaking. **p. 150**

Vagrant

13. **Streak-throated Swallow** *Hirundo fluvicola*
Small with almost square tail. Chestnut cap, buff rump, streaked throat and breast. **p. 150**

1♂
1♂
1♂
1♀
2
2
3
4
4
5
5
6
7
7
8
8
9 (i)
9 (i)
9 (ii)
10
10
11
11
12 (i)
12 (i)
12 (ii)
12 (iii)
13
13

PLATE 39. **Shrikes, Cuckooshrikes and Minivets**

1. Common Woodshrike *Tephrodornis pondicerianus affinis*
Dark mask, off-white eyebrow. Narrow off-white band on rump, dark tail with white outer feathers. **p. 157**

2. **Large Cuckooshrike** *Coracina macei layardi*
Large. Black bill and mask. Pale grey rump. Female barred below. **p. 155**

3. Bar-winged Flycatcher-shrike *Hemipus picatus leggei*
Small and flycatcher-like. Shows white bar on closed wing. White rump. **p. 157**

4. **Small Minivet** *Pericrocotus cinnamomeus*
Male: ash-grey not black on crown, nape, and back. Scarlet breast pales on belly. Female: grey crown and back, scarlet rump. (i) Immature male. **p. 156**

5. Flame Minivet *Pericrocotus flammeus*
Male: black head and back. Scarlet below. Female: unmistakable. (i) Immature male. **p. 156**

6. Black-headed Cuckooshrike *Coracina melanoptera*
Male: black head, white belly and vent. Female barred breast and flanks. Both: black wings, black tail, with conspicuous white tips to outer feathers. Juvenile: barred above and below. **p. 156**

7. Brown Shrike *Lanius cristatus cristatus*
Brown with white face and black mask. (i) First year non-breeding. (ii) Adult Philippine Shrike *L. c. lucionensis*: greyer, especially on head with pale grey crown. **p. 162**

8. Rufous-backed Shrike *Lanius schach*
Grey and white with black mask and rufous rump and rear end. **p. 162**

9. Southern Grey Shrike *Lanius meridionalis*
Large. No rufous. Black wings with large white patch. Graduated white-edged black tail. **p. 163**

10. **Ashy Woodswallow** *Artamus fuscus*
Sturdy. Blue conical bill, black face and throat. Short, square tail. **p. 200**

1 juv
1
2 ♂
2 ♀
3
4 (i)
4 ♂
4 ♀
6 ♀
6 juv
6 ♂
5 (i)
5 ♀
5 ♂
7
7 (ii)
7 (i)
8
10
10 juv
10
8 juv
9

Plate 40. Bulbuls, Leafbirds, Iora and Orioles

1. **Black-headed Yellow Bulbul** *Pycnonotus melanicterus m.*
Black hood, dark tail with white tips to outer tail feathers. Male has red eye, female brown. **p. 158**

2. **Red-vented Bulbul** *Pycnonotus cafer cafer*
Black head with tufted crest, scarlet vent. White rump seen in flight. **p. 158**

3. **Yellow-eared Bulbul** *Pycnonotus penicillatus*
Yellow ear tufts, black and white head markings, white throat. Endemic. **p. 159**

4. **White-browed Bulbul** *Pycnonotus luteolus insulae*
Olive above with white eyebrow. Off-white below with brownish breast band, yellow vent and underwing. **p. 159**

5. **Yellow-browed Bulbul** *Hypsipetes indicus*
Only local bulbul with yellow face. **p. 159**

6. **Black Bulbul** *Hypsipetes leucocephalus humii*
Red bill and legs. Tufted crest. Red-brown eye. **p. 160**

7. **Common Iora** *Aegithina tiphia*
Yellow below, two white bars on wings. Breeding male shown, becomes duller out of season with dark green above. **p. 160**

8. **Jerdon's Leafbird** *Chloropsis cochinchinensis*
Male: yellow-green forehead, dark throat patch only to eye. Female: blue-green throat. **p. 161**

9. **Golden-fronted Leafbird** *Chloropsis aurifrons*
Orange forehead, dark throat extends behind eye. Female has slightly smaller face and throat patch. **p. 161**

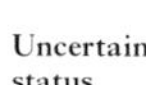

10. **Asian Fairy Bluebird** *Irena puella*
Red eyes. Male: brilliant blue above, black below with blue vent. Female: dull turquoise blue. **p. 161**

11. **Black-hooded Oriole** *Oriolus xanthornus ceylonensis*
Brilliant yellow with black hood. Juvenile: duller with streaked throat. **p. 198**

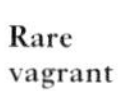

12. **Black-naped Oriole** *Oriolus chinensis*
Black eye-stripe extends to form band across nape. Less black on wing than on Eurasian Golden. **p. 198**

Scarce winter visitor

13. **Eurasian Golden Oriole** *Oriolus oriolus kundoo*
Black stripe from lores continues through eye. Female and juvenile male: greener above and streaked below. (i) Male of vagrant *O. o. oriolus*; eye-stripe stops at eye; less yellow on wing. **p. 197**

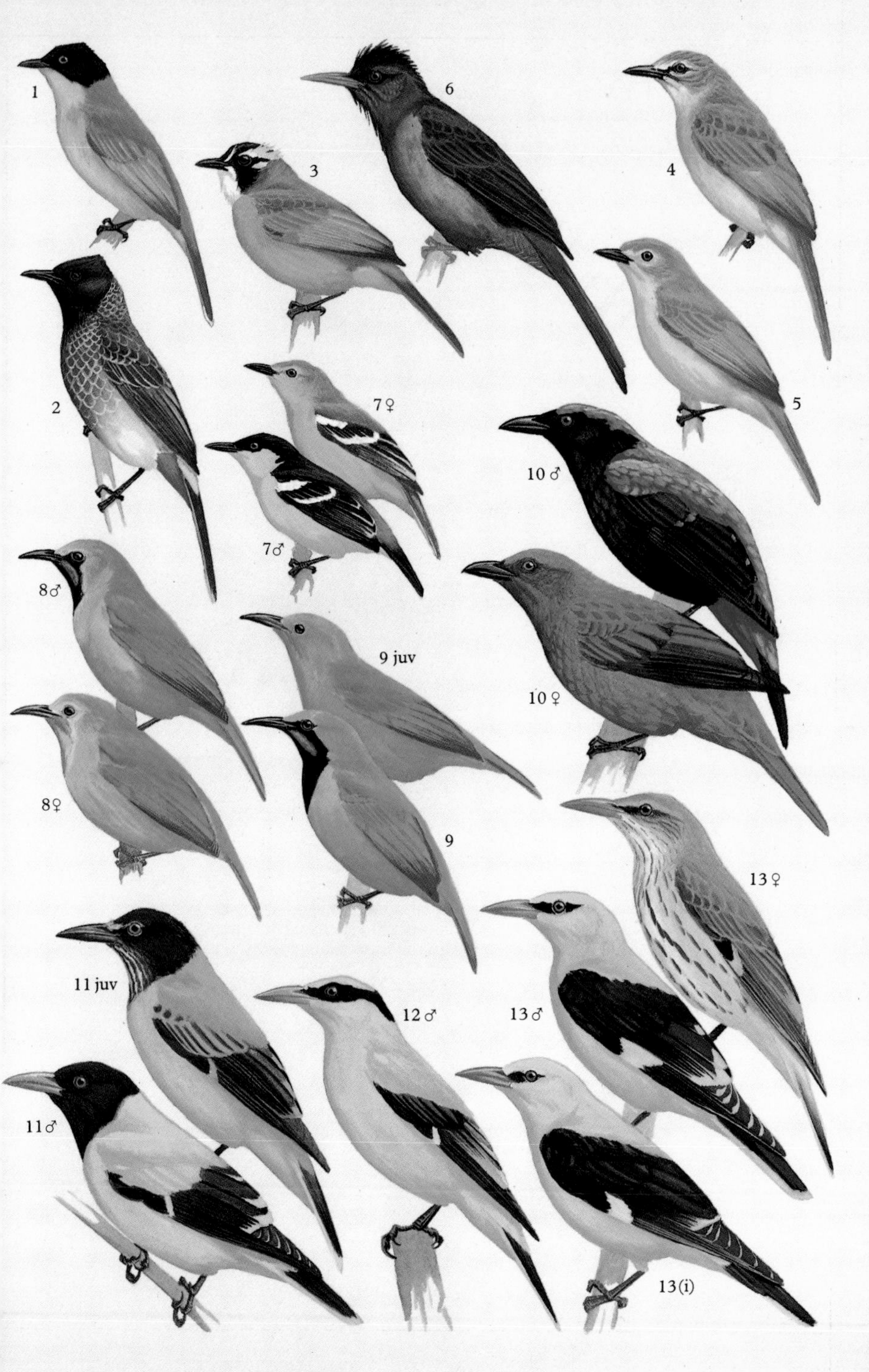
1
6
4
3
2
7♀
5
10♂
7♂
8♂
9 juv
10♀
8♀
9
13♀
11 juv
12♂
13♂
11♂
13(i)

PLATE 41. Chats, Robins and Wheatears

Vagrant 1. **Rufous-tailed Scrub Robin** *Cercotrichas galactotes*
White eyebrow, dark eye-stripe. Rufous tail with dark sub-terminal band and white tips on all but central feathers. **p. 165**

2. **Bluethroat** *Luscinia svecicus*
Vagrant
White eyebrow, black eye-stripe. Rufous edge to base of tail. Female: usually lacks the blue and has less rufous on throat. (i) Non-breeding male. (ii) Breeding male. (iii) First autumn. **p. 164**

3. **Indian Blue Robin** *Erithacus brunneus*
Male: white eyebrow, black face. Orange-rufous below shading to white vent. Female: white below with chestnut on breast and flanks. No white on tail. **p. 163**

4. **White-rumped Shama** *Copsychus malabaricus leggei*
White rump, long white-sided tail, chestnut belly. No white on wing. White under tail with broad black tip. **p. 164**

5. **Oriental Magpie Robin** *Copsychus saularis*
White patch on wing, white outer tail feathers. Female: slaty grey not black head and breast. **p. 164**

6. **Pied Bushchat** *Saxicola caprata*
Male: dull black with white wing patch, white on rump and vent. Female: rufous rump and uppertail coverts. **p. 165**

7. **Black-backed Robin** *Saxicoloides fulicata leucoptera*
Chestnut undertail coverts. Male: blue-black with white on wing coverts (often hidden). Female: dull brown, no white on wing. **p. 166**

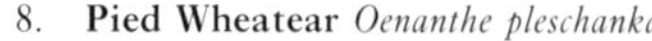

8. **Pied Wheatear** *Oenanthe pleschanka*
Vagrant
White rump extending onto tail to form black inverted T. Darker on scapulars and mantle than in Desert and Isabelline. (i) Fresh adult male, autumn; (ii) Male, first autumn; (iii) Worn male: spring; (iv) Fresh female: autumn;. (v) Worn female: spring. **p. 165**

Vagrant 9. **Isabelline Wheatear** *Oenanthe isabellina*
Very pale and plain. White rump with short stemmed broad topped black inverted T on tail. Pale eyebrow. **p. 166**

Vagrant 10. **Desert Wheatear** *Oenanthe deserti*
White rump, black tail (no T). Pale back and scapulars, dark wing coverts. (i) Fresh male: autumn;. (ii) Worn male: spring; (iii) Fresh female: autumn. **p. 166**

1
2(i)
3♀
3♂
2(ii)
2(iii)
4
6♂
6♀
5♂
7♀
7♂
5♀
8(ii)
9
9
8(i)
10(i)
8
10
8(iv)
8(iii)
8(v)
10(ii)
10(iii)

Plate 42. Thrushes and Pitta

1. **Blue Rock Thrush** *Monticola solitarius*
Long bill. (i) Non-breeding male. (ii) Breeding male. Female: grey-brown with dark fringes and bars below. Faint pale eyebrow. **p. 167**

2. **Sri Lanka Whistling Thrush** *Myophonus blighi*
Bright blue patch on lesser wing coverts, clearly seen in flight, often concealed when perched. Short tail. Male: slaty blue-black with black bill. Female: brown. Endemic and endangered. **p. 167**

3. **Pied Thrush** *Zoothera wardii*
Male: black and white with bold white eyebrow, yellow bill. Female: strong buff eyebrow, buff spots on wing coverts. **p. 167**

4. **Spot-winged Thrush** *Zoothera spiloptera*
Two rows of white spots on wing. Black and white facial pattern, no eyebrow. Black spotted white belly. Endemic. **p. 168**

5. **Scaly Thrush** *Zoothera dauma imbricata*
Brown with dark fringes giving scaly appearance. Endangered. **p. 169**

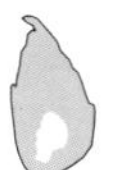

6. **Orange-headed Thrush** *Zoothera citrina*
Orange head, breast and belly. Male: grey above with white shoulder patch: Female: brownish grey above with head usually more clearly marked than male. **p. 168**

Vagrant

7. **Eyebrowed Thrush** *Turdus obscurus*
Grey head, whitish eyebrow, rufous breast, white belly. (i) First year non-breeding. **p. 169**

8. **Eurasian Blackbird** *Turdus merula kinnisii*
Black with orange bill, orange-yellow legs, and longish tail. Sexes almost alike in this race. **p. 169**

9. **Indian Pitta** *Pitta brachyura*
Bold yellow-brown, black and white head pattern. Blue rump. Red vent. **p. 146**

1(i)
1(ii)
2♂
1♀
2♀
6♀
6♂
3♂
3♀
4
5
7(i)
9
7♂
8♂
9
9

PLATE 43. Babblers and Warblers

1. **Brown-capped Babbler** *Pellorneum fuscocapillum*
Dark cap, cinnamon underparts. Endemic. **p. 170**

2. **Indian Scimitar-babbler** *Pomatorhinus horsfieldii melanurus*
Long curved yellow bill. White eyebrow, bib, and breast. **p. 170**

3. **Dark-fronted Babbler** *Rhopocichla atriceps*
Black face and forehead, yellow eye. White throat, breast, and upper belly. **p. 171**

4. **Tawny-bellied Babbler** *Dumetia hyperythra phillipsi*
Pale face and bill. White throat contrasting with rufous-buff below. **p. 171**

5. **Yellow-eÿed Babbler** *Chrysomma sinense nasale*
Black bill, yellow eye with bright orange eye-ring, white eyebrow. White below. **p. 171**

6. **Orange-billed Babbler** *Turdoides rufescens*
Orange bill, rufous plumage. Yellow legs and feet. Endemic. **p. 172**

7. **Yellow-billed Babbler** *Turdoides affinis taprobanus*
Yellow bill, pale eye and face. Drab grey plumage. **p. 172**

8 **Ashy-headed Laughingthrush** *Garrulax cinereifrons*
Black bill, grey head, and pale eye. Dark legs. Endemic. **p. 172**

9. **Sri Lanka Bush-warbler** *Bradypterus palliseri*
Generally dark with rusty-buff throat, dark grey breast. Faint pale eyebrow and eye-ring. Rounded tail. Endemic. **p. 173**

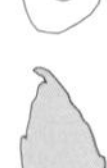

10. **Pallas's Grasshopper Warbler** *Locustella certhiola*
Conspicuous buff eyebrow. More of a rufous tinge than other *Locustella*. Rusty unstreaked rump. Off-white tips to all but central tail feathers. (i) Juvenile/First year non-breeding. **p. 174**

Vagrant 11. **Common Grasshopper Warbler** *Locustella naevia*
Pale, narrow eyebrow. A few dark streaks (variable) on breast, streaked undertail coverts. Plain brown tail. **p. 174**

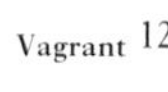

Vagrant 12. **Lanceolated Warbler** *Locustella lanceolata*
Heavy dark streaks on breast and flanks. Well defined pale fringes on dark tertials. **p. 174**

13. **Blyth's Reed Warbler** *Acrocephalus dumetorum*
Smaller and greyer than Clamorous with shortish tail. Short eyebrow. Off-white throat. **p. 175**

14. **Clamorous Reed Warbler** *Acrocephalus stentoreus meridionalis*
Larger and browner than Blyth's with pale buff throat and buff below. Relatively long bill and tail. **p. 175**

1
3
4
2
5
7
6
8
9
13
10(i)
12
14
10
11

Plate 44. Warblers

1. **Zitting Cisticola** *Cisticola juncidis*
Small with short, white-tipped, fan-shaped tail. Buff eyebrow. Dark streaks on crown and mantle. **p. 176**

2. **Grey-breasted Prinia** *Prinia hodgsonii leggei*
Typical long Prinia tail. White below with grey breast band (incomplete in female). Pinky-yellow legs. **p. 177**

3. **Plain Prinia** *Prinia subflava insularis*
Pale with dark eye-stripe and whitish eyebrow. **p. 178**

4. **Ashy Prinia** *Prinia socialis brevicauda*
Ashy grey above, buff below. Red-brown eye. **p. 177**

5. **Jungle Prinia** *Prinia sylvatica valida*
Strong bill. Short, indistinct buff eyebrow not extending beyond eye. Buff below. **p. 177**

6. **Common Tailorbird** *Orthotomus sutorius sutorius*
Rufous crown. Male has extended central tail feathers. **p. 178**

7. **Booted Warbler** *Hippolais caligata*
(i) **Sykes's Warbler** *H. c. rama:* Grey-brown upperparts with a short buff eyebrow. Buff below.
(ii) **Booted Warbler** *H. c. caligata:* Similar to *rama* but darker, more tawny upperparts, finer bill and shorter tail. **p. 176**

8. **Lesser Whitethroat** *Sylvia curruca*
Dusky grey hood and white throat. White on outer tail feathers.
(i) **Hume's Whitethroat** *S. c. althaea:* (ii) First winter.
(iii) **Lesser Whitethroat** *S. c. blythi*: Paler grey hood and warmer brown upperparts. Smaller bill than Hume's. **p. 180**

9. **Bright-green Warbler** *Phylloscopus nitidus*
Palest of possible *Phylloscopus*, each having yellowish eyebrow. Usually shows a second wing bar. (i) Autumn/first winter. (ii) Worn and faded adult, late winter. **p. 179**

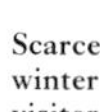

Scarce winter visitor

10. **Greenish Warbler** *Phylloscopus trochiloides viridanus*
Darker than **9**, paler than **11**. Greyish-white below, never yellow. Usually only one wing bar. **p. 179**

11. **Large-billed Leaf Warbler** *Phylloscopus magnirostris*
Stouter and darker than **9** and **10** with dark eye-stripe, bold yellowish eyebrow and larger bill. Usually shows a second wing bar. **p. 179**

1
2 ♂
2 ♀
3
4
5
6 ♀
6 ♂
7 (i)
7 (ii)
8 (iii)
8 (i)
8 (ii)
9 (i)
9 (ii)
10
11

PLATE 45. Monarchs, Paradise-flycatcher and Flycatchers

1. **Black-naped Monarch** *Hypothymis azurea ceylonensis*
Blue with black nape patch (can be erected as crest), white belly. **p. 183**

2. **Asian Paradise-flycatcher** *Terpsiphone paradisi*
(i) Sri Lanka Paradise Flycatcher. Male: blue-black hood, chestnut upperparts, and long tail. (ii) Female: shorter tail, dusky breast.
(iii) Indian Paradise Flycatcher. Male: white with blue-black hood and black and white wings. **p. 183**

3. **White-browed Fantail** *Rhipidura aureola*
Long, broad white eyebrow. Striking white tips to often fanned tail feathers. White breast and belly. **p. 184**

4. **Grey-headed Canary Flycatcher** *Culicicapa ceylonensis*
Grey hood with slight crest, white eye-ring and yellow belly. **p. 183**

5. **Kashmir Flycatcher** *Ficedula subrubra*
White eye-ring. Black tail with white side panels. Male: dark-edged rufous breast and flanks, white belly. Female: white throat, buff breast.(i) First year male: like dull adult male. **p. 181**

6. **Dull-blue Flycatcher** *Eumyias*
Dull blue-grey with brighter blue forehead, dark lores, white belly. Endemic. **p. 181**

7. **Brown-breasted Flycatcher** *Muscicapa muttui*
Rich dark brown above. All pale lower mandible. White throat with dark moustachial stripe, brown-grey tinge on breast and flanks. Flesh-coloured legs. **p. 181**

8. **Asian Brown Flycatcher** *Muscicapa dauurica*
Browny-grey above. Dark-tipped pale lower mandible, white patch on throat. Grey tinge on breast. (i) First winter: pale tips on greater coverts and well marked tertials. **p. 180**

9. **Tickell's Blue Flycatcher** *Niltava tickelliae jerdoni*
Blue above, rufous throat and breast. Female: paler with off-white throat. **p. 182**

Rare winter visitor

10. **Blue-throated Flycatcher** *Niltava rubeculoides*
Male: blue throat, deep rufous breast, white belly. Female: pale eye-ring, buff throat, pale rufous breast. **p. 182**

4
1
2(ii)
2(iii)
5♂
2(i)
5♀
6
3
5(i)
7
9♂
9♀
8(i)
10♀
10♂
8

PLATE 46. **Tit, Nuthatch, Flowerpeckers, Sunbirds and White-eyes**

1. **Great Tit** *Parus major*
Glossy black head, white cheek patch. Black centre line down belly. **p. 185**

2. **Velvet-fronted Nuthatch** *Sitta frontalis*
Bright red bill, velvet black forehead. Lavender blue above, white throat, and pinky-buff below. **p. 185**

3. **Pale-billed Flowerpecker** *Dicaeum erythrorhynchos ceylonense*
Small. Fine pointed bill. Dull olive grey above, pale grey below, no streaks on breast. **p. 187**

4. **Thick-billed Flowerpecker** *Dicaeum agile zeylonicum*
Short, stubby bill. Brown streak on sides of throat, faint brown streaks on breast. White-tipped tail feathers. **p. 186**

5. **White-throated Flowerpecker** *Dicaeum vincens*
Short, stout bill, white throat, white tips on outer tail feathers (less obvious in female). Male: dark blue-grey above. Female: grey-olive above. Endemic. **p. 186**

6. **Purple-rumped Sunbird** *Nectarinia zeylonica zeylonica*
Male: purple throat, yellow breast and belly. Glossy green crown and shoulder patch. Female: pale ashy-grey face with pale eyebrow, warm brown wings, yellow below with whitish flanks. **p. 187**

7. **Long-billed Sunbird** *Nectarinia lotenia lotenia*
Very long down-curved bill. Female: no eyebrow. Buff edged tail. Male: dark brown belly. (i) Displaying male. (ii) Eclipse male. **p. 188**

8. **Purple Súnbird** *Nectarinia asiatica*
Shorter bill than Long-billed. Female: short eyebrow, dull yellow below, white edged tail. Male: dark blue-black belly. (i) Eclipse male. **p. 189**

9. **Oriental White-eye** *Żosterops palpebrosa*
Small with fine, narrow bill. Pale yellow green above and on breast. Only narrow break at front of white eye-ring. **p. 189**

10. **Sri Lanka White-eye** *Zosterops ceylonensis*
Larger than Oriental with heavier bill, darker green above and on breast. Wide gap at front of white eye-ring. Endemic. **p. 190**

1
2
3
5♂
5♀
4
6♂
7♂
7♀
6♀
7(i)
9
7(ii)
8(i)
8♂
8♀
10

Plate 47. Munias, Sparrows and Weavers

1. **White-throated Silverbill** *Lonchura malabarica*
Appears pale. Brown and white with light rufous barring on flanks; white rump and dark brown pointed tail. **p. 190**

2. **White-rumped Munia** *Lonchura striata*
Blackish throat and breast, white belly. Blackish above with some pale streaking, white rump and dark brown pointed tail. Juvenile: browner. **p. 191**

3. **Scaly-breasted Munia** *Lonchura punctulata*
Rich chestnut face and throat. Brown and white scaled breast, belly, and flanks. Juvenile: even brown upperparts. **p. 191**

4. **Black-throated Munia** *Lonchura kelaarti kelaarti*
Black face and throat, pinky-fawn patch on sides of neck; brown and white chequered breast and belly. Black rump with white spots. **p. 191**

5. **Black-headed Munia** *Lonchura malacca*
Very large silver-blue bill. Black hood. Chestnut above; white patch on belly and flanks. Juvenile from juvenile 3 by silver-blue bill, dark lores, wings, and tail. **p. 192**

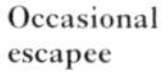

Occasional escapee

6. **Java Sparrow** *Padda oryzivora*
Large red bill, black head with obvious white cheek patch. **p. 192**

7. **House Sparrow** *Passer domesticus*
(i) Breeding male: grey crown, black bib, chestnut nape. (ii) Non-breeding male. Female: dull brown crown, pale eyebrow, dark eye-stripe. **p. 193**

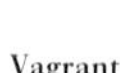

Vagrant

8. **Chestnut-shouldered Petronia** *Petronia xanthosterna*
Appears grey. Unstreaked above with chestnut shoulder patch, yellow throat (paler and smaller in female) and whitish wing bar. **p. 193**

9. **Streaked Weaver** *Ploceus manyar*
Large bill, dark brown streaks below. (i) Breeding male: yellow crown, dark brown face and throat. (ii) Female, non-breeding male and juvenile: obvious pale eyebrow. (iii) Nest. **p. 193**

10. **Baya Weaver** *Ploceus philippinus*
Large bill, unstreaked breast. (i) Breeding male: yellow crown, dark brown face paling on throat. (ii) Female, non-breeding male and juvenile: buff eyebrow. (iii) Nest. **p. 194**

1
2 juv
2
3
3 juv
4
4 juv
5 juv
5
6
7(ii)
7♀
7(i)
8♂
8♀
9(i)
9(ii)
9 (iii)
10(i)
10(ii)
10(iii)

PLATE 48. **Drongos, Starlings, Mynas and Magpie**

1. **Black Drongo** *Dicrurus macrocercus minor*
Black with long forked tail. Pale spot at base of bill. Primaries appear grey-brown in flight. (i) First year. Duller with white fringes on belly. **p. 198**

2. **Grey Drongo** *Dicrurus leucophaeus*
Slate grey with deeply forked tail. Crimson eyes. (i) First year. Dull browny-black. **p. 199**

3. **Greater Racket-tailed Drongo** *Dicrurus paradiseus*
All black with tufted crest above bill.
(i) **Racket-tailed Drongo**: *D.p. ceylonicus:* elongated tail 'rackets', small crest.
(ii) **Crested Drongo**: *D.p. lophorhinus:* long, deeply forked tail, larger crest.
(iii) First year (both races): small crest, white fringes on belly. **p. 200**

4. **White-bellied Drongo** *Dicrurus caerulescens leucopygialis*
Glossy blue-black with white on ventral area. **p. 199**

5. **Sri Lanka Magpie** *Urocissa ornata*
Bright blue with red bill, chestnut head. Long graduated white-tipped tail. Endemic. **p. 201**

6. **Brahminy Starling** *Sturnus pagodarum*
Glossy black crown and nape crest. Reddish-buff below shading to off-white vent. White-edged tail. **p. 195**

Irregular winter visitor

7. **Rosy Starling** *Sturnus roseus*
(i) Adult winter: head and neck dull slate grey with buff fringes, pinky-brown body. Immature: grey-brown with darker wings and tail. **p. 196**

Irregular winter visitor

8. **Chestnut-tailed Starling** *Sturnus malabaricus*
Streaked silver-grey head and neck. Grey mantle becoming chestnut on tail. Rufous belly. Black and grey wings. **p. 195**

9. **White-faced Starling** *Sturnus senex*
Off-white face, dark slaty grey above with white-streaked nape. Pale-streaked lavender grey below. Endemic. **p. 194**

10. **Sri Lanka Myna** *Gracula ptilogenys*
Single pair of yellow wattles on nape. Black-based orange-red bill. Pale grey eye. Endemic. **p. 196**

11. **Hill Myna** *Gracula religiosa*
Yellow wattles on crown, nape, and below brown eye. Orange-yellow bill. **p. 197**

12. **Common Myna** *Acridotheres tristis melanosturnus*
Brown with black head and yellow bill. Triangle of bare yellow skin behind eye. White wing patches and white tips on tail. **p. 196**

1
1(i)
2
3(i)
3(iii)
2(i)
3(ii)
4
5
7 juv
7(i)
6
8
9
10
11
12

FAMILY AND SPECIES DESCRIPTIONS

GREBE Order: Podicipediformes Family: Podicipedidae

MAINLY aquatic birds with pointed bills and stubby tails, the feet are lobed and the legs set at the back of the body. Grebes are expert swimmers and divers but clumsy walkers on the rare occasions when they come onto land. Flight is fast and whirring, often no more than a flutter along the surface of the water but they can fly long distances. There is only one species in Sri Lanka.

LITTLE GREBE *Tachybaptus ruficollis* PLATE 7(1)
(Dabchick) (*Podiceps ruficollis*)

Identification: (23 cm) Smallest Sri Lankan freshwater swimming bird. Breeding plumage: brown with chestnut cheeks throat and foreneck, and a small yellow-white spot at the base of the bill; non-breeding plumage: paler with whitish throat. Sexes alike. Juvenile: pale brown on back and whitish underneath with dark and white stripes on head. Rapid flight with fast wing-beats and legs trailing. Swims low in the water, diving frequently without splash. Often in flocks of a dozen or so but can be solitary. It can be distinguished from Teal and other small ducks by its smaller size, dumpiness, and short, pointed bill.

Voice: Loud whinnying descending trill and a whistling *veet-veet* contact call.

Status and distribution: Resident. Likely on all tanks and lakes in lowland, occasionally in hill country.

Nesting: A large mass of weed by water. December–February and June. Eggs covered in weed when nest left unattended.

Range: Europe, Africa, Asia.

PETRELS AND SHEARWATERS Order: Procellariiformes Family: Procellariidae

BIRDS of the open ocean, normally only coming to land to nest (although not in Sri Lanka) but occasionally straying, especially in bad weather. They have long wings, and fly using a few power strokes alternating with gliding on stiff wings.

Pterodroma species (Gadfly Petrels) fly very fast with big swoops, shearwaters often skim the waves. All swim and can rest on the surface of the sea. They feed on small fish and floating material. They have tubed nostrils on top of a strong, straight bill with a sharply hooked tip, and webbed feet. Sexes alike. Generally silent at sea unless arguing over food.

CAPE PETREL *Daption capense* — Not illustrated

(Pintado Petrel)
(Cape Pigeon)

Identification: (39 cm) Unmistakable. Rather pigeon-like with black head, black dappled white upperparts, white rump and black terminal band on tail; white underparts. Bill and legs black. Sexes and juveniles alike. Stiff winged flight with several wingbeats alternating with glides. Takes food from surface of sea, occasionally diving. Gregarious. Often follows ships.
Status and distribution: Vagrant. One record off north-west coast in 1870.
Range: Southern oceans.

WHITE-HEADED PETREL *Pterodroma lessonii* — PLATE 1 (1)

Identification: (43 cm) White head and belly with black eye-patch, dark underwing, and whitish tail. Pale grey collar and back, white rump and uppertail coverts, blackish upperwing. Sexes and juveniles alike. Typical 'gadfly' flight. Rarely follows ships.
Status and distribution: Possible vagrant. Three unconfirmed sightings off west coast in September 1990.
Range: Southern oceans.

SOFT-PLUMAGED PETREL *Pterodroma mollis* — PLATE 1 (3)

Identification: (34 cm) White underparts with variable grey breast band and grey patterned dark underwings. Forehead and crown grey-brown, black eye-patch, chin and throat white. Sexes and juveniles alike. A rare all-dark form exists. Typical 'gadfly' flight but rather erratic. Sometimes follows ships.
Status and distribution: Possible vagrant. A few unconfirmed sightings in September 1988 off west coast.
Range: Atlantic and southern Indian Oceans eastwards to south of New Zealand, not in south-east Pacific.

BARAU'S PETREL *Pterodroma baraui* — PLATE 1 (2)

Identification: (38 cm) Sturdy with stubby neck, short stout bill, and distinctive underwing pattern. White forehead and dark cap, mantle and upper back appear grey; lower back, rump, and upper tail dark grey; white underparts with distinctive thin black lines across underwing coverts and black flight feathers, under tail has dark tip. Upperwing dark grey showing 'M' pattern across wings. Sexes and juveniles alike. Typical gadfly flight. Rarely follows ships.

Status and distribution: Vagrant. A few records off west coast in most recent years.

Range: Southern Indian Ocean.

BULWER'S PETREL *Bulweria bulwerii* PLATE 1 (6)

Identification: (27 cm) All sooty brown with pale diagonal upperwing bar. Sexes and juveniles alike. Buoyant flight with few wingbeats then glides, close to surface of sea on long wings. Pointed tail, wedge-shaped when turning. Rarely follows ships. Smaller than Jouanin's and has shorter bill and smaller head, also tends to fly lower.

Status and distribution: Vagrant to west, south-west, and south-east coastal waters.

Range: Atlantic, Indian, and Pacific Oceans.

JOUANIN'S PETREL *Bulweria fallax* PLATE 1 (5)

Identification: (30 cm) All brown-black, larger than Bulwer's, with larger head, sturdier bill, broader wings with little or no wing bar. Pointed tail. Sexes and juveniles alike. Strong flight usually at about 15m above surface like a small gadfly petrel. Smaller and sturdier than the Wedge-tailed Shearwater with faster looping flight. Rarely follows ships.

Status and distribution: Vagrant. A few records off west and south coasts, mainly in June.

Range: Open seas from Arabian Sea to Madagascan coast.

STREAKED SHEARWATER *Calonectris leucomelas* PLATE 1 (4)
(White-faced Shearwater) (*Puffinus leucomelas*)
(White-fronted Shearwater)

Identification: (48 cm) Large, grey brown above with whitish face, dark streaked crown, mostly white underwing. Small, slender head with long, thin bill. Browny-grey upperparts, some with whitish band on uppertail coverts; white below with distinctive underwing pattern and dark tip to tail. Pale brown bill with grey tip. Sexes and juveniles alike. Flight slow and effortless, normally low over waves. Often in flocks.

Status and distribution: Vagrant. A few records off west, south and east coasts.

Range: NW Pacific but occasionally in Indian Ocean.

FLESH-FOOTED SHEARWATER *Puffinus carneipes* PLATE 1 (7)
(Pale-footed Shearwater)

Identification: (43 cm) All brown-black, underwing appears dark. Bill horn-coloured with upper ridge and tip black. Flesh pink legs and feet. Sturdier than Wedge-tailed Shearwater and with relatively shorter, rounder tail and pale bill. Larger than both Sooty and Short-tailed and with darker underwing, paler bill, legs, and feet. Sexes and immatures alike. Flies with slow wingbeats and long glides on broad (broader than Sooty), stiff wings. Feeds from surface dipping feet in water, mainly at night. Also dives from surface or by plunging.
Status and distribution: Passage migrant and vagrant. Southerly passage off west coast, June–July, and northerly passage September–October.
Range: Indian and Pacific Oceans.

WEDGE-TAILED SHEARWATER *Puffinus pacificus* PLATE 1 (11)
(Green-billed Shearwater) (*Puffinus chlororhynchus*)

Identification: (43 cm) Long tail only wedge-shaped when turning, normally pointed (beware of moulting birds with short, broad tails). Two morphs: dark: all dark brown with black primaries and tail; rarer pale morph: white on under-parts, underwing white with brown edges. Dark grey bill with pale oval cheek patch, pale pink legs and feet. Sexes and juveniles alike. Distinguish from Flesh-footed Shearwater by more slender build, longer tail, and darker bill. Flies low over waves with slow flaps and glides on broad-based stiff wings.
Status and distribution: Visitor to coastal waters. Most records in summer off west and south coasts.
Range: Tropical areas of Indian and Pacific Oceans.

SOOTY SHEARWATER *Puffinus griseus* PLATE 1 (9)

Identification: (44 cm) Dark brown with sturdy body and long thin wings, often appearing swept-back. Look for conspicuous whitish flashes on under-wing coverts, and dark feet. Longer bill and tail than in Short-tailed. Sexes and juveniles alike. Fast and direct flight, a couple of wingbeats then glides. Attracted to fishing boats, forms large flocks.
Status and distribution: Vagrant mainly to eastern waters. Flock recorded off north-east coast November 1974.
Range: Mainly southern but wanders to most of the oceans.

SHORT-TAILED SHEARWATER *Puffinus tenuirostris* PLATE 1 (8)
(Slender-billed Shearwater)

Identification: (42 cm) Resembles Sooty Shearwater. Dark brown, paler below with grey underwing coverts (not whitish flashes as in Sooty); bill is shorter and legs extend beyond short tail. Crown nearly black with pale chin sometimes giving hooded appearance. Sexes and juveniles alike. Flies fast with stiff-winged glides. Forms flocks. Sometimes follows ships.

Status and distribution: Vagrant. One record from south-east coast, May 1949. One off Colombo 1994.

Range: From seas south and east of Australia to North Pacific.

AUDUBON'S SHEARWATER *Puffinus lherminieri* PLATE 1 (10)

(Dusky Shearwater)

Identification: (30 cm) Small and sturdy with broad wings. White underparts with flesh-coloured legs contrasting with dark undertail coverts. Sexes and immatures alike. Flight fast and whirring between glides, close to surface. Feeds pattering across surface and diving. Forms flocks.

Status and distribution: Vagrant. One record off south-east coast in 1982; another 13 km off west coast in 1994.

Range: Tropical oceans.

STORM-PETRELS

Order: Procellariiformes
Family: Hydrobatidae

SMALL oceanic birds normally only coming to land to nest (not in Sri Lanka) although sometimes driven ashore in bad weather. The nostrils are fused into a single tube on the top of the bill. Sexes alike. Feed from surface of sea. Rarely vocal at sea. Generally a difficult group to identify. Only two species have so far been recorded in Sri Lanka.

WILSON'S STORM-PETREL *Oceanites oceanicus* PLATE 1 (12)

Identification: (18 cm) Dark brown-black and rather swallow-like with a conspicuous curved white band on rump extending onto sides of undertail coverts, a pale bar on upperwing and variable faint pale bar on underwing. Short, triangular wings (broader than Swinhoe's) with very little bend at the wrist and a nearly straight trailing edge. Long legs project beyond square tail when in full flight. Yellow webs on feet only visible when close. Sexes and immatures alike. Flutters just above the sea, often with feet pattering the water, picking food from the surface. Follows ships, sometimes in flocks.

Status and distribution: Regular visitor to coastal waters, more likely off the south and west coasts, June–November.

Range: Southern oceans, tropical seas, and Atlantic, north to 60°.

SWINHOE'S STORM-PETREL *Oceanodroma monorhis* PLATE 1 (13)
(Ashy Storm-petrel)

Identification: (20 cm) All dark brown-black, no white rump, a pale bar on upper surface of longer and narrower wings than Wilson's, with a greater angle at the wrist, and greyish tinge on underwing coverts. Forked tail, not always easy to see. Feet do not project beyond tail in flight. Sexes and immatures alike. Flies faster and higher than Wilson's swooping to surface with an erratic flight of wing beats and glides. Rarely follows ships.
Status and distribution: Vagrant (six sightings to date).
Range: West Pacific, Indian Ocean, and Red Sea.

TROPICBIRDS Order: Pelecaniformes Family: Phaethontidae

MAINLY white marine birds looking rather like sturdy terns. Wedge-shaped tails with, in adults, very long central tail streamers. Bill strong and sharply pointed. Short legs with webbed feet barely adequate for walking. Sexes alike and no seasonal plumage changes. Strong easy flight, plunging into sea to catch small fish or squid. Swim with tail held up. Confident, even inquisitive, flying very close to passers-by. Sometimes follow ships. Usually, but not always, solitary away from breeding area. Only three species world-wide, two of which might appear over Sri Lankan waters. Juveniles have no tail-streamers and are difficult to identify.

RED-BILLED TROPICBIRD *Phaethon aethereus* PLATE 2 (1)
(Short-tailed Tropicbird)

Identification: (98 cm. including 50 cm. of tail streamers) Red bill, barred upperparts, black outer primary coverts and long white tail-streamers. Nape and upper parts finely barred with black but appear white from a distance. White underwing. Sexes alike but male has longer streamers. Juvenile: similar to adult but has broad black eye-stripe continuing behind to meet on nape, more barred upperparts, the black on outer wing extends onto primary coverts, a yellowy-orange bill with blackish tip and no tail streamers. Steady and direct flight with slower wingbeats and broader wings than White-tailed.
Voice: A loud, harsh scream.
Status and distribution: Regular non-breeding summer visitor to south-west coastal waters.
Range: Mainly confined to tropics of Atlantic and Indian Oceans, and seas around America.

WHITE-TAILED TROPICBIRD *Phaethon lepturus* PLATE 2 (2)
(Yellow-billed Tropicbird) (*Phaethon flavirostris*)
(Long-tailed Tropicbird)

Identification: (77 cm including 45 cm of streamers) Yellow bill and obvious diagonal black patches across secondary coverts, and white wing tips on upperwings. Long white tail-streamers and yellow-orange bill. Sexes alike. Juvenile; smaller black patch on primaries than Red-billed, broad barring on upperparts (coarser than on juv. Red-billed), yellow bill with black tip and the eye-stripe does not continue behind the eye. Flight graceful and more buoyant on narrower wings and with faster wingbeats than Red-billed.
Voice: Generally silent at sea.
Status and distribution: Uncommon visitor to west and south coastal waters, possible all year but most likely March–July.
Range: Tropical seas.

PELICANS Order: Pelecaniformes Family: Pelecanidae

VERY large, sturdy birds that have long flattened bills with large pouches used when fishing. Broad wings, short tail, and short, strong legs with webbed feet. Strong and graceful flight, heavy flaps alternating with long glides, the neck curved and the head held back, also often soaring. Usually need a long run across water to take off. Swim well but are ungainly on land with waddling gait. Normally feed early in day then bathe, preen, and rest for long periods. Plumage can vary considerably, often with pink tinges, causing difficulty in identification.

GREAT WHITE PELICAN *Pelecanus onocrotalus* PLATE 3 (2)
(Eastern White Pelican)

Identification: (155 cm) Very large. White with black flight feathers and pink feet. Facial skin: pinkish yellow in male; can be orange in female. Breeding plumage: small crest, yellow patch on lower foreneck and variable pink flush on body, legs tinged with crimson. Distinguish from the Spot-billed by whiter plumage, lead-blue bill with red edges lacking dark spots, pouch colour and black flight feathers. Juvenile: whitish forehead, mottled brown upperparts with white rump and tail; off-white below with brown edges to wings. Legs and feet grey. Larger and generally darker than juvenile Spot-billed. Typical pelican flight. Gregarious.
Voice: Likely to be silent in Sri Lanka.

Status and distribution: Possible vagrant. One unconfirmed sight record at Yala. Normal habitat—fresh water.
Range: SE Europe, parts of Africa, C and SE Asia.

SPOT-BILLED PELICAN *Pelecanus philippensis* PLATE 3 (1)
(Grey Pelican) (*Pelecanus roseus*)

Identification: (145 cm) Smaller than Great White with grey-brown flight feathers and brown legs. Pale fleshy-yellow bill with row of dark spots on upper mandible and an orange tip, flesh-pink pouch with blue spots. Yellow-grey bare skin around eye. Breeding plumage: small brown crest and pink tinges on lower back, flanks, vent, and tail coverts. Sexes alike. Juvenile: brown on head, mantle, and tail. Prefers to fish in shallows sweeping the bill through the water, usually in quite large flocks. Typical pelican flight, often in formation. Swims with wings held high.
Voice: Generally silent but croaks and grunts at nest.
Status and distribution: Resident. On larger tanks or coastal lagoons in dry zone and occasionally in the wet zone. Not in hill country.
Nesting: Colonially, on large bundles of sticks high in trees not far from water; March–May.
Range: Iran, S and SE Asia to Philippines.

BOOBIES — Order: Pelecaniformes Family: Sulidae

LARGE, marine birds which plunge from a height to catch fish. Their bills are strong and pointed; wings long and narrow; tails wedge-shaped. Legs are short with large webbed feet. The sexes are alike. Adulthood is reached after 2–3 years. Flight is direct with several wing-flaps then glide. They tend to fish in flocks. Colonial nesting but none nests in Sri Lanka.

MASKED BOOBY *Sula dactylatra* PLATE 2 (3)
(Masked Gannet)
(Blue-faced Booby)

Identification: (85 cm) Largest of the boobies. Look for white head with blue-grey facial skin appearing as black face mask, black tail and black flight-feathers forming broad band across hindwing. Juvenile; brown head, neck, and upper-parts, with a white collar and a thin black stripe behind leading edge of under-wing; the white collar broadens, the white rump and other white areas extend with maturity. The white collar distinguishes juvenile from adult Brown Booby. Typical booby flight; fishing by plunging nearly vertically.
Voice: A bi-syllabic honk.

Status and distribution: Vagrant to coastal waters. Records from east and west coasts.
Range: Tropical oceans.

RED-FOOTED BOOBY *Sula sula* PLATE 2 (4)

Identification: (71 cm) Occurs in various morphs, all with red feet and a pale blue bill with a pinkish base. White morph has similar plumage to Masked but has a black carpal patch on underwing and white tail. Brown morph is uniform brown (juv. Brown has darker head and pale underwing). See Plate 2 for other morphs. Juvenile: brown with dark brown bill, purple facial skin and yellow-grey legs. Strong flight with regular wingbeats, often in line formation low over the sea. Follows and sometimes perches on ships.
Status and distribution: Vagrant to coastal waters. Three records to date.
Range: Tropical seas.

BROWN BOOBY *Sula leucogaster* PLATE 2 (5)
(Brown Gannet)

Identification: (70 cm) Adult similar to immature Masked but lacks the white collar and shows different underwing pattern. Head, neck, upperparts, and tail brown. Bill and facial skin yellowish, legs and feet yellow-green. Juvenile: like a pale adult but with underparts, buff-brown paling with maturity; bill and facial skin grey. Gregarious, often flying low and in long straggling lines.
Status and distribution: Vagrant to coastal waters.
Range: Tropical oceans.

CORMORANTS

Order: Pelecaniformes
Family: Phalacrocoracidae

MEDIUM to large mainly black aquatic birds that dive and pursue their fish prey underwater. They have long bills hooked at the tips, long necks, medium length tails and webbed feet. Cormorants sit low in the water with their heads up at an angle, lifting themselves up before diving. After feeding, they usually leave the water, often perching with wings held out. They are strong fliers, flying with fast wingbeats and necks extended, often in line or V formation but need a run across water to get airborne. Gregarious, nesting and roosting colonially in trees near water. Sexes alike. Adult plumage is assumed in 2–3 years. Generally silent but have a range of croaks, grunts, and gargling calls at nest or roost. Size is important in identification.

GREAT CORMORANT *Phalacrocorax carbo* PLATE 3 (3)

Identification: (80 cm) Largest cormorant. Usually has yellow or orange facial skin. Mainly black with greeny-blue sheen, a white cheek and throat patch, and grey bill with yellow pouch. There is a slight crest. Breeding plumage: brighter sheen, white patch on thigh and white plumes on the head and neck. Juvenile: crown and neck streaked with brown, white underparts. Second year birds become blacker and lose the white belly. Strong, direct flight, usually low over water, higher over land.

Status and distribution: Rare breeding resident supplemented by winter visitors, sometimes in large numbers. Common on larger dry zone tanks and lagoons in north, less common in south.

Nesting: Platforms of sticks colonially in trees, December–February.

Range: Europe, S Asia, S Africa, Australia, and E coast of N America.

INDIAN CORMORANT *Phalacrocorax fuscicollis* PLATE 3 (5)

(Indian Shag)

Identification: (64 cm) Between Great and Little in size with variable colour facial skin, lacks the white on cheeks of Great. Bigger and sleeker than Little with a long, thin brown bill and a scaly back. Mainly black with a greenish sheen. Wings have a black and brown scaly pattern and the throat is variably speckled white. Brown bill. Breeding plumage: small tuft of white behind the ear-coverts and no speckles on throat. Juvenile: off-white underparts. Sexes alike. Very gregarious.

Status and distribution: Resident. Common on larger tanks in dry zone, moving to smaller ones when fish are short. Less common in wet zone lowlands and lower hills. Prefers fresh water.

Nesting: Colonially on platforms of sticks in trees. October–April.

Range: India and SE Asia.

LITTLE CORMORANT *Phalacrocorax niger* PLATE 3 (4)

(Javanese Cormorant)

Identification: (51 cm) Smallest and commonest of the local cormorants. Smaller than Indian, has shorter, deep-based bill giving it an almost conical head, a relatively long tail and lacks a scaly back. Dull black with white throat, short brown bill with purple base and black tip. Bare skin on face, throat and legs black. Breeding plumage: black with bright greenish sheen, a small tufted crest on the forehead, no white on throat, some white plumes on head and neck, and bare skin on face, throat and legs becomes purple. Juvenile: off-white throat and breast. Direct flight with fast wingbeats. Highly gregarious.

Status and distribution: Very common resident on any fair sized stretch of water in low country, even in paddy, but most numerous in dry zone. Uncommon visitor to hills.

Nesting: Colonially on piles of sticks in trees at edges of tanks. November–May.
Range: India and SE Asia.

DARTER Order: Pelecaniformes Family: Anhingidae

CORMORANT-LIKE, aquatic birds with sharp-pointed bills, long thin necks and longer, more rounded tails than the cormorants.

ORIENTAL DARTER *Anhinga melanogaster* PLATE 3 (6)

(Indian Darter)
(Snakebird)

Identification: (92 cm) Large with very long thin kinked neck. Very thin, pointed bill, short legs, and large feet. Juvenile: mainly brown with pale head and neck, buff and white streaks on back and wing coverts. Sits very low in water with only head, neck, and a bit of mantle showing looking like a snake. Dives by just disappearing below surface. Strong flight with brisk wingbeats and glides, and neck extended showing a bulge at the kink; soars high.
Status and distribution: Resident. Common in tanks and rivers of low country dry zone. Rarely in wet zone or in hills. Not normally in brackish or salt water.
Voice: Generally silent but has a hoarse croak.
Nesting: Colonially on piles of sticks in trees near water, December–March.
Range: S Africa, Middle East, India, SE Asia, Australia.

FRIGATEBIRDS Order: Pelecaniformes Family: Fregatidae

LARGE, dark with green sheen, marine birds with very long, angular wings and deeply forked tails. Bills are long and hooked at the tip, legs short and little used except for perching as they are unable to swim and barely able to walk. Breeding male has large inflatable throat pouch for display. Spend most of the daylight hours in high, soaring flight, swooping down to take marine life from the sea's surface or pirating the catches of other seabirds. Nest and roost colonially in trees on remote islands but not in Sri Lanka. Generally silent away from breeding areas. Sexually dimorphic, immatures taking up to six years to reach adulthood. Identification is very difficult with many plumage variations. Take note of shape and extent of white areas on undersides. For fuller details *Seabirds: an identification guide* by P. Harrison is recommended.

CHRISTMAS ISLAND FRIGATEBIRD *Fregata andrewsi* PLATE 2 (6)

Identification: (94 cm) Male: white patch on lower belly, a pale brown bar across upperwing coverts, blackish bill, legs, and orbital ring. Female: brown-black on upperside with a narrow white collar and the pale bar on wing coverts, white 'star' on belly and axillaries. Pink bill and orbital ring, pale flesh legs. First year birds have dark brown upperparts with pale bar on wing coverts, buff head, white axillary spurs with dark band across breast and white belly. Many variations between first year and adult plumages but all have pale bellies darkening with maturity. Typical frigatebird flight.

Status and distribution: Vagrant to western coastal waters.

Range: Breeds only on Christmas Island (south of Java), wanders Indian Ocean.

GREAT FRIGATEBIRD *Fregata minor* PLATE 2 (7)

Identification: (92 cm) No axillary spurs in any form. Male: mostly black with a green sheen, brown bar across median wing coverts, no white on underwing. Red legs and feet, blue-black bill and black orbital ring. Female: white throat and upper breast, pink orbital ring and legs. First year bird has yellow-white head and breast, dark brown upperside with pale wing bar, dark breast band and white belly patch, the white darkening with maturity. Typical frigatebird flight.

Status and distribution: Vagrant to south and west coastal waters in south-west monsoon.

Range: Tropical oceans.

LESSER FRIGATEBIRD *Fregata ariel* PLATE 2 (8)
(Small Frigatebird)

Identification: (76 cm) Male: white patches on sides of belly and axillaries, dark grey bill, black orbital ring, dark reddy-brown legs and feet. Female: black head and throat, white breast and axillary spur showing a V on the belly, mauve-blue bill, pink orbital ring, legs and feet. First year: rusty head, brown upperparts with pale bar on wing coverts, underside dark brown with variable white breast patch and axillary spurs, sometimes with a dark breast band. Many variations between first year and full adult plumage. Typical frigatebird flight.

Status and distribution: Vagrant to south and west coastal waters, mainly during south-west monsoon.

Range: Indian Ocean and W Pacific.

HERONS, EGRETS, AND BITTERNS

Order: Ciconiiformes
Family: Ardeidae

MEDIUM to large, long necked wading birds with broad, rounded wings and long, straight pointed bills; at rest the head is often hunched back onto the shoulders. They feed by stealth, often standing motionless in water or marsh then thrusting their head down to catch passing fish, crab, frog, or other small animal which is swallowed whole, often with much gulping. Flight is slow with rhythmic wing beats and head drawn back, legs trailing. Herons and egrets nest colonially and roost communally in trees or scrub near water, bitterns are solitary. Sexes alike in herons and egrets.

GREY HERON *Ardea cinerea* PLATE 4 (3)

Identification: (95 cm) White, grey and black heron; can be distinguished from Purple Heron by white head and neck, paler general colouring with no rufous on body, stockier build and thicker, less snake-like neck. Black band from above eye onto crest. Juvenile: dark grey crown, no crest, and more uniformly grey. Flight slow with heavy wingbeats showing contrast between black flight feathers and pale grey coverts. Most active at dawn and dusk. Feeds solitarily or in groups, often in open areas.

Voice: A *kraaaak* in flight, bill clapping at nest.

Status and distribution: Resident. Common around tanks, lagoons, and marshy areas in dry zone. Rarely in wet zone or in lower hills.

Nesting: Colonially on large piles of sticks in trees near water; December–April.

Range: Europe, Africa, Madagascar, Asia.

GOLIATH HERON *Ardea goliath* PLATE 4 (1)
(Giant Heron)

Identification: (140 cm) Largest heron. Much larger than Purple Heron with darker bill, brown crown, plain grey upperwing, dark chestnut underwing, and dark grey legs. **Juvenile**: browner above and generally paler. Flight slow and heavy. Rather inactive and solitary when feeding, stands still waiting for prey.

Voice: Deep raucous squawks and grunts.

Status: Vagrant to marshes, lagoons, shores, near fresh or salt water in dry lowlands.

Range: W, E, and S Africa.

PURPLE HERON *Ardea purpurea* PLATE 4 (2)

Identification: (85 cm) Black crown extending to crest, back of neck rufous with black streaks. Generally a smaller, slighter, and darker bird than the Grey Heron, with a more slender and angular neck. Sexes alike apart from female having shorter crest. Juvenile: more evenly rufous with pale fringed scaly mantle and wing coverts. Slow flight on narrower wings than Grey, showing little contrast between brown and grey flight feathers and wing coverts, with obvious projecting long-toed feet. Often feeds by skulking in cover. Most active at dawn and dusk. Shy and usually solitary away from nest.
Voice: Loud, harsh *kraaak* higher pitched than Grey.
Status and distribution: Resident. Common in marshes, lagoons, and paddy in wet and dry zones. Does not normally stray far from cover.
Nesting: In small colonies with other species on piles of sticks and reeds in bushes or scrub in wet areas; December–February and May–June.
Range: S Europe, Africa, Madagascar, and S Asia.

GREAT EGRET *Casmerodius albus* PLATE 4 (6)
(Large Egret) (*Egretta alba*)
(Great White Egret)

Identification: (91 cm) Large white heron, distinguishable from all other white egrets by much larger size, relatively long bill, and gape line extending behind eye. Breeding plumage: black bill with yellow base, green facial skin, dull black tibia and tarsus (may turn pinky-purple during courtship), and a train of filmy white plumes on the back projecting beyond the tail. Non-breeding plumage: yellow bill, yellow-green facial skin, and brownish tibia. Neck more angular than in other white egrets. No crest. Strong flight with even slow wingbeats, the neck drawn back when fully airborne. Often stands very erect with neck extended. Shy. Solitary or in small flocks with other herons.
Voice: Generally silent but has a low *kraaa*.
Status and distribution: Resident. Common on edges of tanks, lagoons, and paddy in low country.
Nesting: A shallow platform of sticks in a tree by water with others of the heron family; December–May.
Range: South-eastern Europe, Africa, Asia, Australia, southern USA to S America.

INTERMEDIATE EGRET *Mesophoyx intermedia* PLATE 4 (5)
(Median Egret) (*Egretta intermedia*)
(Plumed Egret)

Identification: (66 cm) Smaller than Great but not much larger than Little Egret, bill relatively shorter and less pointed than Great and gape line not extending behind eye, neck curve less angular than in Great. More slender than the dumpy Cattle with longer and more slender bill. No crest. Breeding plumage: yellow bill with dusky tip turning black briefly during courtship, yellow-green facial skin, white plumes on back extending beyond tail and shorter plumes on breast. Non-breeding plumage: yellow bill with dusky tip, variable dark green to brown legs and feet (cf. Little Egret), yellowish facial skin. Usually feeds in small groups.

Voice: Generally silent.

Status and distribution: Resident. Common in wet paddy and marsh in most of low country and the lower hills. Not in the north.

Nesting: Colonially with other herons on platforms of sticks in trees near water; December–May.

Range: Africa, S Asia, New Guinea, Australia.

LITTLE EGRET *Egretta garzetta* — PLATE 4 (7)

Identification: (64 cm) From Intermediate by black legs and yellow feet, and black bill, and slightly smaller size. (Bill can be greyish especially in immatures but not yellow.) From Cattle Egret by black bill and legs. Greeny-yellow facial skin. Breeding plumage: two plumes on the nape, a tuft of plumes on the breast, and more on the back which just project beyond the tail. Feet and facial skin briefly turn pinky-red during courtship. Steady flight on broad rounded wings. Gregarious. More approachable than other egrets.

Voice: A harsh *kraaaak* at nest.

Status and distribution: Resident in low country paddy, lagoons, tank edges, and marshes. Commoner in dry zone and coastal areas but not normally on seashore.

Nesting: Colonially on platforms of sticks in trees near water; December–May.

Range: Southern Europe, Africa, Madagascar, Asia, New Guinea, N Australia.

WESTERN REEF EGRET *Egretta gularis* — PLATE 4 (8)
(Indian Reef Heron) (*Egretta garzetta schistacea*)
(*Demigretta asha*)

Note: There is debate as to whether this and the Little Egret are separate species or races of *E. garzetta*. Here they are treated as separate species.

Identification: (64 cm) Occurs in various morphs, from all grey with white throat through intermediate forms to white with grey patches. White morph sturdier than Little, has more square head and heavier, stouter less pointed bill which can appear slightly decurved. Bill colour is variable; horny brown with some yellow on base of lower mandible, or yellow in dark morph; facial skin yellowish turning greenish in breeding season. Legs as in Little but relatively short greeny-black tarsi (paler than Little), yellowy-brown toes in dark morph and yellow-green in white morph. Habits similar to those of Little with which it associates but more coastal in habitat preference.

Voice: Generally silent but can croak.

Status and distribution: Has bred but no recent records. Now a scarce winter visitor to coastal lagoons and shores, mainly in the north.

Nesting: On a mass of twigs in tree or scrub; May.

Range: N Africa, Middle East, India.

CATTLE EGRET *Bubulcus ibis* PLATE 4 (9)

Identification: (51 cm) From non-breeding Intermediate by smaller size and sturdy build, shorter stout bill, dark olive-grey tibia and feet. From non-breeding Little Egret by stout yellow bill, deep-jowled appearance, sturdier build and slightly off-white plumage. During breeding season the bill becomes more orange, head and neck turn golden-buff, golden dorsal plumes develop and feet become reddish-orange. Flies in parties especially to and from sometimes large communal roosts. Often feeds alongside grazing cattle on the small animals that it disturbs, also scavenges on rubbish. Sometimes perches on cattle. Gregarious. Not shy.

Voice: Generally silent but croaks at nest.

Status and distribution: Common resident wherever cattle graze in low country and lower hills, not confined to wet areas.

Nesting: Colonially on platforms of twigs in trees; December–May.

Range: S Europe, N and C Africa, Asia, Americas.

INDIAN POND HERON *Ardeola grayii* PLATE 5 (1)

(Pond Heron)

Identification: (46 cm) Smallish dark-looking heron commonly seen standing at the edge of water with head hunched on shoulders watching for passing fish or frogs. Bill greenish yellow with dark tip, legs and feet dull green turning yellow or pink in breeding season. Non-breeding and juvenile have streaked head and breast. In flight the rapid wingbeats of white wings and the white tail and white belly are obvious. Solitary during day, forming flocks on way to and from roost. Not shy.

Voice: *Krake* alarm call; various harsh notes at nest.

Status and distribution: Very common resident almost anywhere on water's edge or marsh.

Nesting: Colonially on untidy piles of twigs in trees; December–August.

Range: Middle East, S Asia.

CHINESE POND HERON *Ardeola bacchus* PLATE 5 (2)

Identification: (52 cm) Very similar to Indian Pond in non-breeding plumages but a little larger, more brown and buff on the head and neck, and browner on the back and scapulars. Breeding plumage: head, neck, and long crest chestnut, dark slaty grey back and scapulars, chin and throat white, breast plumes deep chestnut with black tips, rest of body and wings white with brown tips to last few outer primaries.
Status and distribution: Vagrant. First record 1995 in south-east.
Range: China, SE Asia.

STRIATED HERON *Butorides striatus* PLATE 5 (3)
(Little Green Heron)
(Little Heron)
(Green-backed Heron)

Identification: (44 cm) Smaller than Indian Pond and appears generally dark. Glossy black crown with crest. Upper mandible brown, lower one green, darker in breeding season. Juvenile smaller than juvenile Black-crowned Night Heron and has darker crown. Leisurely bobbing flight on wings bent down at wrist. Solitary feeder often with head hunched on shoulders, keeping close to cover. Most active dawn and dusk.
Voice: Alarm call: *kyek-kyek*.
Status and distribution: Common resident in coastal areas, river banks, tank edges of low country, also in lower hills, where cover adjoins water.
Nesting: Platform of twigs low in tree; March–July.
Range: Most of tropics, world-wide.

BLACK-CROWNED NIGHT HERON *Nycticorax nycticorax* PLATE 5 (4)
(Night Heron)

Identification: (58 cm) Stocky. Only Sri Lankan heron with black mantle, pale grey underparts and grey flanks. Breeding plumage: white plumes from rear of crown and the yellowish legs turn red. Juvenile has paler crown than Striated juvenile and has heavy spotting on mantle. Second year birds are closer to adult plumage but greyer on crown and back, variably streaked on underparts. Slow mechanical wingbeats on rounded wings. Usually stands with head hunched on shoulders. Nocturnal, spending the day roosting communally in trees sometimes in towns, but active during the day in the nesting season.
Voice: Hoarse croaks of alarm. *Kwark* contact call in flight.
Status and distribution: Resident in low country, preferring rivers, mangrove fringed lagoons, tree-covered islands.

Nesting: Platform of sticks below tree canopy; December–March and August–September.
Range: Most of tropics, world-wide.

MALAYAN NIGHT HERON *Gorsachius melanolophus* PLATE 5 (5)
(Malay Bittern)
(Tiger Bittern)

Identification: (51 cm) Short, stout bill. Mostly it is the juvenile that is seen in Sri Lanka; black with white tips on crown and nape crest, fine buff barring on dark wings and scapulars (much more so than on juvenile Black-crowned and lacking its whitish spots). Adult: black crown and long nape crest, chestnut upperparts; white below with black streaked sandy fore-neck and upper breast, black and rufous spots on lower breast and belly. Flies, usually briefly, with fast wingbeats. Shy, generally staying in cover during day becoming active at dusk clambering about the branches.
Voice: Generally silent.
Status and distribution: Scarce winter visitor. Arrives on west coast in October–November immediately going to the forests up to 1800 m.
Range: India, SE Asia.

YELLOW BITTERN *Ixobrychus sinensis* PLATE 5 (6)
(Chinese Little Bittern)

Identification: (36 cm) Slender. Paler than the Cinnamon with slaty-black flight-feathers and dark slaty tail. Male has dark crown. Often raises ragged crest. Juvenile paler than Cinnamon and wing coverts much less clearly marked. Nocturnal and crepuscular but can be active in day. Clambers about waterside vegetation, waving slaty tail from side to side, often raising and opening a wing showing black flight feathers. 'Freezes' in true bittern style with bill pointed to the sky when alarmed. Solitary or in pairs. Not shy.
Voice: Generally silent but has a *kak-kak-kak* flight call.
Status and distribution: Resident, supplemented by winter visitors, in reed-beds and waterside vegetation up to 1000 m.
Nesting: A platform of reed stems low in reeds or marshy grass; May–August.
Range: E and S Asia, Japan.

CINNAMON BITTERN *Ixobrychus cinnamomeus* PLATE 5 (7)
(Chestnut Bittern)

Identification: (38 cm) Slightly sturdier than the Yellow and generally darker but lacks contrasting dark flight feathers. White 'moustache' on throat. Male has uniform chestnut upperparts, female has spotting on wing and dark crown. Juvenile darker than Yellow juvenile. Much smaller than Indian Pond Heron. Has some buff-edged black feathers on sides of upper-breast which are normally concealed by breast plumage. All forms appear uniformly cinnamon-coloured in flight. Solitary or in pairs. More likely in grassy marshes than Yellow. Shy. Partly nocturnal.

Voice: A low croak flight alarm call and a quiet *kokokoko*.

Status and distribution: Resident in marshes and reed beds throughout.

Nesting: Pad of grass hidden in reeds or tussocks; June–July.

Range: India, China, Philippines.

BLACK BITTERN *Ixobrychus flavicollis* (*Dupetor flavicollis*) PLATE 5 (8)

Identification: (58 cm) Long dagger-like bill. Dark with characteristic buff-shading-to-white stripe on sides of neck. Male: black with white streaks on throat and breast. Female: generally browner. Juvenile: like female with pale fringes on mantle. Mainly nocturnal but active at dusk. Shy and skulking, climbing in dense vegetation, 'freezing' with neck extended when alarmed. Solitary or in pairs.

Voice: Deep boom in breeding season and croaking flight call.

Status and distribution: Resident, supplemented by winter visitors. Fairly common in marshes and densely vegetated waterside areas in lowlands and lower hills.

Nesting: Small heap of twigs in cover by water; SW monsoon.

Range: India, China, SE Asia, New Guinea, Australia.

EURASIAN BITTERN *Botaurus stellaris* PLATE 4 (4)
(Great Bittern)

Identification: (72 cm) Large and stocky with large feet. Dark crown and moustache, white throat. Sexes alike. Flight has faster wingbeats than heron's on broad, owl-like rounded wings. Generally stays in cover clambering about the vegetation. Often stands head hunched but 'freezes' with neck extended when alarmed. Solitary, nocturnal, and crepuscular.

Voice: Usually silent in Sri Lanka but has a hoarse *kaaark* flight call and a deep boom when breeding.

Status and distribution: Vagrant to marshes and wet areas with cover in lowlands.

Range: Europe, Africa, Asia.

STORKS Order: Ciconiiformes Family: Ciconiidae

VERY large birds with long necks and long bills, more sturdily built than the herons. Wings long and broad, long legs and short tails. Powerful flight with slow wingbeats and glides, neck and legs extended (not Lesser Adjutant which flies with neck held back), often soaring to great height, commonly with other species. Will squat with feet extended in front. Almost mute but clap bills and make various grunts and moans in display. Sexes alike. Gregarious.

PAINTED STORK *Mycteria leucocephala* PLATE 6 (1)

Identification: (102 cm) Large with long, slightly down-curved, sturdy bill and bare orange-pink skin on face. Legs pink-brown but has a habit of excreting on legs making them look white. Non-breeding plumage: generally duller. Juvenile: grey-brown with faint pink flush on scapulars and no breast band. Wades in shallows when feeding with bill in water, raking with feet. Often solitary but also forms flocks. Rests upright with bill held down. Roosts communally in trees.

Status and distribution: Resident throughout lowlands, more frequent in lagoons, tank edges, and marshes of the north and east.

Nesting: Colonially with other wetland birds on small nests high in trees; early in year.

Range: India, China, SE Asia.

ASIAN OPENBILL *Anastomus oscitans* PLATE 6 (2)
(Openbill Stork)

Identification: (81 cm) Smallest of the Sri Lankan storks. Has characteristic gap between mandibles when bill is closed. Breeding plumage: mainly white with black flight feathers and tail. Non-breeding plumage: the white plumage turns grey. Juvenile: grey and brown, very young birds lack the gap in the bill. Wades in shallow water to feed on molluscs, usually but not always in flocks.

Status and distribution: Common resident in swamps and lagoons in wilder parts of lowlands. More frequent in dry zone.

Nesting: Colonially on nests of twigs in tops of bushes and low trees by water; December–March.

Range: India, SE Asia.

BLACK STORK *Ciconia nigra* PLATE 6 (5)

Identification: (96 cm) Glossy black with white belly and undertail coverts; red bill, facial skin, and legs. Juvenile: brown and white (the white parts

being more extensive than in the Woolly-necked), grey-green bill and legs. Typical stork flight. Feeds by stalking invertebrates and other small animals on damp ground. Very shy.
Status and distribution: Vagrant to dry lowlands.
Range: Europe, Africa, India, China.

WOOLLY-NECKED STORK *Ciconia episcopus* PLATE 6 (4)
(Indian White-necked Stork) (*Dissoura episcopus*)

Identification: (81 cm) Look for black crown and white neck. Rest of plumage glossy black except for white undertail coverts. Black bill with red upper ridge, rim, and tip. Juvenile: brown rather than black with fluffy neck feathers. Feeds on grassy areas in small groups, rarely in water. Typical stork flight. Roosts in trees.
Voice: Silent but claps bill at nest.
Status and distribution: Resident in swamps, tank edges, and wet areas of dry low country.
Nesting: Mass of sticks high in tree away from disturbance; February–March.
Range: Africa, India, SE Asia.

WHITE STORK *Ciconia ciconia* PLATE 6 (3)

Identification: (102 cm) White with pointed red bill and black rear scapulars, flight feathers, and greater coverts. Distinguishable from Openbill in flight by larger size, white tail, and red bill. Juvenile: brown not black. Typical stork flight. Walks across wet pasture seeking invertebrate or small vertebrate prey. Roosts in trees. Shy.
Status and distribution: Vagrant to lowlands.
Range: Europe, Africa, C Asia, India.

BLACK-NECKED STORK *Ephippiorhynchus asiaticus* PLATE 6 (6)
(*Xenorhyncus asiaticus*)

Identification: (132 cm) Very large with long, stout bill. Glossy black head, neck, scapulars, greater and median wing coverts, tertials, and tail. The rest of the plumage is pure white. Black bill with dull purple throat pouch and eyelids. Bright red legs projecting beyond the tail in flight. Male has brown iris, female has yellow. Immature: brown and off-white. Flies easily with slow wing beats and long glides with the white wings and black band of the coverts very obvious. Feeds in water or on wet marsh. Solitary or in pairs. Very wary.
Voice: Low boom, also claps bill during courtship.
Status and distribution: Rare breeding resident in wilder parts of the SE dry zone in lagoons and tank edges. Endangered.

Nesting: Mass of sticks at top of tree; September–December.
Range: India, SE Asia, New Guinea, Australia.

LESSER ADJUTANT *Leptoptilos javanicus* PLATE 6 (7)

Identification: (120 cm) Very large with big strong yellow bill with browny-red tinge, naked yellow head, and neck with thin grey down. Non-breeding: bare parts duller. Juvenile has more down on the head. Rests with head on shoulders or stands upright with neck extended. Flies with neck held back (unlike most storks). Stalks small animal prey. Solitary or in pairs. Very wary.
Voice: Generally silent.
Status and distribution: Uncommon resident in wild places by water and paddy in low country dry zone. Endangered.
Nesting: Huge pile of sticks in a big tree; March–April, also September.
Range: India, S China.

IBISES AND SPOONBILLS

Order: Ciconiiformes
Family: Threskiornithidae

MEDIUM sized birds with long necks and legs. Ibises have long down-curved bills and the spoonbill a long, straight, flattened bill with a broad flat 'spoon' at the tip. Strong flight with neck and legs extended, often soaring. Sexes alike. Gregarious. Often perch in trees. Voices are very limited apart from various harsh grunts and wheezes uttered during courtship, at the nest or roost and when alarmed. They will also snap bills at one another.

BLACK-HEADED IBIS *Threskiornis melanocephalus* PLATE 6 (9)
(White Ibis)
(Oriental Ibis)

Identification: (76 cm) Black down-curved bill, bare black skin on head and neck, white plumage except for pale grey tertials. Black legs. Breeding plumage: white filamentous plumes on the breast and scapulars, pale grey ones on tertials long enough to project beyond the tail. Juvenile: dark grey feathers on the head and neck. Shows strip of bare red skin on underwing when flying (black in juvenile). Often flies in formation. Feeds by walking briskly in small groups. Perches in trees. Partly nocturnal.
Status and distribution: Fairly common resident in wilder, marshy parts of the low country, more common in dry zone.

Nesting: Colonially with other species on piles of sticks in trees near water.
Range: India, China, Japan.

GLOSSY IBIS *Plegadis falcinellus* PLATE 6 (8)

Identification: (60 cm) Non-breeding plumage: dull brown-black with purple-green sheen on wing coverts and back, white streaks on head and neck. Darker than Curlew and with sturdier down-curved bill, bare skin on face and broader more rounded wings. Juvenile: pale brown head and neck with whitish streaking, brown breast and belly, grey-brown back and wings, lacking sheen. Often in small flocks feeding in marsh or shallow water with head down nodding from side to side. Flies with fast wing beats and short glides, often with others in a long line. Roosts communally in trees with other species.
Status and distribution: Was breeding resident in dry zone, now a winter visitor to marshes, lagoons, and tank edges in low country, mainly on the west coast near Colombo.
Nesting: Colonially on small piles of twigs high in trees; March–July.
Range: S Europe, Asia, Africa, Australia, C America.

EURASIAN SPOONBILL *Platalea leucorodia* PLATE 6 (10)
(White Spoonbill)

Identification: (84 cm) Ring of bare yellow skin around eye and bare yellow throat, bill slaty-grey turning yellow at the 'spoon'; legs and feet black. Distinguishable from the egrets by the very distinctive bill. Breeding plumage: yellow-orange bushy crest and flush on sides of the breast. Juvenile: like non-breeding but with black-tipped outer primaries. Usually in small flocks resting during day, becoming active at dusk. Feeds communally in shallow water scything the bill through the water. Flies in line formation.
Status and distribution: Fairly common resident in marshes, paddy, tank edges of low country dry zone.
Nesting: Colonially often with herons and egrets on piles of sticks on top of bushes or low in trees near water; December–March.
Range: Europe, Africa, Asia.

FLAMINGOS Order: Ciconiiformes Family: Phoenicopteridae

VERY tall birds with extremely long legs and neck. Bill is large with a sharp downward bend. Feed in shallow water holding head upside down filtering water through the serrated edges of the bill. Frequently rest on one leg with head and neck resting on back. Can swim but usually wade. Fly easily with steady wingbeats, neck and legs fully extended, often in long line or V formation. Highly gregarious. Partly nocturnal.

GREATER FLAMINGO *Phoenicopterus ruber* PLATE 3 (8)

Identification: (127 cm) Pink bill with extensive black tip. Mainly white with a pink flush, upper- and underwing coverts bright pink to red, flight feathers black. Sexes alike. Juvenile: grey with wing coverts mottled brown, underwing coverts and axillaries pale pink. Brown bill, legs grey-brown. Takes three years to reach adulthood. Typical flamingo flight showing red, white, and black pattern.

Voice: Croaking *aaaaa* and various gaggling notes when feeding.

Status and distribution: Winter visitor and summer loiterer, often juveniles. Stretches of shallow open water, preferably salt or brackish, mainly occurring around Jaffna and the salterns of the south.

Nesting: Sometimes builds 'nest' mounds of mud on mud-flats but no record of breeding.

Range: S Europe, S Africa, C Asia, C and S America.

LESSER FLAMINGO *Phoeniconaias minor* (*Phoenicopterus minor*) PLATE 3 (7)

Identification: (95 cm) Smaller and normally darker pink than Greater with dark red bill, only the very tip black. Red iris. In flight has obvious crimson and black wings, shorter legs, and relatively thicker neck than Greater.

Status and distribution: Unconfirmed vagrant. Prefer salterns and brackish lagoons.

Range: S and E Africa, Madagascar, N India.

DUCKS AND GEESE Order: Anseriformes Family: Anatidae

WATER birds with broad flat bills, fairly long necks, pointed wings, short tails, and short legs with webbed feet. Strong swimmers. Flight strong and direct with neck extended and rapid wing beats. Gregarious. Most undergo a moult during which they lose all their flight feathers making them flightless until they re-grow. In some species the males have an 'eclipse' after the moult when they assume a plumage similar to that of the females. Winter visitors might still be in eclipse on arrival in Sri Lanka. Identification of females and males in eclipse is difficult in some species. Large flocks of mixed species occur. Ducks in genus

Dendrocygna commonly perch in trees. Those in *Anas* genus are 'dabbling' ducks which feed on the surface or by 'up-ending', they spring into the air to take off and do not dive to feed but are able to dive when threatened. *Netta* and *Aythya* dive when feeding or threatened and patter along the surface to take off.

FULVOUS WHISTLING-DUCK *Dendrocygna bicolor* PLATE 7 (2)

(Large Whistling-teal)
(Fulvous Tree Duck)

Identification: (50 cm) Has off-white uppertail coverts, a black line down back of neck, a rufous collar and whitish streaks on flanks; larger than the Lesser, otherwise similar. Sexes alike. Juveniles generally duller than adults. Flight faster and stronger than Lesser frequently calling. Sociable, often with Lesser. Perches in trees.

Voice: *Tsoo-eee* flight call and *seee* alarm.

Status and distribution: Winter vagrant to marshes, tanks of dry zone.

Range: E Africa, Madagascar, India, Americas.

LESSER WHISTLING-DUCK *Dendrocygna javanica* PLATE 7 (3)

(Indian Whistling-duck)
(Whistling-teal)
(Lesser Tree Duck)

Identification: (43 cm) Maroon wing coverts contrasting against black flight feathers on broad wings; it is smaller than Fulvous and has chestnut uppertail coverts. Sexes alike. Flight slightly head-down in loose flocks with slower and more laboured wing-beats than in other ducks and frequently calling. Partly nocturnal, often feeds on paddy. Strong swimmer and diver. Perches in trees. Sociable. Shy.

Voice: A shrill cackling whistle frequently uttered in flight.

Status and distribution: Resident. Common in swamps, paddy, and weedy edges of tanks in low country. Not in saltwater. Vagrant to hills.

Nesting: Hidden in waterside vegetation or in holes in trees up to 6 m from ground; December–January and July–August.

Range: India, SE Asia.

GREYLAG GOOSE *Anser anser rubrirostris* PLATE 7 (6)

Identification: (81 cm) Only true goose likely in Sri Lanka. Large. Bill orange or pink, legs and feet pink. Sexes alike. Powerful flight on broad wings with pale silver-grey panel on upperwing coverts, often in V or line formation. Feeds by grazing, often on crops. Partly nocturnal. Sociable in normal range.

Voice: *Yang-ung-ung* and other nasal calls often uttered in flight.

Status and distribution: Winter vagrant to lowlands. One early record.
Range: N Europe, NW Africa, C and E Asia.

RUDDY SHELDUCK *Tadorna ferruginea* PLATE 7 (5)
(Ruddy Sheldrake)

Identification: (**M**66, **F**59 cm) Rather goose-like. Orange-brown with black flight feathers, green speculum, white upper inner forewing and black tail. In breeding season the male has a thin black collar. Female has off-white face. Juvenile: like female but slightly grey on back. In flight the wing beats are slower than in most ducks and the white wing coverts contrast with black flight feathers. Largely nocturnal, resting during day away from cover. In pairs or small groups. Aggressive to other ducks. Shy of humans.
Voice: *Aaonk, aang-aang*, and a rolling *rrowl.*
Status and distribution: Vagrant to open lagoons and tanks.
Range: SE Europe, C Asia, India, S China.

COMB DUCK *Sarkidiornis melanotos* PLATE 7 (7)
(Nukhta)

Identification: (**M**76, **F**66 cm) Large and rather goose-like. Speckled head and neck. Black wings with blue-green sheen and bronze speculum. Black bill with large black comb (knob) in male, females lack the comb. Legs dark grey. Strong flight in small groups, not line formation. Feeds mainly by grazing. Can dive when threatened. Perches and roosts in trees.
Voice: A low quack and a honk in the breeding season.
Status and previous distribution: Was resident in weedy tanks in N and E. Now thought to be extinct in Sri Lanka.
Range: Africa, India, S China, S America.

COTTON PYGMY-GOOSE *Nettapus coromandelianus* PLATE 7 (4)
(Cotton Teal)

Identification: (33 cm) Smallest local duck. Breeding male unmistakable with black collar and obvious white wing bar on upper- and underwing. Female: dark eye-stripe, dingier below and generally duller with narrow wing bar on trailing edge of secondaries. Eclipse male like female but keeps the white wing bar. Bill, legs, and feet black. Juvenile: like female but more brown on head. Agile fast flight with rapid wing beats, usually low. Feeds on surface but can dive if threatened. Rarely comes onto dry land. In pairs when breeding, other times in small flocks.
Voice: *Quack-quackyduck.*

Status and distribution: Resident in tanks and open water of low country, more common in dry zone.
Nesting: In cavities in trees near water; January–March and July–August.
Range: India, S China, Indonesia, NE Australia.

EURASIAN WIGEON *Anas penelope* PLATE 8 (1)

(Wigeon)

Identification: (48 cm) Stocky compact body, round head with slight peak on steep forehead, smallish blue-grey bill, longish wings and pointed tail. Metallic green speculum which often appears black. Male has chestnut head with yellow-buff stripe on crown and white line on sides when wings are closed. Males in eclipse and juvenile are similar to females with dull chestnut to orange flanks but some females may be greyer than the one illustrated. In flight shows white inner wing (pale grey in female), white belly, and dark pointed tail. Forms large flocks. Rests in day on open water (fresh or salt), grazes grass or weed in shallow water at night, often up-ending.
Voice: Male whistles *whee-oo*, female has a low growling *karrr-karrr*.
Status and distribution: Winter visitor to tanks and lagoons in lowlands, more frequently in N and E of dry zone, sometimes in large numbers.
Range: N Europe, N Africa, Asia.

GADWALL *Anas strepera* PLATE 8 (2)

Identification: (51 cm). Squarish head with white speculum. Breeding male: dull grey with white belly, chestnut wing coverts contrast with the white speculum, and black upper- and undertail coverts. Female and non-breeding male: scaly brown with greyer head, white speculum, and dark grey upper mandible with sharply defined orange sides. Larger than Teal and Garganey, superficially resembles Mallard. In flight the male's chestnut upperwing coverts and white belly are obvious as is the speculum (smaller in female) in both sexes. Fast flight with rapid wingbeats making a whistling noise. Rests during day, feeds at night by grazing, dabbling, or up-ending in shallows. Usually in small flocks.
Voice: Male has a nasal *krrek*, female a soft *quack*.
Status and distribution: Winter vagrant to dry zone, mainly in freshwater.
Range: Europe, N Africa, Asia, N America.

COMMON TEAL *Anas crecca* PLATE 8 (7)

(Green-winged Teal)

Identification: (37 cm) Bright metallic green speculum turning nearly black further from body bordered by a prominent white bar to the front. Breeding male: obvious head pattern and a black-fringed buff triangle on undertail coverts. Even smaller than Garganey. From female Garganey by darker upperwing secondary coverts, shorter bill, plainer face pattern lacking obvious eye and cheek stripes, and pale spot at base of bill. Gregarious. Very rapid wader-like flight, twisting and turning in flocks or in long lines. Rests during day, feeds at night by up-ending in shallows or grazing on wet vegetation.

Voice: Male: cricket-like *krik, krik*. Female: a high pitched quack and low *trrr*.

Status and distribution: Winter visitor to coastal lagoons, tanks, and marshes, mainly in north of dry zone.

Range: Europe, N Africa, Asia, N and C America.

MALLARD *Anas platyrhynchos* PLATE 8 (4)

Identification: (58 cm) Purple-blue speculum bordered black and white, obvious in flight. Breeding male: glossy metallic green head, narrow white collar, chestnut breast, grey back and underside. Female and eclipse male: dark line through eye, buff throat and neck, bill brown or brown and orange. Larger than eclipse Gadwall, has different wing pattern and lacks the orange band on upper bill. Fast flight with considerable wing noise. Dabbles and up-ends to feed mainly at night. In small flocks. Shy.

Voice: Female has loud quack and a declining *quack,quack, quack*; male a soft, wheezy *neep*.

Status and distribution: Unconfirmed winter vagrant.

Range: Europe, N Africa, Asia, N and C America.

SPOT-BILLED DUCK *Anas poecilorhyncha* PLATE 8 (5)

Identification: (61 cm) Black bill with chrome yellow patch near the tip, two orange-red spots at the base of the upper mandible and orange-red legs. Pale head with dark crown and eye-line. Metallic green speculum with black and white border. Sexes nearly alike but female smaller and duller with less obvious orange face spots. Flight strong but rather heavy showing speculum, white underwing coverts and black flight feathers. Feeds by dabbling in mud or up-ending in shallow water. In pairs or small flocks.

Voice: Female *quacks*, male has hoarse *neep*, both very similar to Mallard.

Status and distribution: Rare winter visitor to tanks, weedy water, and paddy of dry lowlands. Not normally on salt water.

Range: India, China, Myanmar.

NORTHERN PINTAIL *Anas acuta* PLATE 8(6)

Identification: (M66 cm (including tail feathers); F56 cm) A slender duck with a long neck and obvious white trailing edge to secondaries. Male: long pointed tail, distinctive brown head with white stripe on sides of long, slender neck, longish slim grey bill and bronze-green speculum. Female and eclipse male: pale buff head, longish slender grey bill and indistinct brown speculum. Grey legs. Fast flight showing long neck, set-back wings, and pointed tail. Flocks on open water in day. Feeds at night by up-ending on edges of lagoons or foraging on marsh or paddy. Shy.

Voice: Female has a high pitched *quk, quk.*; male is generally silent.

Status and distribution: Regular winter visitor to lowlands, mostly in dry zone coastal lagoons.

Range: Europe, Asia.

GARGANEY *Anas querquedula* PLATE 8 (8)

Identification: (40 cm) Male: rich brown head with obvious white eyebrow extending down nape, brown breast sharply contrasting with white underparts, pale grey wing-coverts, and grey-green speculum. Female and eclipse male: pale eyebrow, dark eye-stripe, pale spot on lores, often with dark cheek bar, and pure white throat. Slightly larger than Teal and with longer bill. Distinguishable from female Teal by more marked face pattern, thin white bar to the front of the speculum and a thicker white bar on the trailing edge. Fast flight with rapid wing beats, more direct than Teal, usually in flocks with wings looking pale grey from distance. Feeds nocturnally by sifting bits from water surface, sometimes up-ending, and on paddy. Highly gregarious and with other ducks. Shy.

Voice: Female has low *quack*; male a match-in-box rattle but normally silent.

Status and distribution: Regular winter visitor. Common on coastal lagoons of dry zone, rarely on inland tanks.

Range: Europe, Africa, Asia.

NORTHERN SHOVELLER *Anas clypeata* PLATE 8 (3)
(Common Shoveller)

Identification: (51 cm) Dumpy with very obvious large, broad, spoon-like bill, short neck, wings set back on body and orange legs. Eclipse male like dark female. Juvenile similar to female but slightly less speckled. Strong flight with rapid wingbeats showing pale grey-blue wing coverts and green speculum with broad white border to the front of upperwing; white underwing coverts contrasting against chestnut belly in male and dark belly in female. Feeds by swimming with head lowered, bill sieving water at the surface, or up-ending. In small groups often with Teal and Garganey.

Voice: Male has a low double *took*; female a double *quack* but is generally quiet.

Status and distribution: Winter visitor to lowlands, mainly on freshwater lagoons of N and the SE.
Range: Europe, E Africa, Asia, N and C America.

MARBLED TEAL *Marmaronetta angustirostris* PLATE 8 (9)
(Marbled Duck)

Identification: (46 cm) A generally pale duck. Pale brown spotted buff with dusky eye-patch extending down nape, a slight mane-like crest on male, inconspicuous brown speculum, fairly long, narrow, dark bill and brown legs. Sexes alike. Juvenile: like dull adult but with fewer buff spots. Flight usually brief returning to cover on longish wings. Feeds by dabbling, up-ending or diving, in pairs or small groups. Shy.
Voice: A nasal *peep* or a double *peep-peep*.
Status and distribution: Unconfirmed winter vagrant. Prefers weedy water, avoiding open water.
Range: S Europe, Asia Minor, Pakistan, N India.

RED-CRESTED POCHARD *Netta rufina* PLATE 7 (8)

Identification: (55 cm) A stocky diving duck with a large bulbous head and slender bill. Male: orange-chestnut head and crest, crimson-red bill, black neck, breast, and belly, with white patch on flank. Female: brown cap and nape contrasts with pale grey face, dark grey bill with pink tip and edges. Eclipse male: similar to female but browner beneath and retains red bill. Fast direct flight showing mainly white flight feathers. Dives to feed, also up-ends. Prefers deeper fresh water. Shy.
Voice: Usually silent but has a low croak and a *gick*.
Status and distribution: Unconfirmed winter vagrant. Prefers water with submerged vegetation.
Range: E Europe, N Africa, C Asia.

COMMON POCHARD *Aythya ferina* PLATE 7 (9)

Identification: (47 cm) Male: rufous head and neck with high crown and no crest, black breast, rump, and under tail. In eclipse: head duller, black replaced by brown. Female: mainly brown with variable pale eye-stripe and throat. Bill grey-blue with dark base and tip. Fast and direct flight showing no white on wing only an inconspicuous grey wing bar. Swims low in water. Dives to feed, usually in open water. Partly nocturnal. Forms flocks. **Note:** Beware of confusion with Ferruginous Duck *Athya nyroca* (not recorded but possible).
Voice: Usually silent.

Status and distribution: Unconfirmed winter vagrant. Prefers water with submerged vegetation.
Range: W Europe, N Africa, C Asia, S China.

TUFTED DUCK *Aythya fuligula* PLATE 7 (10)

Identification: (43 cm) Stocky. Male: black and white with drooping crest, a pale blue-grey bill with a black tip and yellow eyes. Female: dark brown with very small crest. Eclipse male: dull browny-black, throat pale grey and flanks mottled brown. Both sexes show broad white wing bar in flight. Fast flight with rapid wing beats. Swims low in water. Dives to feed. Forms flocks.
Voice: Mostly silent in winter. Has a *kur-r-r, kur-r-r* flight call.
Status and distribution: Winter vagrant to vegetated freshwater tanks in dry zone.
Range: Europe, Asia, Philippines.

OSPREY Order: Falconiformes Family: Pandionidae

FISH-EATING bird of prey with long angular wings, hooked bill, long legs with bare tarsi. Outer toe reversible. Flies over water plunging feet first to catch fish in claws. There is only one species in the family.

OSPREY *Pandion haliaetus* PLATE 9 (6)

Identification: (M52, F58 cm) Whitish head with dark band through eye to nape, whitish underparts with a variable dark breast band, barred square tail. Long flexible rather pointed wings with dark carpal patch below. Sexes nearly alike but female has more obvious breast band. Juveniles show pale tips and fringes on mantle and upperwing coverts. Gull-like flight with slow wingbeats and glides. Circles or hovers with legs dangling when hunting, plunging into water to take fish prey. Often perches on pole or tree branch near water to rest or eat prey. Solitary.
Voice: Usually silent in Sri Lanka but has sad, high pitched *peewp* and a *kew-kew-kew* alarm.
Status and distribution: Winter visitor to coastal lagoons, estuaries, sometimes on tanks in lowlands. Vagrant to tanks in hill country.
Range: Almost world-wide.

KITES, HAWKS, EAGLES, VULTURES AND HARRIERS

Order: Falconiformes Family: Accipitridae

MEDIUM to large diurnal birds of prey or scavengers with hooked bills, patch of bare skin (the cere) at the base of the upper mandible, large wings, and strong feet. They are powerful fliers often soaring to great heights. The females in many species are larger than the males. Immatures take up to five years to reach full adult plumage. This and the many possible plumage variations can make identification difficult. Nests are often lined with green vegetation.

JERDON'S BAZA *Aviceda jerdoni* PLATE 10 (1)

(Brown Baza)
(Legge's Baza)

Identification: (43 cm) Male: rufous-brown breast and barred belly. Thin dark centre line on throat. White-tipped black crest normally held erect when perched and creamy eyebrow. Broad and rounded wings with narrow bases, appearing white from below with dark trailing edge and dark bars on primaries. Two narrow bars beneath tail and a dark sub-terminal bar. Female: paler rufous on breast and belly. Juvenile: paler, sparsely streaked, not barred on belly and with four or five tail bars. Rather sluggish flight, few flaps then glides, usually just above trees but also soars high, often in pairs. Has deep, stooping display flight with much calling. Spends much time perched. Most active at dusk. Shy.
Voice: *Pee-ow* and a flight call *chip,chip,chip*.
Status and distribution: Uncommon resident in forests of hill country, straying to cultivated land nearby.
Nesting: In shallow cup of leafy twigs high in fork of tree; November–May.
Range: India, Borneo, Sulawesi, Philippines.

BLACK BAZA *Aviceda leuphotes* PLATE 10 (2)

(Black-crested Baza)

Identification: (33 cm) Black crest held erect when perched. Strikingly black, white, and chestnut. Sexes alike. Juveniles are dark grey not black. Much smaller than Jerdon's. Crow-like flight on broad, narrow-rooted, rounded wings with characteristic underwing pattern and unbarred under tail. Solitary or in small groups. Feeds by perching upright on high branch flying out to take insects or small reptiles often well into dusk.
Voice: Not very vocal but has a single, thin *mew*.
Status and distribution: Rare and irregular winter visitor to forests, mainly in low country dry zone.
Range: Himalayas, India, China, SE Asia.

ORIENTAL HONEY-BUZZARD *Pernis ptilorhynchus* PLATE 9 (1)
(Crested Honey-buzzard) (*Pernis apivorus*)

Identification: (66 cm) Small head. Very variable with dark, pale, and intermediate morphs. Typical male: grey face, pale throat, clearly marked dark gorget; broad dark trailing edge, two inner bars and no contrast on carpal area of underwing; two dark bars separated by equal width pale bar near base of under tail. Typical female: browner face and weaker gorget; narrow dark trailing edge with three evenly spaced bars; two narrow dark bars separated by broad pale bar on under tail. Juvenile: faint trailing edge and four or five weak bars on tail. Flies with leading edge of broad wings straight and slots between primaries in powered flight, four or five wingbeats followed by a short glide with wings held slightly down, also soars. Solitary or in pairs.
Voice: Normally silent but has loud *wheeow*.
Status and distribution: Rare breeding resident supplemented by winter visitors in forests throughout.
Nesting: On pile of twigs in a forest tree, probably early in year.
Range: Asia, Borneo, Java, Philippines.

BLACK-WINGED KITE *Elanus caeruleus* PLATE 10 (6)
(Black-shouldered Kite)

Identification: (32 cm) Pale grey and white with bold black tip to underwing and black shoulder patches. Paler and much smaller than the male Pallid Harrier. Sexes alike. Juvenile: browner with obvious pale fringes. Flies quite high like a stocky falcon, strong flaps then glides with wings at an angle, sometimes hovering to drop onto prey. Often perches on exposed branch raising and lowering tail. Solitary but roosts colonially.
Voice: Usually silent but has *wheep,wheep* call.
Status and distribution: Resident. Possible anywhere but less frequent in low country wet zone.
Nesting: Untidy pile of twigs at top of tree in open country; December–March.
Range: Africa, S and SE Asia, Philippines, New Guinea.

BLACK KITE *Milvus migrans* PLATE 9 (5)
(Pariah Kite)

Identification: (60 cm) Dark brown with pale area on upperwing and forked tail but, beware, the tail is continually moving in flight and it can appear square when tail is fanned. Black bill with yellowish base and cere, yellow legs. Sexes alike. Juvenile: paler with buff streaks on head and underparts. Distinguishable from juvenile Brahminy by non-contrasting underwing coverts and darker tip on longer forked tail. Flies easily with long wings held at an angle (Brahminy flies on flat wings). Commonly scavenges on rubbish or feeds in wet areas. Sociable.

Voice: Shrill *keee-kik-kik-kik*.

Status and distribution: Resident, mainly in the coastal areas of the north close to habitation but strays to other coastal areas in the winter.

Nesting: Untidy mass of sticks in canopy of tree or at base of palm fronds. December–April.

Range: Europe, Africa, Asia, Australia.

BRAHMINY KITE *Haliastur indus* PLATE 9 (4)

Identification: (47 cm) Adult distinctive chestnut and white. Sexes alike. Juvenile: dark bown spotted tawny on wings, back and tail; head, breast, and underparts mottled tawny grey with solid, dark underwing coverts and pale patch beneath primaries; very similar to juvenile Black Kite but has shorter, paler, rounded tail. Juvenile can also be confused with the larger Long-legged Buzzard dark morph, or with pale morph Common Buzzard. Easy flight with much soaring on flat wings, swooping onto food or taking insects in mid-air; also scavenges on rubbish. Sometimes alights on water when seeking food.

Voice: A squealing cry.

Status and distribution: Resident. Common in dry zone, less so in wet zone and lower hills. Usually near water. Some movement to coastal lagoons in winter.

Nesting: On pile of sticks in crown of tree; December–April.

Range: India, S China, SE Asia, Borneo, New Guinea, Australia.

WHITE-BELLIED FISH EAGLE *Haliaeetus leucogaster* PLATE 12 (5)
(White-bellied Sea Eagle)

Identification: (70 cm) Closed wings reach to end of tail or beyond. Bill and cere dark grey, strong yellow-grey unfeathered tarsi. Distinguishable from Egyptian Vulture overhead by black base to tail and white head with black bill. Sexes alike. Juvenile: mainly brown, dark underwing secondaries contrast with pale coverts. Flies with strong wingbeats and long glides, wings making a V and with slots between 'fingers' on narrow 'hand'. Frequently soars sometimes to great heights. Perches upright on bare branches near water. Feeds by stooping to grab prey from water without plunging. Also robs other birds. Often in pairs.

Voice: Noisy in breeding season. *Ah-ah-ah-ah* with head extended.

Status and distribution: Resident on coasts, lagoons and tanks of dry zone and lower hills, occasionally straying into wet zone.

Nesting: On large pile of sticks in tree by water; December–March.

Range: India, China, Philippines, Australia.

GREY-HEADED FISH EAGLE *Ichthyophaga ichthyaetus* PLATE 12 (6)
(Tank Eagle)

Identification: (M62, F69 cm) Grey head, white lower belly, short white tibial feathers (no 'trousers') and white undertail coverts, short black-tipped white tail (reverse of White-bellied pattern). Shorter, relatively broader wings than White-bellied. Sexes alike. Juvenile: secondaries normally paler than underwing coverts. Heavy flight shows all dark underwing in adult. Rarely soars. Spends much of its time perched on branch above water watching, swooping down onto its fish prey. Does not plunge.

Voice: Noisy, especially early and late in the day; *Awh-awhrr*.

Status and distribution: Resident by lagoons, tanks and rivers bordered by dense cover in dry zone, always by water. Not common.

Nesting: Big pile of twigs high in tree; December–March.

Range: India, SE Asia, Borneo, Philippines.

EGYPTIAN VULTURE *Neophron percnopterus* PLATE 12 (9)
(Small White Scavenger Vulture)

Identification: (61 cm) From White-bellied Fish Eagle by yellow head and slender bill, and in flight by all white, wedge-shaped tail. Sexes alike. Juvenile: dark with pale head and underwing coverts, becoming whiter over five years of adolescence. Strong flight, often soaring high. Clumsy walk with body nearly horizontal. Scavenges in rubbish or on carrion. Solitary or in small groups.

Voice: Usually silent.

Status and distribution: Vagrant. Possible anywhere but attracted to human settlements. Three records to date.

Range: S Europe, Africa, India.

CRESTED SERPENT EAGLE *Spilornis cheela spilogaster* PLATE 12 (1)
(Ceylon Serpent Eagle)

Identification: (61 cm) Broad rounded wings. Black-tipped flight and tail feathers make characteristic pattern from below. Double band on carpals. Yellow iris, eye-ring, cere, and lores together make a yellow patch at base of slaty bill. Bare yellow tarsi. Has a large black and white ruff-like crest but only raises it when excited. Sexes alike. Juvenile: grey iris, paler than adult with white almost Osprey-like underwing, dark trailing edge and double band on carpals. Soars to great heights with V wings and tail generally closed, often in pairs, calling. Aerobatic display flight. Perches upright and 'narrow-tailed' on high branch to drop onto prey, usually reptiles.

Voice: Frequently heard *kuk-kuk-keer-keer-keer* and *whee-woop-woop* flight calls. *Keer* when perched.
Status and distribution: Endemic race, common throughout where there is forest or tree cover.
Nesting: Mass of twigs hidden in trees; February–May.
Species range: S and SE Asia, Java, Philippines.

PALLID HARRIER *Circus macrourus* PLATE 11 (3)

(Pale Harrier)

Identification: (**M** 46 cm, **F** 50 cm) A typical harrier, slim with long wings, tail, and legs. Slimmer and with more pointed wings than Pied. Male: distinguishable from male Montagu's by paler grey of wings, back, throat, and head, no wing bar, smaller wedge of black on wingtips, and pale, nearly white underwing. Female: obvious pale collar with dark 'moustache' extending below bill. Broader wings and pale underwing primaries more heavily barred in centre (but lighter barring than in female Montagu's except at bases) with only a faint dark trailing edge, weak barring and poorly marked tips on four 'fingers'. Secondaries darker than primaries (cf. female Montagu's), central pale bar tapers away towards body. Coverts heavily marked. Juvenile: similar face pattern to female's with pale collar and usually a darker area behind; heavier underwing primary markings with tawny-buff underparts and underwing coverts. Typical harrier flight, gliding slowly, low over feeding grounds, wings held in a very shallow V with occasional heavy wingflaps, dropping onto prey of small reptiles, small amphibians, and birds, even insects. Perches on ground or not far above it. Solitary but roosts communally.
Voice: Usually silent.
Status and distribution: Winter visitor, occasional summer loiterer, possible in all parts where there are marshes, paddy, grassland, or open scrub. The occasional summer loiterers tend to stay in the hill country.
Range: Europe, Africa, Asia.

PIED HARRIER *Circus melanoleucos* PLATE 11 (4)

Identification: (**M**44, **F**47 cm) Male distinguishable from other local harriers by black head, neck, breast and median upperwing coverts. Female has an obvious ruff, broad wings with five 'fingers' and pale upperwing, more obviously barred than in other harriers, with a pale leading edge; pale barred underwing. Juvenile: much darker than female with brown heavily streaked underparts and underwing coverts, and dark secondaries. Similar in habits to Pallid but has a heavier flight than both the Pallid and Montagu's.
Voice: Usually silent.

Status and distribution: Rare winter visitor possible anywhere, most likely early in the year in paddy of the north or occasionally in hill country grasslands.

Range: Eastern Siberia, India, Myanmar.

MONTAGU'S HARRIER *Circus pygargus* PLATE 11 (2)

Identification: (M43, F48 cm) Slimmer with narrower wings than Pallid showing pointed 'hand' of three 'fingers'. **Male**: from Pallid male by darker grey upperparts, more extensive black on primaries and one black band across upper secondaries, two below; rusty chequering on axillaries and underwing coverts, darker breast, whitish belly with rufous streaks. Female: pale face, indistinct ruff and strong brown streaks on sides and breast, shows strong, even barring under primaries, broad hindmost pale bar across secondaries continues broad to body, pale underwing coverts with rufous chequering usually continuing onto axillaries (diagnostic when present), dark inner primary trailing edge. Juvenile: dark cheek mark only to gape, faint pale collar, the ruff is not obvious, plain underparts varying from coppery-brown to pale ochre but usually darker than Pallid juvenile. Dark underwing 'fingers' and trailing edge. Bases of outer primaries only faintly barred. Hunting flight is a low quartering flight similar to those of the harriers described above but sometimes soars high.

Voice: Usually silent.

Status and distribution: Winter visitor and summer loiterer in low country especially near the northern coasts, sometimes in hills.

Range: Europe, Asia, Africa.

WESTERN MARSH HARRIER *Circus aeruginosus* PLATE 11 (1)

Identification: (M53, F56 cm) Larger with broader wings than other harriers. Male has distinctive silver-grey on wings and tail. A rare adult male dark morph also is possible. Female: variable buff patches on crown, chin, throat, and leading edge. Juvenile: often all dark developing variable patches on crown, nape, and chin similar to the female's. Slimmer than Black Kite but with rounded tail, not forked (Kite's fork is not always obvious) and has dark primaries lacking the pale patches of the Black Kite. Beware of confusion with juvenile Pied. Like the Montagu's, it sometimes abandons the typical harrier low quartering hunting flight to soar high: When it does, the female could be confused with the Black Eagle; however, the eagle is unlikely to be found in Marsh Harrier habitat. Spends more of its time than the other harriers 'loafing' on mudflats or marshes.

Voice: Usually silent.

Status and distribution: Winter visitor. Mainly in lagoons and coastal swamps but occasionally in flat marshy areas in the hill country.
Range: Europe, Asia, Africa, Australia.

CRESTED GOSHAWK *Accipiter trivirgatus layardi* PLATE 10 (3)
(Ceylon Crested Goshawk)

Identification: (M30, F34 cm) A typical *Accipiter,* a short, narrow based and relatively broad-winged hawk with a long tail. Small crest (not always visible). Black centre throat stripe, heavily streaked breast. Barred flight feathers and three dark bars across tail. Sexes alike. Juvenile: buff eyebrow, black central throat stripe, plain buff underparts with a few darker spots. Very agile flight, a few rapid wingbeats and glides: also circles and soars. Hunts by perching in tree darting out to take prey.
Voice: A shrill *he-he-hehehehe.*
Status and distribution: Endemic race. Forests, more frequent in wet lowlands.
Nesting: Large heap of twigs in top of tree. February–July.
Species range: India, China, SE Asia, Borneo, Java.

SHIKRA *Accipiter badius* PLATE 10 (5)

Identification: (M30, F34 cm) Short rounded wings and long tail. Stockier and paler, more finely barred than Besra, grey ear-coverts shading to white throat with a thin pale grey throat stripe. Central upper tail unbarred in adult. Very pale underside with darker wing-tips. Juvenile: from juvenile Besra by white on sides of uppertail coverts and five narrow dark bands on tail. Flies fast (appearing paler than Besra) with glides, often dodging low over scrub in the hope of surprising prey, also soars high in circles. Perches high in tree watching for prey.
Voice: *Iheeya,iheeya,iheeya,* and *titu,titu.*
Status and distribution: Resident throughout. Most common small hawk in most areas. Prefers a mix of open country with trees. Avoids deep forest.
Nesting: On twigs high in tree; March–May.
Range: Africa, Asia.

BESRA *Accipiter virgatus* PLATE 10 (4)
(Besra Sparrowhawk)

Identification: (M28, F34 cm) Similar to Shikra but more slender, more strongly barred but with streaks on breast. Longer legs and toes. Also from Shikra by a sharp division between dark head and white throat, no white on upper tail-coverts, underparts barred a deeper brown. Bold black central throat stripe. Sometimes has white streaking on nape. Long tail with four bars. In flight, shows more well-marked underwing coverts and bolder barring on tail than Shikra. Juvenile very similar to juvenile Shikra but more strongly barred, especially on flanks, flight, and outer tail feathers; has dark rump and uppertail coverts. Typical *Accipiter* flight, fast, weaving between trees.

Voice: Noisy, *tchew-tchew-tchew*.

Status and distribution: Scarce resident in forested areas, more common in wet zone lowlands

Nesting: On untidy mass of twigs high in tree; March–May.

Range: S Asia, Java, Philippines.

COMMON BUZZARD *Buteo buteo* — PLATE 9 (3)

Identification: (M51, F55 cm) Stocky. Variable in plumage, from all dark to very pale but generally greyish brown. Less eagle-like than Honey and Long-legged. Under tail usually more barred than Long-legged. From Honey Buzzard by shorter neck and generally broader build. From Crested Serpent Eagle by lack of wing banding, the tail usually fanned in flight and lack of calls. Sexes alike. Typical juvenile has faint trailing edge to underwing secondaries. Soars high in slow circles on broad rounded wings held in V, showing dark carpal patches in most morphs. Tail is spread when soaring.

Voice: Generally silent in winter but has a *mew*.

Status and distribution: Regular but scarce winter visitor. Possible in all parts near forests and trees.

Range: Europe, E and S Africa, Asia.

LONG-LEGGED BUZZARD *Buteo rufinus* — PLATE 9 (2)

Identification: (60 cm) Heavily built, sluggish, with variable plumage from dark to rufous. Larger, has longer wings and tail, and is more eagle-like than Common. All morphs have pale, almost unmarked under tail. Typical adult: pale head, dark belly and vent contrasting with breast, pale unbarred orange-rufous upper tail, pale patches on upperwing primaries, plain rusty or evenly patterned underwing coverts. Soars high in circles, sometimes hovering on slightly angled wings before pouncing. Also perches looking for prey, then pounces. Solitary or in small groups.

Voice: Generally silent in winter but has a *mew*.

Status and distribution: Winter vagrant to hill country.

Range: C Europe, N Africa, C Asia.

BLACK EAGLE *Ictinaetus malayensis* PLATE 12 (2)

Identification: (**M**69, **F**79 cm) Mostly black with long broad wings with 'fingers' and a long, finely grey-barred tail. Green-grey black-tipped bill, yellow cere, black feathered tarsi, yellow feet. Sexes alike. Juvenile: pale with buff streaking on head, underparts, and underwing coverts, uppertail coverts fringed white and faint barring on tail. Second year: heavily streaked with paler head than adult. Slow sailing flight often only just above tree tops with well separated up-curved 'fingers', inner secondaries shorter than primaries making narrow root to wing. Rarely flaps wings, sometimes trails feet. Stoops onto prey. Usually in pairs.

Voice: Generally silent but has *keee-uuk* call.

Status and distribution: Resident in forest, scrub, and open country in lower hills. Rare in wet zone.

Nesting: Large mass of sticks in crown of tree, preferably on rocky slope. Probably December.

Range: India, S China, SE Asia.

BONELLI'S EAGLE *Hieraaetus fasciatus* PLATE 12 (8)

Identification: (**M**69, **F**74 cm) Slender with a long, square, black-tipped tail, pale patch on upper back. Broad black band across underwing coverts, pale inner leading edge and grey patch at bend of wing. Feathered tarsi. Sexes alike. Juvenile: brown with buff head and rufous-buff underparts and narrow bands on tail but no black tip. Strong flight with relatively fast but shallow wingbeats, soars high showing straight trailing edge to wings, also chases prey or perches and pounces.

Voice: *Klee-klee-klee.*

Status and distribution: Winter vagrant to forested areas.

Range: S Europe, N Africa, S Asia

BOOTED EAGLE *Hieraaetus pennatus* PLATE 12 (7)

Identification: (**M**51, **F**54 cm) Broad wings and a plain square tail. Two morphs: pale has dark underwing with pale coverts; the rarer dark morph has paler inner primaries and pale base to tail. (Distinguishable from Black Kite by square tail; from female Marsh Harrier by lack of cream on head or forewing; from juvenile Marsh Harrier by pale base to tail.) Juvenile: similar to dark phase. Sexes alike. Easy sailing flight taking bird prey on the wing, or pouncing from a perch. Often in pairs. Roosts communally.

Voice: Usually silent.

Status and distribution: Regular winter visitor, possible all areas, even over towns.

Range: S Europe, N Africa, SW and C Asia.

RUFOUS-BELLIED EAGLE *Hieraaetus kienerii* PLATE 9 (7)
(Rufous-bellied Hawk-eagle) (*Lophotriorchis kienerii*)
(Chestnut-bellied Hawk-eagle)

Identification: (M53, F61 cm) Broad winged and relatively short tailed. Rufous underparts often appear dark unless close. Has small crest but not normally erect. Rufous feathered tarsi. Sexes alike. Juvenile: white eyebrow and a dark eye-patch, brownish upperparts, and pale below. Second year; patches of rufous appear on belly and underwing. Distinguishable from juvenile Changeable Hawk and juvenile Crested Serpent by longer wings and shorter tail, pale underwing with dark border, band of dark spots on greater coverts and grey under tail with narrow bars. Buoyant flight with fast wingbeats, often soaring and circling on straight wings taking bird prey on the wing, falcon-like, by stooping. Also takes small mammals and reptiles. Very upright stance when perched.
Voice: Normally silent but is said to have a scream.
Status and distribution: Resident, scarce in hills, rare elsewhere. Endangered.
Nesting: Large pile of sticks in tree; December–March.
Range: Asia south of Himalayas, Java, Philippines.

CHANGEABLE HAWK EAGLE *Spizaetus cirrhatus ceylanensis* PLATE 12 (4)
(Ceylon Hawk-eagle)
(Crested Hawk-eagle)

Identification: (60 cm) Slender build, broad wings (but less so than Mountain Hawk Eagle), long tail and white-tipped crest usually obvious. Off-white underparts with a narrow black throat stripe and a few streaks on the breast and belly. Legs feathered to yellow feet. Sexes alike. Juvenile: off-white head and very pale underparts. Rarely soars. Often perches upright on exposed perch, such as telegraph pole, looking out for prey upon which it pounces. Has an aerobatic and vocal display flight.
Voice: A ringing *k'lee-kle-k* and *pew-pew-pew-pew… pew-pewheep* often uttered while perched and in flight.
Status and distribution: Endemic race. Common in open woodland in lowlands and hills up to 1500 m.
Nesting: On a large mass of sticks in a tall tree; June–July.
Species range: India, Borneo, Java, Philippines.

MOUNTAIN HAWK EAGLE *Spizaetus nipalensis kelaarti* PLATE 12 (3)
(Hodgson's Hawk Eagle)

Identification: (M70, F76 cm) Very broad winged. Dark brown hood with long thin black crest. Distinguishable from Changeable by creamy upper breast becoming barred rufous on belly. Flanks, undertail coverts, and tibia barred rufous and white. Overhead: fingered, broad wings narrowing at the bases, plain buff coverts and prominent bars on flight feathers and tail. Legs feathered to large, powerful dull-yellow feet. Sexes alike. Juvenile: very pale underparts with almost unmarked wing coverts, narrow barring on tail. Soars high on shallow V wings, tail normally spread, usually alone. Hunts by perching in cover to pounce onto small mammal or bird.

Voice: Usually silent but has shrill *tlueet-weet-weet.*

Status and distribution: Endemic race. Scarce in forests of hill country above 600 m, occasionally straying to villages and cultivation. Endangered.

Nesting: Large mass of sticks in tall tree in forest; December–March.

Species range: India, SE China, Japan.

FALCONS — Order: Falconiformes Family: Falconidae

SMALL to medium sized birds of prey with hooked bills, narrow pointed wings and long tails. Flight is fast and they perch with an upright stance. Well feathered tibia and bare strong tarsi. Juveniles can be difficult to identify.

LESSER KESTREL *Falco naumanni* — PLATE 13 (6)

Identification: (30 cm) Smaller than Common. Wing-tip reaches sub-terminal tail band when perched. Male: unspotted mantle, blue-grey greater coverts on upperwing, buff-white underwing, no moustachial stripe and rather less streaking on breast than Common. Female difficult to separate from female Common, look for lack of black eye-stripe, more contrast between upper primaries and secondaries, pale underwing compared with coverts and, if very close, fine streaking on crown and pale claws (Common has black claws). Second year male lacks the grey on inner upperwing. Hovers with faster wingbeats than Common, also glides more often than Common. Drops onto insects on ground, also takes insects in flight. Often gregarious.

Voice: Has high pitched *ki-ki-ki-ki*, or *kirri-kirri* but likely to be silent in Sri Lanka.

Status and distribution: Vagrant. One record to date. Prefers open country.

Range: S Europe, Africa, Asia.

COMMON KESTREL *Falco tinnunculus* — PLATE 13 (7)
(European Kestrel)

Identification: (35 cm) Pointed wings, somewhat rounded tail. Wing-tip does not reach sub-terminal tail band when perched. Legs and feet yellow-orange with black claws. Male: grey head with dark moustachial stripe, spotted mantle, breast, and belly. No grey on upperwing. Female and juvenile: more heavily barred and spotted on underwing than Lesser. Frequently hovers or perches on high branch looking down for small animal prey. Stoops to carry off prey in claws, often eating on wing. Solitary.

Voice: A loud *kee-kee-kee-kee*.

Status and distribution: Scarce breeding resident in drier parts of the eastern side of the mountains supplemented by winter visitors in open or thinly wooded country throughout.

Nesting: Sparse nest on ledge of cliff; March–June.

Range: Europe, Africa, Asia, Japan, Philippines.

AMUR FALCON *Falco amurensis* PLATE 13 (5)

(Eastern Red-legged Falcon) (*Falco vespertinus amurensis*)
(Eastern Red-footed Falcon)

Identification: (29 cm) Relatively longer wings and shorter tail than Common Kestrel. Reddish cere, orange-yellow eye-ring, orange legs and feet. Male: slaty grey with white underwing coverts. Female: whitish underparts, streaks and arrows on body with pale orange thighs and undertail coverts, barred underwing. Juvenile: more heavily barred underwing especially on lesser coverts, and no orange on thighs. Hovers, but less often than Common Kestrel, takes insects in mid-air or perches on branch or post and pounces on prey. Active well into dusk.

Voice: Usually silent but has *kiwee-kiwee*.

Status and distribution: Winter vagrant to low country.

Range: E and S Africa, E and S Asia.

RED-NECKED FALCON *Falco chicquera* PLATE 13 (4)

(Red-headed Merlin)

Identification: (34 cm) Only local falcon with a chestnut head. Appears pale with dark outer upperwing. Sexes alike but female slighty larger. Juvenile: duller head, heavier barring below and some black barring on back. Flight very fast and direct, usually hunts in pairs, dashing through cover taking small birds by surprise. Will also take small prey from ground.

Voice: Probably silent in winter but has *kee-kee-kee* call.

Status and distribution: Vagrant to northern dry zone.

Range: Africa, S Asia.

ORIENTAL HOBBY *Falco severus* PLATE 13 (3)

(Indian Hobby)

Identification: (28 cm) Like small Shaheen but with unmarked rufous underwing coverts. Narrow wings, shortish tail. Black hood; throat and cheek-patch white. Sexes alike. Juvenile: browner above, paler rufous below with black streaks on underparts and barred underwing coverts. Very fast dashing swift-like flight takes insect prey and occasionally small birds on the wing; sometimes takes small animals from ground. Most active dawn and dusk. Perches in trees (not on rocks) unlike Peregrine and Shaheen. Forms small flocks.

Voice: A rapid, high pitched *kee-kee-kee.*

Status and distribution: Rare winter visitor. Possible anywhere but prefers forests.

Range: E Himalayas, SE Asia, Philippines, New Guinea.

PEREGRINE FALCON *Falco peregrinus*

NB The Peregrine is represented in Sri Lanka by two distinct races:

EASTERN PEREGRINE FALCON *F. p. calidus* (*F. p. japonensis*) PLATE 13 (1)

Identification: (**M41**, **F48** cm) Heavy bodied, broad-based pointed wings, relatively short tail. Blackish hood with white cheeks and dark moustache stripe, finely barred underparts. Sexes alike but female much larger. Juvenile: browner above and streaked below. From Shaheen at all ages by paler, more fringed upperparts and barred whitish underparts but both forms vary in coloration. Very strong flight with rapid wingbeats and glides on longish wings, shortish barred tail normally closed, chasing or stooping in long, fast, diagonal dive onto bird prey which it takes to a perch to eat. Soars in circles to great heights. Most active at dawn and dusk. Solitary.

Voice: A shrill *kek-kek-kek-kek.*

Status and distribution: Scarce winter visitor throughout. Sometimes comes into towns roosting on ledges of buildings.

Species range: Almost world-wide.

SHAHEEN *F. p. peregrinator* PLATE 13 (2)

(Shaheen Falcon)

Identification: (**M38**, **F44** cm) Smaller than *F. p. calidus* with darker upper plumage and rufous underparts with weak barring on body. Beware, plumage variable. From Rufous-bellied Eagle by smaller size, pointed wings and white patch behind the cheek. From Hobby by much larger size and lacks the chestnut underwing coverts. Sexes alike but female larger. Juvenile: streaked body. Habit is similar to that of *F. p. calidus.*

Voice: A loud scream *hehehehe.*

Status and distribution: Scarce resident, preferring steep hills with cliffs and forest but not above 1200 m.

Nesting: On inaccessible cliff ledge; December–April.
Range of Shaheen race: India, S China.

PARTRIDGES, QUAILS, SPURFOWL, JUNGLEFOWL, AND PEAFOWL Order: Galliformes Family: Phasianidae

RATHER plump birds with short, rounded wings, small heads and powerful, bare legs and feet. Males and, in some species, the females have spurs. Mainly vegetarian, spending much of their time skulking and feeding on the ground for which they have short, strong bills. Flight is heavy and whirring with legs retracted, usually dropping into cover after a short distance. Juveniles develop quickly assuming plumage similar to that of female. Often in small groups.

PAINTED FRANCOLIN *Francolinus pictus watsoni* PLATE 14 (1)
(Ceylon Painted Partridge)

Identification: (30 cm) Male: chestnut face, spotted underparts, black outer tail feathers. Female and juvenile generally duller, rump and tail browner with whitish throat and finely barred below. Usually in cover, most likely to be seen at dawn and dusk when feeding, and during breeding season when the male will perch on a boulder and call. Shows black and white spotted plumage, black outer tail feathers and rufous on the wings when flying to cover. In pairs or small groups.
Voice: *Kuserk-kuserk-kuserk.*
Status and distribution: Endemic race. Scarce in dry grasslands of eastern foothills of Uva up to 1400 m. Endangered.
Nesting: Well hidden grass-lined hollow in ground under tussock; March–June.
Species range: India.

GREY FRANCOLIN *Francolinus pondicerianus ceylonensis* PLATE 14 (2)
(Ceylon Grey Partridge)

Identification: (31 cm) Brown head with broad pale eyebrow and obvious black-edged rufous throat patch. Broadly barred with pale shaft streaks above, finely barred below. Dark red legs and feet. Sexes alike. Juvenile has paler head and less obvious throat patch which lacks black edging. Keeps to ground, running from danger or making short whirring flight showing mainly chestnut tail. Feeds by scratching ground for seeds. Walks upright. Usually in small groups except in nesting season when in pairs. Noisy, especially at dawn and dusk.

Voice: *Ka-tee klar-ka, ka-tee klar-ka* like a rusty pump. Also *keeyakok, keeyakok* and *kito, kito, kito*.
Status and distribution: Endemic race. Dry scrub and rough pastures of coastal lowlands of N and NW.
Nesting: Grass-lined scrape under small bush or tussock; April–August.
Species range: Iran, Pakistan, India.

RAIN QUAIL *Coturnix coromandelica* PLATE 14 (3)
(Black-breasted Quail)

Identification: (18 cm) Male: characteristic face pattern and breast with heavy black streaking. Female: cream eyebrow and brown streaking on breast below a buff throat. Runs when threatened, only flies with whirring wings as last resort. Solitary, in pairs, or occasionally in small groups.
Voice: A repeated *which-which, which-which*, mainly heard at dawn or dusk.
Status and distribution: Rare winter visitor to grassland, scrub, and dry cultivation of lowlands and lower hills.
Range: India, Myanmar.

BLUE-BREASTED QUAIL *Coturnix chinensis* PLATE 14 (4)
(Indian Blue Quail) (*Excalfactoria chinensis*)

Identification: (14 cm) Very small with bright yellow legs. Male: black throat with bold white cheek and necklace, blue-grey breast, chestnut belly. Female: from other quail by pale throat and barred underparts. From male buttonquails by uniform upperwing colour. Stays on ground unless really threatened when flies briefly in a straight line to cover. Small groups, or pairs during nesting season.
Voice: *Tee-tee-tew*.
Status and distribution: Resident in damp grassy areas, swamps, paddy, and tank edges up to 1800 m; throughout.
Nesting: Grass-lined hollow hidden in vegetation on damp ground; May, August–September, and December–January.
Range: E and S Africa, S and SE Asia, Borneo, New Guinea, Australia.

JUNGLE BUSH QUAIL *Perdicula asiatica* PLATE 14 (5)

Identification: (16 cm) Striking brown, white, and buff facial pattern with a rufous eyebrow stripe continuing down neck, brick-red throat patch. Underparts barred in male, rufous in female. Juvenile: more generally brown with buff mottling. In small groups, pairs during nesting season. Normally keeps in cover bursting into brief flight if observers get too close. Comes into the open to feed on seeds especially after rain.
Voice: A piping call *whee-whee-whee*, and a low chuckling alarm.

Status and distribution: Resident in grass and scrub of dry eastern hills and nearby lowlands.
Nesting: March–April.
Range: S Asia.

SRI LANKA SPURFOWL *Galloperdix bicalcarata* PLATE 14 (8)

Identification: (34 cm) Male: red bill and orbital skin, heavily spotted white above and below, black tail. Bright red legs and feet with two or more spurs. Female: reddish brown with white throat. One or two spurs. Bill and orbital skin a duller red than in the male. Very secretive, keeps on ground in deep cover in the forest, scratching for food. Rarely flies, usually runs from danger. Roosts in trees.
Voice: Noisy choruses of *yuhuhu, yuhuhu, yuhuhu, yuhuhu, yuhuheeya*, each syllable rising in pitch, often setting off a chorus from other Spurfowl.
Status and distribution: Endemic species. In forests of wet zone low country and in hills up to 1800 m. Also in forests of dry zone.
Nesting: Scrape in ground beneath bush or rock; November–March and July–September.
Range: Sri Lanka.

SRI LANKA JUNGLEFOWL *Gallus lafayettii* PLATE 14 (9)

Identification: (M69, F36 cm) Close relative of wild ancestor of domestic hen. Male like a small rooster. Female: smaller, dull brownish, bare face, spotted and streaked below, heavily barred on wing. Similar in habit to domestic hen. Mainly on ground, scratching for food, flying up to branch when threatened, clucking. Male crows at dawn. Wings flapped noisily when challenged. Roosts high in trees, solitarily or in small groups. Shy where persecuted, can be tame in deep forest.
Voice: Male: a high pitched rooster-like crow *cor-cor-chow*, at dawn often from a tree branch. Female: *kwikkuk, kwikkukkuk*.
Status and distribution: Endemic species. In jungle and dense scrub throughout but now mainly in reserves.
Nesting: In scrape in cover on ground or on a pile of vegetation just off the ground; mostly in December–April and August–September, but possible any time of year.
Range: Sri Lanka.

INDIAN PEAFOWL *Pavo cristatus* PLATE 14 (10)
(Common Peafowl)
(Blue Peafowl)

Identification: (M175, F96 cm) Both sexes have crest of bare shafted feathers but only the male has the train. Walks long distances in search of food with the male's train held parallel to ground. Usually in small groups. Scratches ground when feeding. Wary, runs for cover when threatened. Generally stays on ground but will fly with tail fanned (male's train held in a bundle) to cross obstacles or to go to roost. Roosts in trees. Male erects and spreads train in display, fluttering wings.

Voice: Very loud *peehawn, peehawn*. Female has *kwikkuk, kwikkukkuk...* and a hen-like *kra, krark*. Alarm: a squawk plus a loud hollow grunt.

Status and distribution: Resident. Open areas and scrub of low country dry zone, mainly in reserves.

Nesting: Slight hollow in ground hidden in dense cover; December–May.

Range: India.

BUTTONQUAILS — Order: Gruiformes Family: Turnicidae (Bustardquails)

SMALL, rounded game birds with very short tails and lacking a hind toe. Similar to quails in form and behaviour but distinguished from them in flight by contrast between sandy upperwing coverts and dark flight feathers. Very secretive, often only showing their presence by small scrapes where they have been dust-bathing. Females are bigger and more brightly coloured than the males, taking the dominant role in courtship and driving off rivals. The males incubate and rear the young.

SMALL BUTTONQUAIL *Turnix sylvatica* PLATE 14 (6)

(Andalusian Hemipode)
(Little Bustardquail)

Identification: (14 cm) Very small with a pointed tail. Brown crown with a white central stripe, spotted buffish breast. From female Barred by spots not bars below. Skulks, usually staying on ground running in zig-zags from danger. Scratches ground in search of food. If it flies, keeps low, landing after a few metres. In pairs or solitary. Very shy.

Voice: Female has deep repeated hoot, like a distant cow.

Status and distribution: Winter vagrant to open country of dry lowlands.

Range: Iberia, Africa, S and SE Asia, Java, Philippines.

BARRED BUTTONQUAIL *Turnix suscitator leggei* PLATE 14 (7)

(Ceylon Bustardquail)

Identification: (M13, F14 cm) From Small Buttonquail by barred (not spotted) breast and upper belly. Female: dark brown crown with an indistinct pale central line, black throat, rufous belly. Male generally duller than female, pale not black throat, barred breast, and tawny belly. Keeps in cover on ground but will fly short distances showing buff patches on 'shoulders'. Very jerky walk. Most likely to be seen at dawn and dusk. In pairs or solitary.

Voice: Female has loud, low pitched, sustained *purr*.

Status and distribution: Endemic race. Grass, scrub of lowlands and lower hills, preferring dry zone.

Nesting: On dry grass in well concealed hollow at base of shrub or tussock; most of year but most likely January–March and July–August.

Species range: S and SE Asia, Java, Sulawesi, Philippines.

Rails, crakes, and coots

Order: Gruiformes
Family: Rallidae

Medium to small water birds with short, rounded wings, short tails and long legs. Feet not webbed. Swim well. Trail legs in whirring, laboured flight but rarely fly, usually running through vegetation away from danger. Constantly flick tail when walking. Generally secretive, skulking in swampy, weedy places, and often nocturnal. Noisy, more often heard than seen. Young active soon after hatching.

SLATY-BREASTED RAIL *Rallus striatus* Plate 15 (1)
(Blue-breasted Banded Rail) (*Gallirallus striatus*)

Identification: (27 cm) Chestnut crown and nape, rest of upperparts banded brown and white. Slate-grey cheeks and breast. Juvenile: brown breast and duller with less distinct barring. Heavy flight with slow flaps and legs trailing. Skulks in vegetation. Walks upright with head and tail bobbing. Can swim. Less shy than others in the family. Solitary or in pairs.

Voice: Generally silent but has a staccato double *cluck* and a grunt.

Status and distribution: Resident, possibly also a winter visitor. Scarce in wet areas up to 1800 m.

Nesting: Pile of grass stems on swamp; July–October, December.

Range: S and SE Asia, Borneo, Java, Philippines.

WATER RAIL *Rallus aquaticus* Plate 15 (2)

Identification: (28 cm) Relatively longer bill than in other rails and with red on lower mandible. Slate-grey face including eyebrow, white throat, slate-grey breast, black and white broadly barred flanks. Pinkish legs and feet. Sexes alike. Juvenile: paler bill, lacks grey on face and breast, is generally duller with underparts tinged chestnut and buff, white bars on wing coverts. Very difficult to see because of skulking habit. Fluttering flight with legs dangling. Can swim. Solitary.

Voice: Mainly silent in winter but has various calls including a *kik, kik, kik*.

Status and distribution: Winter vagrant to marshes, lowland paddy, mangroves in lowlands.

Species range: Europe, NW Africa, N and C Asia.

SLATY-LEGGED CRAKE *Rallina eurizonoides* PLATE 15 (3)

(Banded Crake)

Identification: (25 cm) Chestnut head, neck, and breast. Uniform brown back. Boldly barred black and white belly and flanks, slaty legs and feet. Juvenile: brown head and breast. Heavy flight. Will fly up to perch in trees. Runs with a jerky gait, tail flicking. Skulking and largely nocturnal. Most likely to be seen when arriving on migration.

Voice: A long drumming croak, *krrrrrrr-ar-kraa-kraa-kraa*.

Status and distribution: Regular winter visitor to swampy wet areas in lowlands but more frequent in hill country up to 1500 m.

Range: India, SE Asia, Philippines, Sulawesi.

CORNCRAKE *Crex crex* PLATE 15 (4)

Identification: (26 cm) Short thick bill. Blue-grey eyebrow, face, and breast, brown barred buff flanks and undertail coverts, chestnut wings with darker flight feathers. Flesh-coloured legs and feet. Sexes alike. Juvenile has buff breast. Clumsy flight with legs dangling showing chestnut wings. Reluctant to fly, preferring to skulk in cover. If flushed, returns to cover almost immediately.

Voice: Mostly silent in winter. Has rasping *crex-crex*, and a mew.

Status and distribution: Winter vagrant to wet areas in lowlands.

Range: Europe, N Africa, C Asia.

BAILLON'S CRAKE *Porzana pusilla* PLATE 15 (5)

Identification: (19 cm) Smallest local rail. Brown upperparts with white and dark brown streaks on back; blue-grey face, throat, neck, and upper breast; barred black and white flanks and belly. Red iris, short green bill with dark tip, greenish (or pinkish) legs and feet. Female is duller with brown ear coverts. Immature has buff where adult is grey. Skulks in deep cover. Typical rail flight, quickly returning to cover. Tail-bobbing walk.

Voice: A loud *crek* sometimes repeated in an accelerating run.

Status and distribution: Scarce winter visitor. Dense vegetation in swampy areas of lowlands.
Range: Europe, Africa, Asia, New Guinea, Australia, New Zealand.

RUDDY-BREASTED CRAKE *Porzana fusca* PLATE 15 (6)
(Ruddy Crake) (*Amaurornis fuscus*)

Identification: (21 cm) Only local crake with orange red legs (Water Rail has pinkish legs). Chestnut head and breast, plain brown nape and upperparts; belly and rear flanks weakly barred. Red iris, greenish bill with yellow tip to lower mandible, orange-red legs and feet. Sexes alike. Juvenile: duller, lacks chestnut and finely barred below. Distinguishable from juvenile Slaty-legged by shorter bill and pale eyebrow. Flight slow and clumsy with red feet dangling. Less shy than other crakes sometimes feeding away from cover.
Voice: Usually silent but has a repeated *Keek*.
Status and distribution: Scarce resident and winter visitor. Swamps, paddy, and wet areas of lowlands or by streams up to 1400 m.
Nesting: On pile of reed stems and grass on swampy ground; June–September.
Range: India, China, Japan, Philippines, Sulawesi.

WHITE-BREASTED WATERHEN *Amaurornis phoenicurus* PLATE 15 (7)

Identification: (31 cm) Characteristic white face, throat, breast, and belly. Red iris, pale green bill with a red patch at base of upper mandible. Sexes alike. Juvenile: brown-grey above, off-white face and underparts. Distinguish from Common Moorhen by lack of streaking on flanks and no white under tail. Feeble flight with legs trailing. Flicks tail when walking showing rufous undertail coverts. Swims well but rarely. Often emerges from cover to feed early and late in day. Sometimes clambers over vegetation. Usually in pairs.
Voice: Noisy when breeding with an excited *quaarr, quaarr, korowakwak, korowakwak* and *kor, kor, akcow*, even during night. Mostly silent at other times.
Status and distribution: Common resident. Swamps, paddy, wet areas with dense vegetation up to 1800 m.
Nesting: Mass of weed in vegetation on wet ground or in low bush. June–October.
Range: India, SE Asia, Philippines, Sulawesi.

WATERCOCK *Gallicrex cinerea* PLATE 15 (8)
(Kora)

Identification: (M42, F36 cm) Breeding male: slaty-black with scaling on mantle and buff-white undertail coverts. Yellow bill with striking bright red base and horn-like shield. Dull red legs. Female and non-breeding male: brown upperparts with buff fringes; buff below with fine dark bars across breast and belly. Yellowish bill (male's shield is reduced and loses the 'horn'), dark green legs. Appears dark and nondescript. Typical rail flight. Tail-bobbing walk. Very secretive, mainly crepuscular and nocturnal. Aggressive in courtship.

Voice: Deep, repetitive, booming calls made with head held upright; *kok, kok, kok…, oodoomp, oodoomp, oodoomp…* or a repeated clucking.

Status and distribution: Resident. Swamps, paddy, reed beds in lowlands.

Nesting: Mass of weed well hidden in dense vegetation; July–August.

Range: India, China, Japan, Philippines, Sulawesi.

COMMON MOORHEN *Gallinula chloropus* PLATE 15 (9)

(Common Gallinule)

Identification: (32 cm) Sooty black with red shield on yellow-tipped bill; white stripe on side, white undertail coverts with central black line. Red iris. Greenish-yellow legs and feet with orange band just below tibial feathers and long toes. Sexes alike. Juvenile: brownish and lacks red shield. Distinguish from juvenile Coot by white line on side and white under tail. Spends much time on the water but usually near cover. Sits high in water. Jerks head and tail, showing white undertail coverts when swimming and walking. Laboured flight, needs to run across water to take off. Can dive to avoid danger. In pairs or small flocks.

Voice: A loud *kirrik* and a *kirrik, kek, kek, kek*. Noisy in breeding season, even at night.

Status and distribution: Resident. Fresh water with vegetation in lowlands, more common in dry zone.

Nesting: Heap of weed on tussock at edge of water; March–July.

Range: Europe, Asia, Americas, and many oceanic islands.

PURPLE SWAMPHEN *Porphyrio porphyrio* PLATE 15 (10)

(Purple Coot) (*Porphyrio poliocephalus*)

(Purple Gallinule)

Identification: (43 cm) Large, green-blue with pale head, greenish wings, no pale line on flanks, white undertail coverts. Bill duller out of breeding season. Sexes alike except female has smaller shield. Juvenile: duller and grey with reduced shield. Heavy flight with feet extending beyond tail, usually of short duration but can make long flights. Flicks tail showing white undertail coverts when walking, clambering over vegetation or swimming. Gregarious. Swims well and spends a lot of time chasing others. Sometimes feeds by pecking pith from vegetation held in claws. In groups. Shy, staying in cover where persecuted, less so when undisturbed.

Voice: Various cackling, clucking, and hooting noises; also a soft *cluck-cluck*, contact call.
Status and distribution: Common resident. Reed-beds, swamps, and weedy tanks of low country.
Nesting: On heap of vegetation in reed-bed or swamp; February–May, possibly July–August.
Range: Europe, Africa, Asia, New Guinea, Australia.

COMMON COOT *Fulica atra* PLATE 15 (11)
(Black Coot)

Identification: (38 cm) Slaty black with narrow white tips to secondaries and broad white forehead shield and bill. No white under tail. Lobed toes, dull green feet and tarsi, orange tibia. Sexes alike. Juvenile: lacks the juvenile Moorhen's white line on side and white undertail coverts. Very young birds have rufous heads. Heavy flight with fast wingbeats and feet trailing, needing long, pattering take-off from water. Swims well jerking head. Dives frequently to feed. Gregarious and argumentative, especially in the breeding season.
Voice: Loud, explosive *kik* or *kewk* calls, also heard at night.
Status and distribution: Scarce resident in tanks and water bounded by vegetation around Mannar, Anuradhapura, and Chilaw in northern lowlands. Appears to be spreading southwards.
Nesting: On large heap of vegetation in cover at edge of water; January–April, possibly longer.
Range: Europe, N Africa, Asia, New Guinea, Australia.

JACANA Order: Charadriiformes Family: Jacanidae

WETLAND birds with long legs and very long, slender toes and claws enabling them to walk on floating vegetation. There is a hard spur at the bend of the wing which becomes enlarged in the breeding season.

PHEASANT-TAILED JACANA *Hydrophasianus chirurgus* PLATE 15 (12)

Identification: (30 cm increasing to 50 cm or more (with tail) in breeding season, females somewhat bigger and longer tailed than males.) Brown, white, and yellow head pattern. Bluish legs and feet with very long thin toes. Sexes alike. Juvenile: more scaled above, lacks white wing coverts, has only a pale breast band and dirtier white on head. Weak, flapping flight, normally low with legs trailing, showing black-edged white wings, black body, and long tail when breeding. Can swim but usually walks gracefully on the water weed. Sociable. Not shy.

Voice: Nasal *tew, tew, tew* and a cat-like *miuu*....

Status and distribution: Common resident. Weed covered water in low country.

Nesting: On small pile of water weed on wet vegetation; February–July.

Range: India, SE Asia, Philippines, Java.

Painted-snipe Order: Charadriiformes Family: Rostratulidae

Brightly coloured snipe-like birds, although not closely related to them, with short, broad wings and slower flight than the true snipes. Long bill, though shorter than in most true snipes, slightly down-curved at the tip. There is a sexual role reversal: the females are larger, more strikingly marked than the males and they lead the courtship; the males incubate the eggs and rear the young.

GREATER PAINTED-SNIPE *Rostratula benghalensis* Plate 22 (1)
(Painted Snipe)

Identification: (**M**25, **F**28 cm) Look for white eye-ring (off-white in male) merging into short stripe towards nape, white 'harness', white belly and long bill curving down slightly and thickening at tip. Female: brown eyebrow and buff crown stripe, chestnut cheeks and throat, glossy dark olive back, white belly and barred wings. Male: smaller, much less boldly marked and greyer about the head and breast, more spotted and barred on scapulars and wings than female. Juvenile: like pale male with smaller spots on grey wing coverts. Mainly crepuscular or nocturnal, resting in cover during the day. If flushed, flies from beneath feet with slow, flapping flight on broad and rounded wings with legs dangling, showing white on belly continuing onto underwing coverts, returning to cover a short distance away. Usually in pairs or small groups.

Voice: A low *ooop,ooop*..., a purring, and a whistle.

Status and distribution: Resident. Swamps, marshes, and undisturbed paddy in low country and lower hills.

Nesting: Small heap of grass and reeds on tussock at edge of marsh or paddy; November–May.

Range: Africa, S Asia, Java, Philippines, Australia.

CRAB-PLOVER Order: Charadriiformes Family: Dromadidae

MEDIUM sized shore birds with strong, heavy bills and long legs with front three toes webbed.

CRAB-PLOVER *Dromas ardeola* PLATE 16 (1)

Identification: (40 cm) Large black bill and sturdy, blue-grey legs. White underwing with darker tips to primaries. Sexes alike. Juvenile: like adult but has grey upperparts and grey streaks on crown and neck. Rather tern-like flight on long pointed wings, legs extending well beyond tail. Often flies in formation, calling. Can swim. Feeds wading or walking along shore. Solitary or in small flocks. Partly nocturnal.
Voice: *Krook* and a flight call *cherruk*.
Status and distribution: Scarce resident. Beaches, estuaries, and lagoons of N and NW coasts, occasionally in south.
Nesting: Digs a burrow in a sand bank by the shore; May–June.
Range: Shores of Indian Ocean.

OYSTERCATCHER Order: Charadriiformes Family: Haematopodidae

MEDIUM-LARGE, sturdy wading birds with long, straight, brightly coloured bills.

EURASIAN OYSTERCATCHER *Haemotopus ostralegus* PLATE 16 (2)

Identification: (43 cm) Black with white rump, tail coverts, and tail except for black terminal band, and white belly. Broad white wing bar. Long, sturdy, straight, orange-red bill, legs pink-purple. Mostly seen in non-breeding plumage with a white band across throat. Lacks the white band in breeding plumage. Sexes alike. Juvenile: as non-breeder but the black has brown tinge, the bill is narrower with a dusky tip and the legs are duller. Usually in small groups, often with other waders. Fast and direct flight with fast, shallow wingbeats. Feeds by probing on rocky shores, rest on rocks or remote sand bars. Wary.
Voice: Has a loud, two syllable piping call *klee-peep, klee-peep*..., but usually silent in Sri Lanka.

Status and distribution: Scarce winter visitor to reefs, sand-bars, lagoons of dry zone coasts.
Range: Europe, N Africa, Asia, Japan.

Avocet and stilt

Order: Charadriiformes
Family: Recurvirostridae

Graceful black and white waders with very long legs and slender bills closely associated with wet areas. Gregarious and often very noisy.

BLACK-WINGED STILT *Himantopus himantopus* Plate 16 (3)
(Sri Lanka Stilt) (*Himantopus ceylonensis*)

Note: There is debate on the taxonomy of this species. Some authorities consider *H. (h.) ceylonensis* with a paler grey crown to be a separate and endemic species.
Identification: (38 cm) Very long, bright red legs and long, thin, tapering black bill are distinctive. Black mantle with glossy sheen in male, dull dark brown in female, the sexes otherwise alike. Breeding: blackish area on crown variable (in extent and density) sometimes extending down nape, turning grey out of breeding season. Juvenile: grey crown and neck, brown mantle with pale fringes and white trailing edge on wings. Flies with slow regular wingbeats, the legs trailing far behind the tail. Wades with deliberate strides usually lifting the feet clear of the water. Gregarious.
Voice: Noisy, *ik-ik-ik-ik...* and *gnreet.*
Status and distribution: Resident on coasts, lagoons, marshes, and tanks of dry zone. Possibly supplemented by winter visitors to wet and dry lowlands.
Nesting: Small colonies in scrapes at edge of tank or lagoon; June–July.
Range: Europe, Africa, Asia.

PIED AVOCET *Recurvirostra avosetta* Plate 16 (4)

Identification: (44 cm) Long, thin, tapering, upturned black bill and bold black and white pattern on wings in flight. Bluish legs with partially webbed feet. Sexes alike but female's bill can be shorter and more up-curved than male's and female may show faint eye-ring. Juvenile: dull brown in place of black and the white can be mottled brown. Flies with fairly fast wingbeats, legs trailing well beyond tail. Can swim. Wades, scything bill from side to side in water or mud when feeding, sometimes up-ending. Gregarious.
Voice: A loud *klueet-klueet...* and a grunting flight call.
Status and distribution: Irregular winter visitor to coasts, marshes, and tidal flats of dry zone.
Range: Europe, Africa, Asia.

THICK-KNEES (Stone Curlews) Order: Charadriiformes Family: Burhinidae

MEDIUM sized plover-like birds with long legs, large heads, strong bills and big eyes. Strong flight on long, pointed wings. Mainly nocturnal or crepuscular. Terrestrial and preferring arid, open country, scrub or shores. Food is mainly invertebrates.

EURASIAN THICK-KNEE *Burhinus oedicnemus* PLATE 16 (5)
(Stone Curlew)

Identification: (41 cm) Staring yellow eye, chunky head, short neck, dark and white bar on closed wing and pale grey panel on greater coverts. Yellow bill with black tip, yellow legs with sturdy knees. Sexes alike but male shows a more prominent black bar above the white on the closed wing. Juvenile: less obvious face pattern and wing markings, warm brown upperparts. Well camouflaged, tends to sit tight when danger threatens or runs with head held low. If pressed, will run and fly a short distance with stiff wing beats. Direct flight, sometimes with long glides showing characteristic white patches on primaries and two white wing bars. Sometimes sits with tarsi resting on ground. Usually in pairs or small flocks. Mainly crepuscular and nocturnal, resting in shade during day.

Voice: A curlew-like *coo-ree* and a descending piping whistle often heard in the dark.

Status and distribution: Resident. Mainly on coasts and scrubby areas of dry zone. Rarely in wet zone.

Nesting: A shallow scrape on ground; June–August.

Range: Europe, N Africa, Middle East, S Asia.

GREAT THICK-KNEE *Esacus recurvirostris* PLATE 16 (6)
(Great Stone Plover) (*Esacus magnirostris recurvirostris*)

Identification: (51 cm) Much larger than Eurasian Thick-knee and with a much larger, heavier, slightly upturned black bill turning yellow towards tip and pale grey-green legs. Large squarish head, big yellow eye with bold black and white face pattern. Wing pattern similar to Eurasian but with larger white patches, clearly visible in flight. Flies with stiff, jerky wingbeats on less pointed wings than Eurasian, neck extended looking a bit duck-like. Runs well and can swim, sitting high in water. Mainly nocturnal and crepuscular, resting in open during day. Usually in pairs or small flocks. Wary.

Voice: A curlew-like wailing cry and a descending piping whistle, often heard at night.

Status and distribution: Resident. Coasts, lagoons, estuaries, and tank shores of dry lowlands.

Nesting: Eggs laid on ground on remote shingle strand or shore; January–August.

Range: India, Myanmar.

COURSER AND PRATINCOLES

Order: Charadriiformes
Family: Glareolidae

SMALL to medium sized somewhat plover-like birds which can be distinguished from them by the slightly down-curved bills. The courser is a mainly terrestrial bird with long legs and a thin bill. The pratincoles have short legs and short bills, and are largely aerial, feeding on the wing. All prefer open country, the pratincoles are usually found not far from water on dried river flood plains, tank, and lagoon edges.

INDIAN COURSER *Cursorius coromandelicus* PLATE 17 (1)

Identification: (25 cm) Chestnut crown, white eyebrow and black eye-stripe meeting on nape, and grey-brown mantle. White chin, chestnut throat and breast, centre of belly black, white lower belly and undertail coverts. Black primaries and dark grey secondaries. Long white legs. Sexes alike. Juvenile: pale eyebrow and lores, faint dark eye-stripe behind eye, upperparts strongly barred and spotted brown and buff; white underparts with slightly spotted rufous-buff breast. Spends much time on ground running around in short bursts, dipping then standing upright, sometimes pecking at invertebrate prey. Runs to avoid threat, eventually taking to air for a short, low flight on narrow, pointed wings. Usually in pairs or small groups.

Voice: Generally silent but has clucking flight call.

Status and distribution: Resident in arid coastal areas of N and NW, occasionally in SE.

Nesting: Lay on open bare ground; May–June.

Range: India.

COLLARED PRATINCOLE *Glareola pratincola* PLATE 17 (2)
(Common Pratincole)

Identification: (24 cm) Similar to Oriental but has longer, deeply forked tail, is paler above, has thin white trailing edge on secondaries and slightly narrower wings. The black edge to the throat patch is less pronounced and the longer outer-tail feathers usually protrude a little beyond the folded wing. Non-breeding birds briefly become duller and the throat patch is fringed with dark streaks during moult. Feeds on flying insects with swallow-like flight, often high. Also takes insects on ground. In flocks, often with other pratincoles. Most active dawn and dusk.

Voice: Noisy, *kee-ik* tern-like calls.

Status and distribution: Rare winter visitor to coastal areas of south-east.

Range: Mediterranean, Africa, NW India.

ORIENTAL PRATINCOLE *Glareola maldivarum* PLATE 17 (3)

(Eastern Collared Pratincole)
(Large Indian Pratincole)

Identification: (24 cm) Brown upperparts, white uppertail coverts and forked tail, shorter than Collared. Black-edged sandy throat, brown breast becoming white on belly. All dark upperwing, no white on trailing edge; chestnut underwing coverts and black primaries. Closed wings reach well beyond tail. Short legs. Non-breeding birds briefly become duller and the throat patch is fringed with dark streaks during moult. Sexes alike. Juvenile: similar to non-breeding but upperparts fringed buff with dark marking especially on scapulars. When feeding on flying insects the flight is swallow-like, on long, narrow, pointed wings, showing the forked tail when turning. Also feeds by running after insects on ground. Most active dawn and dusk, spending much of the day resting on the ground in scattered flocks. Roosts communally, sometimes in reed beds.

Voice: *Krrree, krrree…*

Status and distribution: Resident, mainly in coastal areas and tank edges in dry lowlands.

Nesting: No nest, eggs laid on bare ground or on old cow-pat; March–July.

Range: C, E, and SE Asia.

SMALL PRATINCOLE *Glareola lactea* PLATE 17 (4)

(Little Pratincole)

Identification: (17 cm) Smaller, paler, and more compact than other local pratincoles, also lacks black-edged throat patch and tail is hardly forked. White wing bar on upper- and underwing. Sandy grey above with black loral stripe (often absent in winter), brown forehead shading to grey on nape and central sub-terminal black patch on white tail. Buff throat and breast, white belly and undertail. Long, narrow wings with black primaries and their coverts, broad white bar and black trailing edge on secondaries; black axillaries and underwing coverts, often with a white primary patch. Black bill and

legs. Non-breeding birds are duller briefly during moult. Sexes alike. Juvenile: scaly upperparts and dark spots on throat.
Voice: A repeated *took, took* and a *kirrit* flight call.
Status and distribution: Resident in dry lowlands, mainly in arid coastal areas and on tank edges.
Nesting: In shallow scrape on sand or grit in open; March–June.
Range: India, SE Asia.

Plovers Order: Charadriiformes Family: Charadriidae

Small to medium sized waders of shores and open ground, usually near water. More compactly built with larger, rounder heads, thicker necks and shorter, sturdier bills than in the sandpipers. Plumage often boldly marked. Plovers have fast flight on sharply pointed wings, lapwings fly slower and have more rounded, flapping wings. Feed on invertebrates with characteristic movements; walk or run, pause, stand upright, bob head, thrust down at food, move on. Usually in flocks, often of mixed species. Nest on ground. Look for wing-bars and listen for calls.

YELLOW-WATTLED LAPWING *Vanellus malabaricus* Plate 17 (5)
(*Lobipluvia malabarica*)
(*Hoplopterus malabaricus*)

Identification: (27cm) Lemon-yellow wattles, black crown and white eye-stripes meeting at nape, black chin and sandy-brown upperparts, white tail with central black sub-terminal patch; sandy-brown breast separated from white belly by black band. Sandy-brown upperwing separated by white bar from black primaries and their coverts. Black trailing edge to secondaries. Long yellow legs but shorter than Red-wattled. Can be confused with Courser, look for yellow wattles and straight bill. Sexes alike. Juvenile: pale fringes, dark markings on upperparts and a streaked brown crown turning black with maturity. Easy flight, often low, showing conspicuous white wing-bar on dark wings, feet extending beyond black-banded tail. Solitary, in pairs or small flocks sometimes with the Red-wattled.
Voice: Persistent *tee-ee, tee-ee* .... and *kit, kit, kit* ... anxiety calls.
Status and distribution: Common resident. Arid areas, dry paddy and stony pastures of dry lowlands. Less dependent on water than Red-wattled.
Nesting: In shallow scrape on stony ground; May–July.
Range: India.

SOCIABLE LAPWING *Vanellus gregarius* PLATE 17 (6)
(Sociable Plover) (*Chettusia gregaria*)

Identification: (29 cm) From Red- and Yellow-wattled by lack of wattles, obvious eyebrow from forehead to nape and white secondaries. Non-breeding plumage: grey-brown crown, pale buff eyebrow, sandy brown back and white tail with black sub-terminal centre patch. Buff throat, brown breast, white belly and tail. Sandy brown upperwing with white secondaries, black primaries and their coverts; white underwing with black primaries. Short black bill and blackish legs projecting beyond tail in flight. Breeding plumage: black crown, white eyebrow, black line from bill through eye, rufous tinge on cheeks and black belly turning chestnut at rear. Sexes alike. Juvenile: similar to non-breeding adult but grey-brown throat, neck, and breast, streaked on head and breast, and pale fringes on mantle, scapulars, and wing coverts. Typical lapwing flight. Forms mixed flocks with other waders.
Voice: Generally silent in Sri Lanka but has a short high pitched whistle.
Status and distribution: Scarce and irregular winter visitor to open areas of low country.
Range: NE Africa, C Asia.

RED-WATTLED LAPWING *Vanellus indicus* PLATE 17 (7)
(*Lobivanellus indicus*)
(*Hoplopterus indicus*)

Identification: (33cm) Larger and longer winged and legged than Yellow-wattled. Red wattle and ring around eye. Black crown and nape, white ear-patch, white rump and tail with black sub-terminal band. Black throat and central upper breast, broad white stripe from eye down sides of neck. Red bill, tipped black, long yellow legs projecting beyond tail in flight. Black wing-tips separated from brown inner coverts by broad diagonal white bar. Non-breeding; duller with brown streaks on crown and white spots on throat. Sexes alike. Juvenile: duller and greyish on sides of face and throat. Slow and flapping flight. Feeds in typical plover fashion, usually on dry ground. In pairs or small groups. Mainly active dawn and dusk, even at night, resting in day. Wary.
Voice: A loud and persistent *did he do it* anxiety call.
Status and distribution: Common resident. Edges of tanks, dry paddy, or any open land not far from water in the lowlands and lower hills.
Nesting: In shallow scrape in open on stony ground; April–September.
Range: Middle East, S and SE Asia.

PACIFIC GOLDEN PLOVER *Pluvialis fulva* PLATE 17 (8)
(Asiatic Golden Plover) (*Pluvialis dominica fulva*)

Identification: 24 cm. Non-breeding plumage: mottled gold and brown on upperparts but appears brown, yellow-buff eyebrow, breast mottled brown and buff. Brown upperwing with faint wing bar, pale grey-brown underwing (Grey has white with black 'armpit'). Breeding plumage: black belly and under-tail (sometimes with white marks on under tail), gold on back brighter; black face, throat, and breast bordered by a white line from eyebrow to flank. Black bill and legs. Sexes nearly alike. Juvenile: like non-breeder but more yellow spotted above and more yellow on breast. Fast flight on sharp pointed wings with feet projecting beyond tail, usually in compact flocks. Runs in short spurts, standing tall when stopped. Wary.

Voice: A liquid *til-wee* flight call and a *chooo-it, chooo-it.* (Grey has three syllables.)

Status and distribution: Common winter visitor to open pasture near water, mud-flats, shores of lagoons and tanks, and dry paddy of lowlands.

Range: N, NE, and SE Asia, Australia, Alaska.

GREY PLOVER *Pluvialis squatarola (Squatarola squatarola)* PLATE 17 (9)

Identification: (28 cm) Larger than Golden with large head, sturdy black bill, shorter legs, white underwing with black 'armpit' and hunched stance. Non-breeding plumage: pale eyebrow, darker patch on ear, white patch on rump and black and white barred tail, appearing grey at a distance. White wing-bar, largely white underwing, and obvious black 'armpits'. Breeding plumage: black face, throat, breast, and upper belly with broad white edging, spotted black and silvery white above. Sexes almost alike but breeding female is generally a little browner. Juvenile: mottled golden buff above resembling Golden Plover but duller and has the black 'armpits'. Fast and direct flight on long pointed wings well bent at the 'wrist' appearing pale and showing the wing bar and white rump. Sluggish on ground, often resting on sand spit or mud bank. Usually solitary or in small groups with other waders. Wary.

Voice: A slurred, whistling *klee-oo-ee*, the middle syllable lower pitched (Golden has two syllables).

Status and distribution: Winter visitor to coasts, lagoons, and estuaries of both zones, normally by salt or brackish water. More common in north and east.

Range: Europe, Africa, Asia, Australia, America.

COMMON RINGED PLOVER *Charadrius hiaticula* PLATE 18 (1)

Identification: (19 cm) Larger and thicker set than Little Ringed with black-tipped orange bill, inconspicuous drab eye-ring (Little Ringed has obvious yellow one), bright orange to orange-yellow legs (beware of mud stains) and white wing bar. Non-breeding plumage: buffish forehead and eyebrow, brown crown, bold white collar and brown mantle. Dark breast band (sometimes broken in centre), white belly and undertail. Yellow-orange legs and feet. Female has less clearly marked breast band. Breeding plumage: black and white face pattern, bolder black breast band and more orange on base of bill. Juvenile: paler and has brown head markings with narrow white forehead and eyebrow, black bill, white collar, incomplete brown breast band and buff fringes on mantle and wing coverts. Fast flight with regular wingbeats. Active feeder, running, pausing, and pecking at food usually on ground, not in water. Gregarious. Wary.

Voice: A rising *kooo-eep*.

Status and distribution: Uncommon winter visitor to mud-flats and shores throughout.

Range: Europe, Africa, Asia, N America.

LONG-BILLED PLOVER *Charadrius placidus* PLATE 18 (2)

(Long-billed Ringed Plover)

Identification: (20 cm) Similar to Common Ringed and Little Ringed but slightly larger. It has a longer and thinner bill, is broader winged, longer tailed (extending beyond closed wings), and longer legged. Faint narrow wing-bar. Inconspicuous yellow eye-ring, longish black bill, brown tinge on ear coverts (not black as in Common Ringed), and pale yellow legs. Non-breeding are briefly duller during moult. Solitary or in small groups.

Voice: *Peewee*.

Status and distribution: Winter vagrant. Prefers coasts, estuaries, river banks, and tank edges.

Range: E Asia.

LITTLE RINGED PLOVER *Charadrius dubius jerdoni* PLATE 18 (3)

Identification: (16 cm) Similar to Common Ringed but smaller and slimmer. From breeding Common Ringed by lack of prominent wing-bar, legs dusky yellow to pinkish, short dark finer bill with some yellow at base of lower mandible, clear yellow eye-ring, and distinctive call. From Kentish by complete black chest band. Female has less clearly marked breast band. Juvenile: dull brown head above a white collar, all dark bill, pale fringed scapulars, incomplete brown band on chest, generally buffer on throat and forehead than Common Ringed juvenile. Fast and usually low flight in tight flocks, calling. Feeds in scattered flocks often with other waders. Has faster movements than Common Ringed.

Voice: A falling *pee-oo* and a flight call, *hwee*.

Status and distribution: Resident. Open pastures, mud-flats, drying paddy and tank edges of the dry zone supplemented by winter visitors of race *curonicus* in lowlands (see below).

Nesting: In a small scrape on gravely shore of a tank or a sandy beach; May–July.

Range: Europe, Africa, Asia, New Guinea.

Note: Race *C. d. curonicus* is similar to but larger (18cm) than *jerdoni* and has a slightly longer bill with less yellow at base of lower mandible. Has a more marked non-breeding plumage than *jerdoni*, the black on the head and breast band is replaced by brown and the white on the head by buff.

KENTISH PLOVER *Charadrius alexandrinus seebohmi* (*Leucopolius alexandrinus*) PLATE 18 (4)

Identification: (16 cm) Dumpy with large head, black bill, longish usually black legs (can be paler) set further back than on other plovers, incomplete breast band showing as spurs on sides of breast, broad white wing-bar and shortish tail. Male breeding plumage: white forehead sometimes with slight dark brow and variable amounts of white on face, grey-brown crown, white collar, grey-brown mantle, and white underparts with the breast spurs. Non-breeding male, female, and juvenile; slightly paler on head. Fast flight. Runs in short bursts. In pairs or small flocks, often with other waders. Not shy.

Voice: *Twit-twirrit* and a fast *crwair, crwair-a-wair.*

Status and distribution: Endemic race. Sand and mud beaches, salt flats, lagoon, and tank edges of dry lowlands.

Nesting: In a depression on short grass near water; March–August.

Species range: Europe, Africa, Asia.

Note: The resident population of *C. a. seebohmi* can be supplemented in the lowlands by race *alexandrinus,* an uncommon winter visitor which differs mainly by being slightly larger (17 cm) and having a rufous tinge on the crown in breeding plumage.

MONGOLIAN PLOVER *Charadrius mongolus* PLATE 18 (5)
(Lesser Sand Plover)

Identification: (20 cm) Similar to but smaller than Greater Sand Plover, both being larger than Kentish and lacking the white collar (beware—Kentish collar can be hidden when hunched). From Greater Sand by relatively smaller, more rounded head with steeper forehead; shorter, slimmer, less pointed bill and darker grey-green legs with shorter tibia and longer tarsi, the legs set further back than Greater Sand. Black bill and usually dark grey legs. Closed wings reach tip of tail. White wing-bar even width across primaries, white underwing, white edges to rump, white outer tail feathers. Non-breeding plumage: grey-brown above with white forehead and eyebrow, grey cheek-patch. White below with a grey-brown patch on side of breast. Breeding male: black band from forehead through eye to ear (Lesser Sand is never all black), white throat, chestnut breast. Breeding female: similar to male but forehead band is brown. Fast flight in tight flocks with legs not projecting beyond tail, alternately showing dark upper and white underwings as they bank, calling as they fly. Upright stance when relaxed, usually in flocks, sometimes with Greater Sand.

Voice: A *twip* flight call, a *chittik*, and a trill similar to Greater Sand Plover's.

Status and distribution: Winter visitor. Common on shores, mud-flats, salt marshes and open pasture of both zones.

Range: E Africa, C and SE Asia, Japan, Australia.

GREATER SAND PLOVER *Charadrius leschenaultii* PLATE 18 (6)

(Large Sand Plover)

Identification: (23 cm) Similar to Mongolian but larger, with relatively larger, flatter head and longer more pointed bill often with a swollen tip, and paler legs with long tibia. Wing bar broadens across primaries. Non-breeding plumage: like Mongolian but with faint eyebrow. Breeding male: black band from bill through forehead to eye and ear-coverts with a variable white patch on forehead (never all black), chestnut-tinged brown crown and a broad chestnut band across the breast. Fast flight on pointed wings, legs projecting well beyond tail. Usually adopts a more horizontal stance than Mongolian. Solitary or in twos or threes, sometimes with Mongolian.

Voice: Usually silent in winter apart from a trilling *kirrrr* or *trrrri* flight call.

Status and distribution: Winter visitor. Mainly coastal on shores, lagoons, and estuaries of dry zone, occasionally in wet zone.

Range: Africa, Asia, Australia.

CASPIAN PLOVER *Charadrius asiaticus* (*Eupoda asiatica*) PLATE 18 (7)

Identification: (19 cm) Tall and thin with long, pointed wings. Narrow wing-bar, white underwing with dark brown flight feathers, feet just projecting beyond tail in flight. Closed wings extend well beyond tail. From Greater Sand and Mongolian by slimmer bill, longer neck, slimmer body with an elongated rear end, less of a wing bar, less white on sides of tail. From Oriental by bolder eyebrow, darker cap and white underwing coverts. Non-breeding plumage: whitish eyebrow, brown eye-stripe, brown upperparts with white edges to rump; pale buff throat, complete grey-brown breast-band, white belly and undertail. Black bill, variable green or grey-brown legs. Breeding male: white eyebrow, cheeks and throat, broad chestnut band across breast with variable black line edging the white belly. Breeding female: grey-brown breast. Juvenile: as non-breeding with more buff fringes to upperparts. In flocks, not shy.

Voice: *Cheeup* and a shrill *quit.*
Status and distribution: Rare winter visitor to dry lowlands often away from water, occasionally in wet lowlands.
Range: Africa, S Asia.

ORIENTAL PLOVER *Charadrius veredus* PLATE 18 (8)
(Eastern Sand Plover)

Identification: (24 cm) Non-breeding plumage: similar in most ways to non-breeding Caspian but considerably larger, with relatively longer neck and wings, and only a very faint wing bar, all dark underwing and longer yellow-pink legs. Folded wings extend well beyond tail. Breeding male has paler head than Caspian. Fast flight, often high and twisting with feet projecting well beyond tail. Runs fast, stopping to bob head when alarmed. Solitary or in flocks, shy.
Voice: *chip, chip, chip* flight call.
Status and distribution: Winter vagrant to dry lowlands, often away from water.
Range: E Asia, Australia.

CURLEWS, SANDPIPERS, AND SNIPE — Order: Charadriiformes, Family: Scolopacidae

SMALL to medium sized waders, generally smaller headed than the plovers with angular, pointed wings and swift flight. Bills medium to long and slender; down-curved in the curlews. All are migrant to Sri Lanka and some are highly gregarious on wintering grounds. Mainly invertebrate feeders, prodding bills into mud or sand to feed. Identification of non-breeding birds can be a problem; look for bill length and shape, wing bars, rump colour, tail markings, and leg length. Identification of snipe presents many problems because they appear so similar in the field. Full descriptive notes are beyond the scope of this guide, *Shorebirds. an identification guide*, by Hayman, Marchant, and Prater is recommended.

BLACK-TAILED GODWIT *Limosa limosa limosa* PLATE 19 (2)

Identification: (M37, F43 cm) Tall and slim. Long straight tapering bill, orange-pink at base with black tip. Bold broad white wing-bar, white rump and black tail band, black-edged white underwing, legs project well beyond tail in flight. Non-breeding plumage: narrow white eyebrow, pale grey upperparts with poorly marked pale fringes on mantle, unstreaked breast, white belly and undertail. Breeding male plumage: head, neck, and breast become rufous with darker bars on belly; breeding female is paler rufous. Juvenile: like breeding female with pale cinnamon on neck and breast, buff fringes on mantle. Fast flight in tight, wheeling flocks showing black and white wing and tail pattern. Feeds by walking about in flocks probing mud or shallow water, lifting food forward (Dowitcher prods up and down). Shy.

Note: Race *L. l. melanuroides* is thought to be a less frequent winter visitor. It is smaller. Non-breeding plumage is darker above; breeding plumage shows a rufous neck but not breast.

Voice: Usually silent in winter but has a *wik-wik-wik*... flight call.

Status and distribution: Winter visitor and occasional summer loiterer to lagoons, estuaries, and tank edges of dry lowlands.

Range: Europe, N Africa, Asia, N Australia.

BAR-TAILED GODWIT *Limosa lapponica* PLATE 19 (3)

Identification: (M36, F41 cm) Long, slightly up-curved, orange-pink based bill with a black-tip. Distinguishable from Black-tailed by lack of white wing-bar, finely barred not black banded tail, more stocky appearance and slightly shorter legs (short tibia); from Whimbrel by slightly up-curved bill. Non-breeding plumage: creamy eyebrow, dark eye-stripe, pale fringes and dark shaft streaks on upperparts; pale streaked sandy-brown breast, white inverted V rump and barred tail, creamy belly and under-tail. No wing bar. Breeding male plumage: chestnut head and underparts. Breeding female: duller and often lacks chestnut resembling non-breeder. Juvenile: like breeding female but upperparts and breast are streaked brown and buff. In flocks, usually with other waders. Fast flight in tight flocks. Feeding similar to Black-tailed.

Voice: Generally silent in winter apart from a *kekak* call.

Status and distribution: Scarce winter visitor to dry zone coastal areas.

Range: Europe, Africa, Asia, Australia.

WHIMBREL *Numenius phaeopus phaeopus* PLATE 19 (5)

Identification: (43 cm) Smaller than Eurasian Curlew, with relatively shorter bill, dark crown with pale central stripe, buff eyebrow and dark eye-stripe. Long bill, down-curved at tip and long legs. White back and rump showing as an inverted V in flight (but see note below), and brown barred tail. White underwing coverts, barred flight feathers. Sexes alike. Juvenile: like adult but darker brown on upperparts with pale buff spots and fringes. Direct flight with faster wingbeats than Curlew, feet trailing behind tail. Feeds by poking and probing with long bill, singly or in small parties. Roosts in flocks, sometimes in trees.

Note: *N. p. variegatus,* with brown and white underwing coverts, back and rump, is thought to be an occasional winter visitor to the dry lowlands.

Voice: Fairly quiet in winter but has a characteristic rapidly whistled *pipipipipipi*... and a similar call to the Curlew.

Status and distribution: Regular winter visitor to coastal areas of lowlands, more common in dry zone.

Range: Almost world-wide.

SLENDER-BILLED CURLEW *Numenius tenuirostris* PLATE 19 (6)

Identification: (38 cm) Smaller and paler than other curlews with shorter all dark, finer-tipped bill, generally colder tones, dark crown and only a faint eyebrow. White back and rump showing as white V in flight, and white tail with thin brown barring. Underparts mainly white with brown streaks on neck and breast, dark spots on flanks (Eurasian Curlew has fine streaks) and white underwing coverts. Juvenile: like adult but with stronger contrast between dark outer primaries and coverts, and paler inner wing; very pale tail and uppertail coverts.

Voice: Similar to Eurasian Curlew but shorter and higher in pitch.

Status and distribution: Unconfirmed winter vagrant. Prefers coastal areas in winter. Highly endangered.

Range: Was E Europe, Iran, N Asia but declining. Possibly now only N Asia.

EURASIAN CURLEW *Numenius arquata* PLATE 19 (4)

Identification: (58 cm) Larger than Whimbrel, lacks the head pattern and has longer more evenly down-curved bill. Non-breeding plumage: grey-brown upperparts with whitish back and variably brown barred lower rump and tail. Pale throat, buff breast with brown streaks, cream belly, cream flanks with fine dark streaks, and usually white underwing. Upperparts are buff and brown in breeding season. Sexes alike. Juvenile: more buff below with fewer streaks on breast and flanks. Fast flight with slower wingflaps than of smaller curlews, often in line or V formation. Feeds by picking over pasture or probing in mud. Singly or in flocks, often with other waders. Roosts in flocks. Wary.

Voice: Winter calls of a rolling *cur-lee* and a repeated *coo-lit*.

Status and distribution: Winter visitor to lowlands, more common in north.

Range: Europe, Africa, Asia.

SPOTTED REDSHANK *Tringa erythropus* PLATE 20 (2)

Identification: (31 cm) More elegant and with longer, finer bill than Common Redshank, only has red on base of lower mandible, lacks white on secondaries and has longer and darker red legs. From non-breeding and juvenile Common by short dark eye-stripe and short white eyebrow, neither extending behind eye. Non-breeding plumage: grey upperparts with white back and rump, white tail with grey barring. Pale grey breast and white belly, white under-tail finely barred grey near tip. White underwing becoming grey on primaries. Breeding plumage: mainly black, some white spots on scapulars and wing coverts, white back, grey and white tail, white underwing contrasting with black body. Can look blotchy when moulting. Sexes alike. Juvenile: like non-breeding adult but browner and the breast and belly are dark with variable barring. Fast and direct flight with red feet trailing beyond tail and showing white back. Feeds in mud or in water sometimes almost swimming, singly or in flocks. Wary.

Voice: *Tew-it.*

Status and distribution: Rare winter visitor to tanks and lagoons of dry zone lowlands.

Range: Europe, W and N Africa, Asia.

COMMON REDSHANK *Tringa totanus* PLATE 20 (1)

Identification: (28 cm) Shorter, stouter bill than Spotted, longer than Ruff, with orange base and dark tip. Narrow white eye-ring, bright orange legs, white secondaries contrasting with dark upperwing. Non-breeding plumage: grey-brown upperparts, white back and rump showing white inverted V in flight and white tail barred brown (often appears all white). Off-white underparts with fine dark streaks, white underwing with grey primaries. Breeding plumage: cinnamon and brown tinges on upperparts and breast, and bolder streaks on breast. Juvenile: like non-breeder but more clearly spotted upperparts, thin dark streaks on flanks and belly and often yellowish bill and legs. Fast and erratic flight showing white back and secondaries. Feeds in mud or shallow water. Can swim. Solitary or in small groups with other waders. Noisy, excitable, and wary.

Voice: Noisy whistled *tew-tew-tew* alarm and *tew-oo-oo*, the first syllable slurred and descending.

Status and distribution: Regular winter visitor. Fairly common in coastal areas of dry zone, less so in wet zone.

Range: Europe, Africa, Asia, Sulawesi.

MARSH SANDPIPER *Tringa stagnatilis* PLATE 20 (3)

Identification: (24 cm) Tall and long necked with long thin, needle-like, straight bill and long greenish or dull yellow legs. Smaller, slenderer and finer-billed than Greenshank. Non-breeding plumage: white fringed pale grey-brown upperparts, white back and rump with barred tail. Grey eye-stripe, white eyebrow, forehead and face giving pale-headed appearance, white underparts. Dark upper wings without wing bar. Breeding plumage: finely dark-brown streaked crown and nape, white eyebrow, brown strongly notched and barred grey and cinnamon upperparts; brown spotted breast becoming chevrons on flanks. Sexes alike. Juvenile: like non-breeder but browner streaking on head and fine dark sub-terminal barring on upperparts. Very fast flight with head drawn back and feet trailing well beyond tail. Probes mud or wades in shallows to feed sometimes even swimming, singly or in flocks with other waders. Wary.

Voice: A high pitched, soft *tew* or *tew-tew*, and a more chipping *tyip tyip*.

Status and distribution: Regular winter visitor. Common in lagoons, coastal areas and sometimes tanks of dry lowlands. Also in wet zone.

Range: Europe, Africa, Asia, Australia.

COMMON GREENSHANK *Tringa nebularia* PLATE 20 (4)

Identification: (32 cm) A large pale greyish 'shank. Much larger than Marsh Sandpiper and has sturdier, slightly upturned bill. Non-breeding plumage: grey fringed white upperparts, white back and rump with brown barring on uppertail; underparts white. Dark upperwing with no bar, white underwing with faint brown barring on coverts. Breeding plumage: crown and nape heavily streaked with brown, upperparts grey-brown or black notched and fringed white, tail barred brown. White heavily streaked brown breast and flanks, white belly and undertail. Grey-green legs, feet, and base of bill. Sexes alike. Juvenile: like browner non-breeding adult with more contrasting notching and fringing on upperparts and more streaking on breast. Fast and twisting flight showing dark upperwing, inverted white V on back and legs just trailing behind a pale tail. Feeds singly in mud or shallows, sometimes dashing after prey, but roosts in flocks.

Voice: A ringing *tew-tew-tew* flight call.

Status and distribution: Regular winter visitor. Common on coasts and tanks of dry zone, less so in wet zone.

Range: Europe, Africa, Asia, Australia, New Zealand.

NORDMANN'S GREENSHANK *Tringa guttifer* PLATE 20 (5)

(Spotted Greenshank)

Identification: (30 cm) Very similar to Common Greenshank but has much shorter, sturdier, yellower legs which only reach the tip of the tail in flight, not beyond; a paler underwing and a slightly heavier bill. Non-breeding plumage: paler head and neck with less marking and generally paler above than Common; white underparts and underwing. Breeding plumage: head, neck, and upper breast streaked dark brown, dark grey and brown white-fringed scapulars with fewer and larger white spots than on Common. Juvenile: duller than Common and browner above with more pronounced cap.

Voice: *Keyew*, more piercing than Common.

Status and distribution: Unconfirmed winter vagrant to coastal areas of north.

Range: E Siberia, India, SE Asia.

GREEN SANDPIPER *Tringa ochropus* PLATE 21 (1)

Identification: (22 cm) Plump and rather hunched, dark above and white below when on ground. Short eyebrow (only to eye, Wood Sandpiper has longer) connecting to narrow white eye-ring. Shortish green-brown legs. Non-breeding plumage: grey-brown head and neck, dark olive-brown back and upperwings (darker than Wood Sandpiper) with faint white spots; white underparts with brown streaks on well defined breast band. Breeding plumage: eyebrow and ring more obvious, upperparts show obvious white spots, bolder brown streaks on face, throat, and breast. Sexes alike. Juvenile: darker buff and bronze on upperparts. Rapid and twisting flight with shallow, clipped wing-beats, dark upperparts without wing bar contrast with white rump and barred tail, dark underwing, legs barely projecting beyond tail. Moves about sedately, body parallel to ground, on mud or in shallow water picking or probing for food. Bobs when anxious. Solitary or in very small groups. Wary.

Voice: A shrill *chweet-chwit-chwit* flight call, a *tu-tu-weet* and variations.

Status and distribution: Regular but uncommon winter visitor to rivers and freshwater pools near trees. More common in north but can be found anywhere, even in hills.

Range: Europe, Africa, Asia, Borneo, Philippines, Japan.

WOOD SANDPIPER *Tringa glareola* PLATE 21 (2)

Identification: (20 cm) Smaller, slimmer, more elegant, longer necked, and longer legged than Green with pale underwing, longer and much more obvious white eyebrow extending behind eye. Non-breeding plumage: faintly white spotted brown upperparts, no wing bar, white rump and brown barred tail. White underparts with a pale greyish wash across breast and pale grey underwing. Yellow-green legs appearing pale. Breeding plumage: upperparts become boldly speckled white, breast streaked with brown and brown barring on flanks. Sexes alike. Juvenile: like breeding adult but has brown spotted buff upperparts and finely streaked breast. Very fast flight on narrow based, angled wings, smaller and less contrasting white rump than Green, legs showing well beyond finely barred tail. Feeds in mud or at water's edge, often in flocks.

Voice: A fast *chiff-chiff-chiff* and a *pee-pee-pee*.

Status and distribution: Winter visitor and scarce summer loiterer. Common in lowland marshes and paddy, preferring fresh water. Less common in hills.
Range: Europe, Africa, Asia, Australia.

TEREK SANDPIPER *Xenus cinereus* (*Tringa cinerea*) PLATE 21 (3)

Identification: (24 cm) The only small to medium-sized wader with long, slightly up-curved bill. Brown bill with a yellow-orange base. Broad white trailing edge to secondaries, shortish orange-yellow legs and very active feeding habit. Non-breeding plumage: plain grey-brown upperparts with dark shoulder patch, white forehead, and short eyebrow; white underparts. Breeding plumage: often has dark streaks on upper scapulars showing as dark line; face, neck, and breast band finely streaked brown. Sexes alike. Juvenile: like breeding adult but somewhat darker upperparts with dark bars and bright buff fringes. In flight, shows white trailing edge on secondaries and pale grey rump. Often feeds in small groups with other sandpipers by dashing about, head down, poking and probing, sometimes scything bill sideways through mud, washing food before eating it.
Voice: Flight call a rising, fluty *tweeweewit*, softer than Redshank, also *weet-ee-wit* and a sharp *too-lee*.
Status and distribution: Regular but scarce winter visitor to lagoons and estuaries of dry zone.
Range: E Europe, E Africa, Asia, Australia.

COMMON SANDPIPER *Actitis hypoleucos* (*Tringa hypoleucos*) PLATE 21 (4)

Identification: (20 cm) Shortish legs; white on belly continuing up to form line between wings and breast patch. Characteristic flight with brief glides, usually low with fluttering stiff wings held downwards showing broad white wing bar. Bobbing stance. Non-breeding plumage: olive brown upperparts with faint white eye ring and eyebrow, white outer tail feathers; white underparts with grey-brown breast patch, white underwing with dark trailing edge and tip with two dark bars on coverts. Breeding plumage: darker with some streaking and barring on upperparts and breast. Sexes alike. Juvenile: like non-breeding adult but with buff barring on wing and buff notches on tertials. Feeds by picking over rocky shores, sometimes pasture, bobbing tail. Will perch on posts or branches. Solitary or in small groups.
Voice: Flight call a loud and descending: *tswee-wee-wee*.
Status and distribution: Winter visitor and scarce summer loiterer. Common almost anywhere with water and rocks or gravel. Avoids sand.
Range: Europe, Africa, Asia, Australia.

RUDDY TURNSTONE *Arenaria interpres* PLATE 21 (6)
(Turnstone)

Identification: (22 cm) Stoutly built with short pointed bill, white rump, striking black and white wing pattern, and short orange legs. Non-breeding plumage: mottled dark brown and black upperparts with white back and uppertail coverts; white underparts with off-white chin and dark breast band. Breeding plumage: bold black and white head, throat, and breast pattern, black and chestnut upperparts; white underparts with black breast. Breeding female is somewhat duller with less white on head. Juvenile: like non-breeding but has warm buff fringing on head and back. Fast direct flight, often in close formation, showing distinctive black and white pattern with white rump and black band on tail. White underwing with black trailing edge. Feeds by turning over stones and other debris for what is hidden beneath. Solitary or in small groups. Not shy.
Voice: A flight call: *tuk-e-tuk* and a sharp *tchit-ik* alarm.
Status and distribution: Winter visitor. Common on coasts, lagoons, and estuaries of dry zone, preferring rocky or stony areas. Less common in wet zone.
Range: Europe, Africa, Asia, Australia, S America.

RED-NECKED PHALAROPE *Phalaropus lobatus* PLATE 21 (7)

Identification: (19 cm) Slender with prominent black eye-patch and very thin black bill, usually seen swimming on sea or fresh water. Most likely in non-breeding plumage: very pale grey crown, grey upperparts with white fringes and faint white lines on mantle, white patches on sides of rump; white underparts. Breeding female plumage: dark grey upperparts with white spot above eye, white chin and chestnut patch from foreneck extending up sides of neck to behind eyes, and chestnut mantle lines. Breeding male similar but duller. Juvenile: dark brown head, neck, and upperparts with bright buff mantle lines; buff eyebrow continuing down sides and front of neck to buff breast (but most migrating juveniles have moulted head and neck to adult plumage). Fast twisting flight showing white wing bar and white on sides of rump, often in flocks, also patters along surface of water. Feeds by swimming, picking food off surface of water, darting and spinning as it goes, occasionally 'up-ending'. Also feeds on ground. Gregarious. Very tame.
Voice: Generally silent in winter but has a *kitt* flight call.
Status and distribution: Scarce winter visitor, mainly to coasts and coastal waters of SE dry zone.
Range: N Europe, Asia, Borneo, New Guinea.

EURASIAN WOODCOCK *Scolopax rusticola* PLATE 22 (2)

Identification: (35 cm) A stocky woodland wader appearing like a large brown snipe. Quite long, straight bill, short legs, characteristic head shape with dark crown and nape transversely barred with buff. Buff face and forehead, dark loral stripe. Upperparts mottled black, brown, and chestnut, grey tip to tail; brown and buff barred underparts continuing onto breast. Dark underwing. Sexes and juveniles alike. Owl-like twisting flight on broad wings with bill held down but explodes from cover when threatened and flies away rapidly in zig-zags. Prefers damp areas in woodland or thick cover on hills. Walks with steady gait and probes mud when feeding. Mainly nocturnal and crepuscular. Solitary or in pairs.

Voice: Generally silent in winter, even when flushed, but has *chaak* call.

Status and distribution: Rare winter visitor. Passes through wet zone lowlands to damp glades in hill country woods.

Range: Europe, N Africa, Asia.

WOOD SNIPE *Gallinago nemoricola* (*Capella nemoricola*) PLATE 22 (3)

Identification: (30 cm) Chunky woodland snipe with broad rounded wings, smaller than Eurasian Woodcock with buff central crown stripe and eyebrows (not buff transverse bars on crown) and very little white on corners of tail. Only local snipe with the belly all barred. Dark brown upperparts (darker than Great Snipe) with buff fringes; streaked breast, dark underwing. Sexes and juvenile almost alike but juvenile's mantle is more scaled with less obvious parallel lines. Slow, meandering flight on broad, rounded wings. Sits tight and 'explodes' from hiding when threatened, soon returning to cover. Solitary.

Voice: Generally silent, even when flushed, but has a *tok-tok* call.

Status and distribution: Probable rare winter visitor. Prefers damp glades in upland woodlands.

Range: India, Myanmar.

PINTAIL SNIPE *Gallinago stenura* (*Capella stenura*) PLATE 22 (4)

Identification: (27 cm) Dumpy with relatively short (for a snipe) straight bill, small head and shortish legs. Distinguish from Common Snipe by indistinct very narrow grey fringe on trailing edge of wings, pale median coverts showing as pale mid-wing panel and plain secondaries with faint pale tips; plain dark underwing, shorter bill and tail (and from Swinhoe's) with very little white on corners. Very similar to Swinhoe's but has shorter bill, the central buff crown stripe usually reaches the bill. Fore-part of buff eyebrow broader than eye-stripe. Parallel buff lines on mantle, buff breast with brown streaks, brown barred flanks, white belly. 'Pin' feathers at sides of tail not normally visible in field. Sexes and juveniles nearly alike. Well camouflaged on ground, often explodes from beneath feet with alarm call to zig-zag up high, then circles, with a rather slow, heavy flight on rounded wings, the inner wing contrastingly pale, toes showing beyond tail in flight, before dropping to ground. Less erratic flight than Common. Feeds by probing in mud. Solitary or in small groups. Mainly nocturnal.

Voice: Nasal slurred high-pitched *scape* alarm call.

Status and distribution: Winter visitor. Common in lowland paddy and swamps, less common in hills to 2000 m.

Range: C, E, and SE Asia.

SWINHOE'S SNIPE *Gallinago megala* (*Capella megala*) PLATE 22 (5)

Identification: (28 cm) Very similar to Pintail Snipe but is noticeably larger in flight with larger almost square head with central buff crown stripe not always reaching bill. Longer bill, deeper chest, more pointed wings and longer tail showing a little more white on the corners than in Pintail but very difficult to separate in field. Tail extends beyond closed wing. Tends to sit tight but when flushed out flight is heavier and less zig-zagging than Pintail with toes projecting less beyond tail.

Voice: *Scape* alarm call lower pitched, less harsh and less slurred than Pintail. Rarely calls and then normally only once.

Status and distribution: Winter vagrant to lowlands, preferring drier areas than other snipe.

Range: C and SE Asia, Philippines, N Australia.

GREAT SNIPE *Gallinago media* (*Capella media*) PLATE 22 (7)

Identification: (28 cm) Similar to Pintail, Swinhoe's and Common Snipe but is stouter, thicker, and stubbier billed, has less clearly defined mantle stripes. It has broad white tips on greater and median coverts making prominent white bars on wing, more extensively and heavily barred flanks and belly, a very small white belly patch and more extensive white on outer tail feathers. Sexes alike. Juveniles show less white on tips of wing coverts. Appears heavy and dark in slower and more horizontal flight when flushed than other snipe and does not zig-zag. White pattern on upperwing and tail corners obvious in flight. Solitary or in small groups with other snipe.

Voice: A low croak when flushed.

Status and distribution: Winter vagrant to damp areas, possibly pasture, in lowlands.

Range: N Europe, N and E Africa, S Asia.

COMMON SNIPE *Gallinago gallinago* PLATE 22 (6)
(Fantail Snipe) (*Capella gallinago*)

Identification: (27 cm) Relatively slim and long-billed with more extensive white belly than on other similar sized snipe. Distinguish from Pintail Snipe by darker upperwing with broad white trailing edge to secondaries, white bars on underwing, white on outer tail feathers and toes showing further beyond shorter tail in faster jinking flight. Brown crown with central buff stripe and buff eyebrow contrasting with paler cheek, broad eye-stripe in front of eye, strong parallel buff lines on mantle and broader fringes on outer webs than inners of lower scapulars showing as diagonal lines, brown barred flanks. Tail protrudes beyond closed wings. Sexes and juveniles alike. When flushed, explodes from cover climbing very steeply to circle high in erratic flight. Has a circling display flight with steep dives, the outer tail feathers making a bleating noise, possible in spring. Probes in mud to feed, mainly at night. Often in flocks.

Voice: Rasping and urgent *scape* alarm call. Also a vocal *chipper chipper* call.

Status and distribution: Winter visitor to swamps, paddy, and tank edges in lowlands.

Range: Europe, Africa, Asia, N and C America.

JACK SNIPE *Lymnocryptes minima* PLATE 22 (8)

Identification: (21 cm) Much smaller than other snipe and relatively short billed. Normally only met when flushed when it bursts from beneath feet, usually without calling, to jink briefly and return to cover nearby. Dark crown (no central buff stripe), buff double eyebrow divided around dark stripe. Glossy dark brown mottled and barred buff upperparts; white with brown streaks (not bars as in other snipe) on throat, breast, flanks, and undertail. Dark, wedge-shaped tail. Mainly nocturnal or crepuscular but will feed in day. Has comic bobbing habit when feeding. Usually solitary.

Voice: Generally silent in winter.

Status and distribution: Winter visitor to swamps and paddy in lowlands, occasionally in hills.

Range: Europe, N and E Africa, Asia.

ASIAN DOWITCHER *Limnodromus semipalmatus* PLATE 19 (1)

Identification: (35 cm) Similar to but smaller bodied than Bar-tailed Godwit with a more parallel and blunt-tipped mostly black bill, sometimes with pink at base of lower mandible. Chevron pattern on flanks. Non-breeding plumage: off-white eyebrow, dark loral eye-stripe, white barred brown rump and tail. White underparts with brown streaks on neck and breast, brown chevrons on flanks, and undertail coverts. No clear wing bar, white underwing. Breeding plumage: upperparts dark brown with rufous fringes; face, throat, and breast rufous, lower belly white, white flanks barred rufous. Breeding female duller and paler than male. Juvenile: like non-breeding adult but with streaked orange-buff neck and breast, and darker above with neatly fringed mantle and scapulars. Strong flight with feet extending beyond tail. Feeds in flocks probing mechanically often with godwits and other waders.

Voice: A *chep-chep* contact call, a humanoid *kiaow* and *chewsk*...

Status and distribution: Winter vagrant to lagoons, estuaries, and muddy coasts of dry zone.

Range: C and SE Asia.

RED KNOT *Calidris canutus* PLATE 23 (1)

(Knot)

Identification: (24 cm) A large *Calidris* stocky and rounded in appearance with short grey-green legs. Relatively short straight bill (as long as the head). Non-breeding plumage: grey upperparts with grey and white barred rump (usually appears grey), white underparts with grey streaks on breast and flanks (breast often appears uniform grey). Breeding plumage: rufous and black spots on back and rufous underparts. Juvenile: like non-breeding adult but scalier with buff wash on upperparts and pale buff wash on breast and flanks. Strong flight showing white wing bar. Head-down feeding posture on short legs. In flocks in normal range.

Voice: Likely to be silent but has a *wit-wit* and *knut-knut*.

Status and distribution: Uncommon winter visitor to lagoons and coasts of dry zone.

Range: Europe, Africa, Asia, Australia, America.

GREAT KNOT *Calidris tenuirostris* PLATE 23 (2)

(Eastern Knot)

Identification: (27 cm) Largest Calidris, larger and sturdier than Red Knot with longer, more pointed bill, more streaky head and upperparts, wings projecting beyond tail and a white rump. Non-breeding plumage: grey upperparts with dark streaks on head and mantle, white underparts with band of narrow streaks and spots across breast and flanks (usually darker than in Red Knot). Breeding plumage: more streaked head and neck, chestnut patches on scapulars, the breast band more heavily streaked with black spots and crescents on flanks and undertail. Sexes alike. Juvenile: similar to non-breeders but have darker more scaly upperparts (darker than in Red Knot) and a buff tinge on breast band. Fast and direct flight showing narrower bar on longer wings and whiter underwing than in Red Knot, and white rump. Feed by probing rather slowly, usually with other waders.

Voice: Usually silent but has a *nyut-noot* call similar to Red Knot.

Status and distribution: Rare winter visitor to dry zone coasts, preferring mud or sand.

Range: E, S, and SE Asia, Australia.

SANDERLING *Calidris alba* (*Crocethia alba*) PLATE 23 (3)

Identification: (20 cm) Rather sturdy with a straight bill a little shorter than the head, no hind toe and characteristic habit of busily following waves up and down beaches when feeding. Non-breeding plumage: very pale grey upperparts with a dark patch at the bend of the wing; all white underparts. Breeding plumage: much darker than non-breeding with mottled chestnut and black upperparts, sometimes with chestnut breast with brown streaks (but variable), white belly and undertail. Sexes alike. Juvenile: mottled black, buff and white upperparts, white below. Fast flight, showing broadest white wing bar on a small wader and dark trailing edge. Forms flocks. Very mobile when feeding, sometimes with other waders. Not shy.

Voice: Very sharp *plick* and *plick-plick* flight calls.

Status and distribution: Winter visitor, likely on all coasts.

Range: Europe, Africa, Asia, Australia, Americas.

RUFOUS-NECKED STINT *Calidris ruficollis* PLATE 24 (4)

(Red-necked Stint)
(Eastern Little Stint)

Identification: (14 cm) Very similar to Little Stint in non-breeding plumage but slightly paler grey above, has a slightly thicker tip to bill, longer wings, and shorter legs. Breeding plumage: usually more extensively reddish on face, breast, and often throat, pale eyebrow behind eye and white chin; reddish breast-band with dark streaks on breast below the band. Sexes alike. Juvenile: lower scapulars and tertials less extensively black-centred, contrasting with upper scapulars. Behaviour similar to Little Stint.

Voice: *Chreet chreet*... flight call and a trill when flushed.

Status and distribution: Winter vagrant. Two records in SE to date.

Range: NE and E Asia, Australia, NW America.

LITTLE STINT *Calidris minuta* PLATE 24 (3)

Identification: (14 cm) Very small and dark-legged with a finely tipped bill. Non-breeding plumage: grey upperparts (paler than Temminck's) with white eyebrow and dark streaks on crown, dark centres on mantle and scapulars (darker than Rufous-necked); white underparts with grey streaks on sides of breast sometimes forming a complete band. Breeding plumage: rufous head, neck, and breast with brown streaks on breast; white eyebrow, chin, throat, and belly. Sexes alike. Juvenile: rufous crown with brown streaks, whitish eyebrow, grey nape, dark brown scapulars and wing coverts with dark centres and variable white lines on mantle and scapulars. Very fast flight in flocks showing white wing bar and white sides of rump and upper tail. Runs busily when feeding, picking, and probing usually out in open. Gregarious.

Voice: *Twit-twit* flight call and a low trill.

Status and distribution: Winter visitor. Common on dry zone tidal lagoons, mud-flats, and tank edges. Less common in wet zone.

Range: Europe, Africa, Asia.

TEMMINCK'S STINT *Calidris temminckii* PLATE 24 (2)

Identification: (15 cm) Like a small Common Sandpiper but size of Little Stint. Distinguish from Common Sandpiper by duller plumage, only a faint pale eyebrow, streaked breast band right across breast, white on sides of rump continuing onto outer tail feathers, tail usually projecting beyond wing tips when at rest. Non-breeding plumage: more uniform grey-brown upperparts and breast-band than Little or Long-toed, white belly. Breeding plumage: grey upperparts with scattered black centres and brighter orangey-fringed feathers. Sexes alike. Juvenile: brownish upperparts with thin neat buff fringes, buff breast band. Fast, erratic flight showing short wing bar and white outer tail feathers when turning. Often climbs high when flushed. Less busy when feeding than Little, picking food from surface of mud in slightly crouched posture not far from cover. Prefers fresh water but not exclusively. Usually in small groups, or solitary with other waders.

Voice: *Tirrirrirrirri* when flushed.

Status and distribution: Scarce winter visitor to dry zone creeks and wet muddy coastal areas where there is cover.

Range: Europe, N Africa, Asia.

LONG-TOED STINT *Calidris subminuta* PLATE 24 (5)

Identification: (14 cm) Relatively long, yellowish legs with long toes which project beyond tail in flight (not easy to see in field), longer neck than Little, only a thin wing bar on secondaries, white on sides of rump and pale brown outer tail feathers. Non-breeding plumage: faint pale eyebrow, dull grey-brown upperparts with dark centres on mantle and scapulars; grey-brown streaked breast band and white belly. Breeding plumage: brown and rufous streaked crown, brown forehead, pale eyebrow; brown, rufous and white mantle showing pale lines, white underparts with brown streaks on breast-band. Sexes alike. Juvenile: brown crown with rufous streaks, pale broad eyebrow; black, rufous and buff upperparts with white lines on mantle; white underparts with brown streaked buff breast-band. Fast and erratic flight on fluttering wings. Often flies high when flushed. Feeds busily by picking from surface of mud usually in small groups, often with Little and Temminck's and other waders, sometimes 'stands tall' with neck outstretched. Less shy than other stints.

Voice: *Chrreep.*

Status and distribution: Winter visitor and occasional summer loiterer on paddy, marshes, and wet areas near dry zone coasts, especially in N.

Range: E S and SE Asia, Philippines, Australia.

WHITE-RUMPED SANDPIPER *Calidris fuscicollis* PLATE 24 (1)

Identification: (16 cm) Small and long-tailed, appearing grey-brown. White band across upper tail and short, slightly down-curved bill. Long wings extend beyond tail. Dark legs. Non-breeding plumage: grey-brown upperparts with white eyebrow; pale grey breast with brown streaks, white belly with spots and short streaks on flanks. Faint, short wing bar (weaker than Curlew Sandpiper) and white underwing. Sexes alike. Juvenile: chestnut cap, buff ear coverts, dark scapulars with chestnut fringes, finely streaked grey breast. Strong flight on long wings. Feeds actively on mud, marshes, and wetlands both salt and fresh.

Status and distribution: Unconfirmed vagrant.

Range: Americas but strays widely.

SHARP-TAILED SANDPIPER *Calidris acuminata* PLATE 23 (4)

(Asian Pectoral Sandpiper)

Identification: (21 cm) Rufous tinged brown crown and long pale eyebrow suggest a cap being worn. Bill the length of head, white eye-ring. The tail is not sharply pointed, despite the name, only the tail feathers. Non-breeding plumage: creamy eyebrow widens behind eye, scaly grey-brown upperparts; white chin, throat, and belly with lightly streaked grey breast. Breeding plumage: darker upperparts with orangey fringes; orangey throat and breast with dark spots, white below with dark chevrons on belly, flanks, and under-tail coverts. Pale legs. Sexes alike. Juvenile: like clearly marked breeding adult above, brown streaked rich buff breast-band and white belly. Fast flight showing white sides to tail but no wing bar. Takes food from mud or fringe vegetation with other sandpipers. Can be tame.

Status and distribution: Winter vagrant to lagoons and wetlands of southern dry zone coasts.

Range: E and SE Asia, Australia.

DUNLIN *Calidris alpina* PLATE 23 (5)

Identification: (19 cm) Slightly smaller and shorter legged than Curlew Sandpiper with shorter and straighter bill slightly down-curved at tip, white sides to rump with dark central line and less obvious eyebrow. Larger than the Stints. Black legs. Non-breeding plumage: grey-brown upperparts; white underparts with fine grey streaks on throat and breast. Breeding plumage: chestnut crown with dark streaks, upperparts scalloped black, chestnut and white; white underparts with dark streaks on breast and obvious black patch on belly. Sexes almost alike. Juvenile: buff on head, lines of dark spots on buff-white breast and white belly. Fast flight, usually in flocks with other small waders, twisting and turning in air showing clear white wing bar. Feeds by running on mud, picking and probing in hunched posture as it goes. Gregarious.

Voice: *Krroo-eep* flight call.

Status and distribution: Rare winter visitor to muddy coasts, avoids sand. Occasionally inland.

Range: Europe, N Africa, Asia, Australia, N America.

CURLEW SANDPIPER *Calidris ferruginea* (*Calidris testacea*) PLATE 23 (6)

Identification: (20 cm) Long, thin, down-curved black bill, white rump and fairly long (longer than Dunlin) black legs. Non-breeding plumage: grey-brown upperparts with clear white eyebrow; white below with grey-brown patches on sides of breast (usually paler and less streaked than on Dunlin). Breeding plumage: brick-red head, neck, breast, and belly with variable pale fringes (especially female) and dark streaks on crown (fresh plumage in spring can have white fringes); white chin, mottled brown, rufous and white scapulars. Sexes alike apart from female having paler underparts. Juvenile: scaly dark grey-brown upperparts with buff fringes and buff wash on neck and breast. Fast flight, often in tight flock, showing white wing bar, white rump and toes trailing beyond tail. Feeds busily by picking and probing, running head down. Gregarious.

Voice: A liquid *chirrup*.

Status and distribution: Winter visitor. Common in lagoons, mud flats, and saltings of dry zone coasts, rarely in wet zone.

Range: Europe, Africa, Asia, Australia.

SPOONBILL SANDPIPER *Eurynorhynchus pygmeus* PLATE 24 (6)

Identification: (15 cm) Similar to Little Stint, but has characteristic 'spoon' on its bill, appearing to be a drip on lower mandible from a side view.

Non-breeding plumage: grey-brown upperparts with white forehead and double eyebrow, and white sides to rump. Underparts white with grey-brown patch on sides of breast. Breeding plumage: mottled brown, chestnut and white upperparts with reddy-brown head, neck and breast shading to white below with dark spots on upper belly. Sexes alike. Juvenile: dark streaked crown, creamy eyebrow and broad dark eye-mask, dark upperparts with buff fringes; white below with variable buff tinge and streaking on sides of breast. Shows spoon bill and white wing bar in flight. Feeds by scything the 'spoon' from side to side across the mud, often with stints.

Voice: *Preep* contact call.

Status and distribution: Winter vagrant to coastal areas.

Range: NE and SE Asia.

BROAD-BILLED SANDPIPER *Limicola falcinellus* PLATE 24 (7)

(Broad-billed Stint)

Identification: (17 cm) Short legged and long billed, the bill down-curved towards tip (the broadness is not usually visible in the field). Smaller and shorter-legged than Dunlin. Non-breeding plumage: grey-brown upperparts with two parallel white eyebrows the upper being indistinct, white below with finely streaked grey breast and throat. Breeding plumage: head pattern becomes more obvious, white lines show at edges of scapulars and mantle (but appears much darker in worn plumage, often almost black when fringes wear off); streaks on breast become bolder and continue onto flanks. Sexes alike. Juvenile: like breeding adult with lightly streaked buff breast and no streaking on flanks. Fast flight showing narrow wing bar and white sides to rump, white underwing coverts and black leading edge. Probes deliberately into mud to feed, often with stints.

Voice: A trilling *chrreek*, flight call.

Status and distribution: Winter visitor to dry zone coasts.

Range: Europe, Asia, Australia.

BUFF-BREASTED SANDPIPER *Tryngites subruficollis* PLATE 21 (8)

Identification: (19 cm) Much smaller than female Ruff and lacks a wing bar. Buff face, breast, and belly with short black bill and yellow legs. Brown and buff upperparts with dark streaked crown giving a capped appearance. Sexes alike but female slightly smaller. Juvenile: very similar to adult with more scaly upperparts. Flight slower than most sandpipers with no wing bar; dark outer wing, brown and buff inner; no white patches on sides of rump; dark edged white underwing with dark bar on primary coverts, underwing contrasting with buff body. Picks food from grass. Can be quite tame.

Voice: A low *preeet* flight call.

Status and distribution: Winter vagrant to dry lowlands, preferring grassy areas.
Range: Americas.

RUFF *Philomachus pugnax* PLATE 21 (5)
The female is sometimes called a Reeve

Identification: (M31, F25 cm) Small head, long neck and plump body with medium short, slightly down-curved bill. Long legs. Usually appears in non-breeding plumage: scaly grey-brown upperparts with dark spots and two white oval patches on sides of rump, white underparts mottled grey-brown on breast. Much variation, sometimes showing white on head and neck, more rarely on back or belly. Non-breeding sexes alike but male is larger. Juvenile: grey-brown upperparts with black fringed chestnut and white on mantle and scapulars; buff underparts with white lower belly and vent. Fast and direct flight in flocks on long wings with narrow white wing bar and white underwing. Feeds by probing the mud or in quite deep water, sometimes swimming. Gregarious, also with other waders.
Voice: Generally silent but has a croak.
Status and distribution: Rare and irregular winter visitor to freshwater marshes, paddy, salterns, sometimes creeks of dry zone; mainly in SE. Occasionally in wet zone.
Range: Europe, Africa, Asia.

SKUAS (Jaegers)

Order: Charadriiformes
Family: Stercorariidae

RATHER gull-like sea-birds with hook-tipped bills, webbed feet and some with slightly or greatly elongated central tail feathers which are moulted in winter. Mainly brown in plumage usually showing a white flash on the wing. The sexes are alike. They breed in the far north or south, roaming the oceans out of the breeding season. The flight is fast and direct on long, narrow, angled wings. Feed in winter mainly by chasing other sea-birds until the victim disgorges its food which is then caught by the skua. Commonly rest on the water. Generally silent in winter. There is continuing debate on the taxonomy of the family.

Identification of the Skuas is complicated by the polymorphism shown by some species. Also, intermediate morphs, juvenile and immature plumages present a bewildering array of possibilities which space does not allow to be shown. For more detail, *Skuas and Jaegers* by Olsen and Larsson, is recommended.

SOUTH POLAR SKUA *Catharacta maccormicki* PLATE 25 (1)
(MacCormick's Skua)

Identification: (53 cm) Smaller and slimmer than Antarctic. Occurs in range of morphs from pale to dark. Pale morph: contrast between pale grey-buff head and underbody, and blackish underwing. Dark morph: generally dark grey-brown often showing a contrast between the underbody and darker underwing, pale hind collar and forehead. A range of intermediates is possible but the darker morphs usually have pale collar and forehead, and are never warm brown. Follows fishing vessels.
Status and distribution: Summer vagrant, mainly to western coastal waters.
Range: Antarctica, Pacific, and Southern Oceans.

ANTARCTIC SKUA *Catharacta antarctica* PLATE 25 (2)
(Brown Skua) (*Catharacta lonnbergi*)
(Southern Skua) (*Stercorarius skua*)

Identification: (63 cm) Largest and sturdiest local skua, lacking the pale collar of South Polar. Mainly dark brown with yellow streaks on nape, rufous and buff tinges on upperparts; slightly paler underparts with yellow mottling on breast, no obvious contrast between belly and underwing. Bold white patches on bases of primaries on upper- and underwing. Central tail feathers not noticeably elongated. Follows fishing vessels.
Status and distribution: Rare summer visitor to western coastal waters.
Range: Antarctica, southern Atlantic Ocean.

POMARINE JAEGER *Stercorarius pomarinus* PLATE 25 (3)
(Pomarine Skua)

Identification: (Approximately 70 cm including tail streamers.) Larger, bulkier and deeper billed than Parasitic with broad, rounded, elongated tail feathers. Wings broad at base narrowing at 'hand'. Occurs in two morphs, more likely is pale morph. Non-breeding plumage: browny-grey crown and chin, pale buff collar, dark brown upperparts (darker than Parasitic) with brown and white barred tail coverts, white below with brown barred breast band, bars on flanks and undertail coverts. Dark morph; mostly dark brown. Juvenile: very variable, grey-brown with pale barred uppertail coverts and rump (paler than nape—opposite to Parasitic); barred underwing coverts and often with double pale patch on underside of primaries. Follows fishing vessels.
Status and distribution: Regular summer visitor to S and W coastal waters.
Range: Arctic, Pacific, Atlantic, and Indian Oceans.

PARASITIC JAEGER *Stercorarius parasiticus* PLATE 25 (4)
(Arctic Jaeger)
(Arctic Skua)

Identification: (Approximately 50 cm including tail streamers.) Smallest of the likely Skuas and has finely pointed elongated tail feathers. Slimmer and thinner billed than Pomarine with narrower wings of even breadth and longer tail (ignoring central feathers). Occurs in dark, pale, and intermediate morphs. Dark morph most likely: dark hood not reaching below bill, sometimes with buff collar, generally warm, dark tawny brown with slight barring on tail coverts. Pale morph: brown cap, white collar, buff mottling on upperparts, more obvious barring on tail coverts, white underparts with variable mid-grey breast band and ventral patch. Juvenile: warmer brown than juvenile Pomarine, pale rusty orange nape darker than upper tail (opposite to Pomarine), warmer underwing coverts with less obvious barring than on Pomarine and no obvious pale double patch on underside of primaries. Flight more dashing than in other local Skuas with jerky wingbeats and glides.
Status and distribution: Winter vagrant to NE coastal waters.
Range: Arctic, Atlantic, Pacific, and Indian Oceans.

GULLS AND TERNS Order: Charadriiformes Family: Laridae

GULLS are robust seabirds with long wings, powerful and easy flight, strong bills, short usually square tails and webbed feet. They are mainly found in coastal areas but some species come well inland, usually not far from water. The plumage is generally white with some grey, brown, or black. The sexes are alike but there are seasonal changes in plumage. Some species take up to four years to reach maturity, with a succession of usually brown becoming whiter and greyer immature forms, making identification difficult. Look for relative darkness of upperwing inner primaries and greater coverts, underwing pattern and tail bands. Gulls feed on carrion and small fish, and most follow fishing vessels, while some 'pirate' the catches of other sea-birds. All swim, rest on water, and walk easily on land with body held near to horizontal. Calls are rarely useful in identification. No gulls are known to breed in Sri Lanka.

Terns are slimmer and more aerobatic than gulls, with long, narrow, pointed wings and forked tails, some deeply so with long streamers. They mostly feed by plunging or by swooping down to pick from the water surface. Their legs are short and weak, normally used only to perch when resting or nesting. Look for bill and leg colour, crown and face markings, also wing patterns, including white patches or 'mirrors' on the wing tip.

SOOTY GULL *Larus hemprichii* PLATE 26 (1)

Identification: (45 cm) Relatively long, strong, bright to dull yellow-green bill with a black band and red at the very tip, and long wings. Adult: sooty brown head, throat, and bib, small white crescent over eye, white hind half-collar, sooty brown upperparts, white rump and tail; mainly white below with a grey-brown breast band. Greeny-yellow legs. White trailing edge on wings. Non-breeding birds are slightly duller with a paler hood. First winter immature has a black-tipped blue-grey bill, grey-brown head, scaly brown and buff upperparts, white rump and black tail with white base and tip; underparts mainly white with pale brown breast band and grey legs. Second year: more like adults with dark bar on secondaries and thin dark band near tip of tail. Adulthood reached after three seasons. Scavenges around harbours and follows fishing vessels. Also robs other birds of their catches.
Voice: Usually silent but has mewing call.
Status and distribution: Winter vagrant most likely on W coast.
Range: Coastal waters of Middle East and E Africa.

HEUGLIN'S GULL *Larus heuglini* PLATE 25 (5)
(Lesser Black-backed Gull) (*Larus fuscus heuglini*)
(Herring Gull) (*Larus argentatus heuglini*)
(Siberian Gull)

Note: There is debate about the taxonomy of this and the next species.
Identification: (55 cm) Large with blackish upperparts. Non-breeding plumage: white head with dark grey streaks on nape. Blackish upperwing with white trailing edge on secondaries and inner primaries, one or two 'mirrors'; white underwing with blackish flight feathers. First winter from Yellow-legged and Great Black-headed first winters by all dark primaries, secondaries, and greater coverts; extensive dark barred tail and dark underwing coverts. Second winter: dark upperwing approaching that of adult. Scavenges in harbours, follows fishing vessels or paddles the tide line, sometimes goes inland.
Voice: Generally silent in winter but has a deep *kiaoow*... and *kekekek*.
Status and distribution: Regular winter visitor to coasts and lagoons of N and NW, rarely in S.
Range: Black Sea, Middle East, W and C Asia.

YELLOW-LEGGED GULL *Larus cachinnans* PLATE 25 (6)
(Herring Gull) (*Larus argentatus cachinnans*)
(Steppe Gull)

Note: There is debate about the taxonomy of this and the previous species.

Identification: (62 cm) Large, robust white gull with similar grey upperparts to Great Black-headed, darker than in Common Black-headed and Brown-headed. Much paler grey upperwing than Heuglin's. Distinctive black and white wing-tip pattern with two mirrors, the black largely restricted to the outer webs. Darker underwing flight feathers than Great Black-headed. Yellow iris, yellow bill with red spot on side of tip and yellowish or pink legs. Non-breeding plumage: pale grey streaking on nape; white rump and tail. Breeding plumage: no grey streaking on nape. First winter immature; blackish bill becoming pale at base, brown iris, dull flesh legs. Shows paler inner primaries than first year Heuglin's and a dark greater covert bar (Great Black-headed has even grey), narrow black band on tail. Takes four years to reach adulthood; white gradually replacing grey-brown below; second year has broad tail band; third year a faint band. Settles on water and swims well. Confident on ground. Scavenges around ships, ports, and rubbish dumps. Roosts communally on sand bars or sheltered water, sometimes inland.

Voice: Has a *kiaoow, kiaoow*... and a *kekekekek*.

Status and distribution: Rare winter visitor to W and NW coasts.

Range: E Mediterranean, Red Sea, Black Sea, S and C Asia.

GREAT BLACK-HEADED GULL *Larus ichthyaetus* PLATE 25 (7)

(Pallas's Gull)

Identification: (69 cm) Very large with heavy bill and long sloping forehead. Long thin wings. Grey upperparts with faint white fringes. Yellow bill with black and red bands just before tip, white crescents above and below eye. Yellow legs. Non-breeding plumage: dark ear coverts and brown streaks on lower hind neck. Grey upperwing with white leading edge which broadens to cover most of the outer primaries and distinctive wing-tip pattern, white underwing with similar black wing-tip pattern as on upperwing. Breeding adult (often from January); only large gull with bold black hood, the hood emphasizing white crescents around eye. First year immature: largely grey upperparts but can retain scaly brown pattern early in winter, brown-black upperwing with pale patch on central midwing; white underparts, black band on tail (beware of confusion with Brown-headed and Common Black-headed first winters and second winter Yellow-legged). Second winter: like non-breeding adult with blackish tips and outer webs to primaries and coverts, black band on tail. Scavenges and hovers to dive onto fish like clumsy tern, also robs other seabirds of their catches.

Voice: A raucous *kraaa*.

Status and distribution: Winter visitor to tidal flats, sand spits of N and NW coasts and lagoons.

Range: E Africa, southern central Asia.

BROWN-HEADED GULL *Larus brunnicephalus* PLATE 26 (2)
(Indian Black-headed Gull)

Identification: (44 cm) Most common Sri Lankan gull. Much smaller than Great Black-headed, larger than Common Black-headed and with a more obvious eye-ring, pale iris, and distinctive black wing tip pattern usually with two white mirrors. Non-breeding adult plumage: mainly white head with dark patches on crown, ear coverts, and in front of eye and a dark-tipped red bill; mid-grey upperparts, pale grey underwing with black and white wing tip pattern. Has brown hood in breeding plumage, usually from March. First winter: like non-breeding but with largely dark flight feathers and tail band. (All three hooded gulls show variable pale grey on nape, hind neck, and to breast-sides). Three years to adulthood. Scavenges in harbours and picks from water surface. Follows coastal ships. Gregarious, not shy. Swims and walks well.

Voice: *Kraaek, kraaek*... and a *gegeg*.

Status and distribution: Winter visitor and summer loiterer. Common during winter on coasts and lagoons of north, less so in SE and SW. Some summer loiterers in dry zone coastal areas.

Range: C and S Asia.

COMMON BLACK-HEADED GULL *Larus ridibundus* PLATE 26 (3)

Identification: (40 cm) Slightly smaller and slimmer than Brown-headed with distinctive white leading edge of upperwing broadening to a white wedge on outer primaries and their coverts; black trailing edge on primaries. Dark iris (yellow in Brown-headed). Non-breeding plumage: mainly white with a dark spot on ear coverts, pale grey upperparts. Dark-tipped red bill. Red legs. Has dark brown hood in breeding plumage (from March) but only to nape. First winter immature: flesh coloured bill with black tip and flesh to orange legs; scaly pattern on median coverts declining as winter progresses (less black on primaries and more white, especially on primary coverts, than in Brown-headed), dark band across tail. Two years to adulthood. Lighter more tern-like flight than Brown-headed on slender, pointed tipped wings (Brown-headed has broader, more blunt tipped). Scavenges as Brown-headed. Gregarious, also with other gulls. Not shy.

Voice: *Kreeah, kreeah, kreeah*....

Status and distribution: Winter visitor to coasts.

Range: Eastern N America, Greenland, Europe, N Africa, Asia, Philippines.

SLENDER-BILLED GULL *Larus genei* PLATE 26 (4)

Identification: (42 cm) Similar to Common Black-headed but slightly bigger, longer legged, and longer billed (not slender despite name), has a flat forehead and faint to absent ear spot, long neck and pale yellow iris. Non-breeding dark red bill and legs. Mainly white with pale grey upperparts and faint grey ear spot. Breeding plumage: white head, usually pink tinged below. First winter: from Black-headed first winter by faint ear spot, long bill, and pale iris. Appears hump-backed in flight. Not a scavenger, feeds on small fish at sea, comes to land to rest on sand spits.

Voice: A nasal *kao, kao, kao...*

Status and distribution: Winter vagrant to western coastal waters.

Range: S Europe, N Africa, Middle East, Pakistan.

WHISKERED TERN *Chlidonias hybridus* PLATE 29 (1)

Note: *Chlidonias* terns are marsh terns with shorter, less deeply forked tails lacking streamers, and shorter and more rounded wings than marine terns.

Identification: (26 cm) The commonest Sri Lankan tern and largest of the genus. Non-breeding plumage: appears pale. Blackish eye-stripe extends to meet on nape (but does not drop behind eye as in other *Chlidonias* species), streaky crown and pale unmarked grey upperparts and tail; white below sometimes with faint grey patch on sides of breast; black bill and red-brown legs. Breeding plumage: (possible from February on) *Sterna*-like glossy black cap, obvious white cheek stripe, blue-grey breast and darker belly with white vent and undertail coverts. In flight the grey body contrasts with white collar, rump and pale underwing. First year immature: like non-breeding adult but has brown and buff mottled upperparts with a grey saddle and rump contrasting with pale upperwings, and white underparts sometimes with grey breast patch. Distinguish from juvenile White-winged by slightly longer bill, paler leading edge on inner wing and grey rump. Flies low with head down, swooping to pick food. Solitary or in flocks. Rests on paddy bund or fence post.

Voice: A shrill *kreeik, kreeik*.

Status and distribution: Winter visitor and summer loiterer. Common on marshes, tanks, and paddy, occasionally lagoons, of low country especially near coasts. Also in lower hills.

Range: S Europe, Africa, Asia, New Guinea, Australia.

WHITE-WINGED TERN *Chlidonias leucopterus* PLATE 29 (2)

(White-winged Black Tern)

Identification: (23 cm) Relatively short dull red bill, white to pale grey rump. Dull orange legs. Non-breeding plumage: similar to non-breeding Whiskered but has very pale head, black eye-stripe dropping behind eye and no breast patches; upperwing has faint dark carpal bar and dark tips to secondaries. Breeding plumage: (possible from April); distinctive pattern of black head and body with white rump, vent, and tail, grey wings paling to white on the upperwing coverts which shows as a conspicuous white patch on the folded wing. First year immature: similar to Whiskered first year but has whitish rump, no breast patches, and dark carpal and secondary bars on upperwing. Flight and feeding similar to those of Whiskered with which it associates.

Voice: A *weeick, weeick...*, a throaty *krrrr* and *kek*.

Status and distribution: Winter visitor to marshes, paddy, tanks, and lagoons of low country.

Range: SE Europe, Africa, Asia, Australia.

BLACK TERN *Chlidonias niger* — PLATE 29 (3)

Identification: (23 cm) Grey rump. Black bill and red-tinged black legs. Non-breeding plumage: very similar to non-breeding Whiskered but has longer bill and a darker cap which extends further forward on the head with a lobe behind and below eye; the upperparts and rump are the same grey, and more obvious dark grey patches on sides of breast. Dark carpal and secondary bars on upperwing. Distinguish from non-breeding White-winged by grey rump. Breeding plumage: dark grey body and white vent. Grey upperwing, grey underwing with paler coverts. First year immature: from very similar Whiskered immature by larger cap, uniformly dark upperparts with rump only slightly paler, dark grey patches on sides of breast; faint carpal and secondary bars on upperwing. Erratic flight, often hovering before swooping down to surface or making shallow plunge. More marine in winter than other possible local *Chlidonias* terns.

Voice: Has a *keek, keek...*

Status and distribution: Winter vagrant most likely on W coast.

Range: Europe, W coast of Africa, W Asia, N America, W coast of S America.

GULL-BILLED TERN *Gelochelidon nilotica* (*Sterna nilotica*) — PLATE 27 (5)

Identification: (38 cm) Largish and rather stocky with a short, deep, black, gull-like bill and no crest, appearing almost white in distance. Relatively long black legs. Wings extend well beyond tail when folded. Non-breeding plumage: mainly white with dark eye-patch, some dark streaking on nape, pale grey upperparts and narrow black trailing edge on outer primaries. Breeding plumage: (possible from February): black cap extending from bill to nape. Juvenile: like non-breeding but with less distinct eye-patch and brown spots on upperparts. Generally keeps inshore, flying low and swooping to pick from surface, rarely plunging. Also hawks for insects over land. Singly or in flocks. Rests with other terns and gulls on shore.

Voice: Generally silent but has a *kwak, kwak, kwak*..., *chrr-wuk*, and *wik, kuwikkeewik*.

Status and distribution: Winter visitor, summer loiterer, and possible breeder on sandy islets of Adam's Bridge. Common in coastal areas of dry zone, less so in wet zone.

Nesting: Colonially, in shallow scrape in sand; April–June.

Range: S Europe, Africa, S Asia, Australia, tropical and sub-tropical Americas.

CASPIAN TERN *Hydroprogne caspia* (*Sterna caspia*) PLATE 27 (1)

Identification: (51 cm) The largest tern and much larger than any other local tern, with thick red bill with dark band before a pale tip. A short crest giving an angular shape to the head and extensive blackish outer underwing primaries. Non-breeding plumage: mainly white with white-streaked black cap, pale grey back, upperwings and tail. Breeding plumage: dense black cap. First year immature: like non-breeding with brown flecks on upperparts. Fast, powerful gull-like flight. Flies singly or in pairs a couple of metres above water when hunting with head held down, then hovers with legs dangling before plunging. Sometimes settles on water. Roosts with other terns on sand banks.

Voice: *Kraak, kraa* and variations.

Status and distribution: Breeding resident on Adam's Bridge islets. Common winter visitor to dry zone coasts, rarely in wet zone.

Nesting: Singly or in small groups in shallow scrape in sand; May–June.

Range: Europe, Africa, Asia, N America, Australasia.

COMMON TERN *Sterna hirundo* PLATE 28 (1)

Identification: (35 cm) Grey upperparts, grey upperwing with dark wedge on wing tip (not always during moult) and black tips on underwing primaries. Non-breeding plumage: black bill sometimes with some red at base, white forehead, black hind crown, grey upperparts (darker than on Roseate), white rump and tail, tail without streamers; white underparts. Usually has darker carpal and secondary bars on upperwing than Roseate. Breeding plumage: red bill usually with black tip, shiny black cap and very pale grey on lower underparts. Tail streamers. First year immature: like non-breeding but has dull grey cap, buff tinge on upperparts, scaly mantle, and shows a strong carpal bar on upperwing. Very graceful flight, plunging from up to 10 m onto prey. In flocks with other terns. Mainly marine in winter.

Voice: Has a screaming *kee-yar* and *kik, kik, kik*....

Status and distribution: Winter visitor and summer loiterer to coastal waters. Possible breeding resident on islets off E coast.

Nesting: Colonially in shallow scrape; May.
Range: Europe, Asia, Africa, Australasia, Americas.

ROSEATE TERN *Sterna dougallii* PLATE 28 (2)

Identification: (38 cm) Slender and very pale. Paler than Common. Breeding plumage: black bill with red tinge on base, longer and thicker bill than in Common, shiny black cap which persists into autumn, very pale grey upperparts, white rump and tail with long streamers which project well beyond wing tips when perched; white underparts with variable rosy tinge. Pale grey upperwing with dark leading edge on wing tip (beware during moult), white underwing. Deep red legs. Non-breeding plumage: black bill, white forehead and fore crown, variable rosy tinge on belly, shorter tail streamers and dark red legs. First year immature has dark brown cap, scaly grey and buff back and mantle, pale grey upperwing with white trailing edge. Graceful flight, plunging from height onto prey. Gregarious. Strictly marine.
Voice: *Chew-it* and a rasping *aaaark* alarm.
Status and distribution: Summer breeding visitor and partial resident on islets off E and SW coasts.
Nesting: Colonially, often with other terns, in shallow scrape with a few scraps of weed or on vegetation; March–June.
Range: British Isles, W Africa, Indian Ocean, SE Asia, Australasia, Caribbean, and W Atlantic.

WHITE-CHEEKED TERN *Sterna repressa* PLATE 28 (3)

Identification: (35 cm) Non-breeding plumage: distinguish from very similar non-breeding Common by darker grey upperparts, including rump and tail, and dark underwing secondaries. Breeding plumage: black cap and nape, white cheek stripe and mauve-grey underparts. Long tail streamers. First year immature: like non-breeding but has brown flecks on upperwing. Graceful flight, plunges onto catch. Strictly maritime.
Voice: Has a *kee-leek*.
Status and distribution: Vagrant to W coastal waters.
Range: Coasts of E Africa, Red Sea, Gulf, W India.

BLACK-NAPED TERN *Sterna sumatrana* PLATE 28 (4)

Identification: (32 cm) Appears white at distance. Black band through eye continuing to nape and deeply forked tail. **Adult**: mainly white with pale grey upperparts and black bill and legs, sometimes has rosy tinge on underparts. Pale grey upperwing with dark line on edge of outer primary, showing on folded wing. No seasonal change. First year immature: like adult but eye-stripe less distinct, grey streaks on crown, upperparts flecked brown, no tail streamers. Can be confused with immature Little but is larger with steadier flight. Flies low when feeding, taking food from surface, sometimes plunging.

Voice: Has a *keeeik, keeeik, keeeik* and a *kikik*....

Status and distribution: Winter vagrant to W coastal waters.

Range: Indian Ocean, SE Asian waters, W Pacific.

BRIDLED TERN *Sterna anaethetus* PLATE 28 (5)

(Brown-winged Tern)

Identification: (37 cm) Dark brown and white with a deeply forked tail. Adult: black bill, white forehead continuing as eyebrow over eye (Sooty stops above eye), black cap, black loral stripe continuing through eye to join cap (the bridle), dark brown upperparts with white outer tail feathers. White cheeks and throat, pale grey underparts. Dark brown upperwing, pale grey underwing with buff-brown flight feathers. No seasonal variations. First year immature: brown upperparts with pale fringes (darker than other terns except Sooty), grey on flanks and shorter tail streamers. Takes food from surface by skimming, rarely plunging. Sometimes soars high. Rests on water. Sociable but can be solitary. Oceanic.

Voice: A *kerk, kerk* not unlike a distant barking terrier.

Status and distribution: Passage migrant through seas off W and S coasts. Large numbers possible in September but likely any time between May–October or, rarely, later.

Range: Indian Ocean, seas off SE Asia, C America and W Africa.

SOOTY TERN *Sterna fuscata* PLATE 28 (6)

(Wideawake Tern)

Identification: (43 cm) Similar to but larger and darker than Bridled and the white eyebrow does not continue behind the eye. Very dark sooty brown upperparts, white below. Sooty brown upperwing, white underwing with brown flight feathers. No seasonal variation. First year immature: sooty brown head, sooty brown body flecked with pale buff, white tips on upperwing coverts. From noddies by white vent and undertail. Feeds by swooping to pick fish from sea. Sometimes soars high. Gregarious. Oceanic.

Voice: Has a *wideawake, wideawake*... call, hence its alternative name.

Status and distribution: Summer passage migrant through W coastal waters.

Range: Tropical seas world-wide.

LITTLE TERN *Sterna albifrons* PLATE 29 (5)

(White-shafted Little Tern)

Identification: (23 cm) Smaller and slimmer than Whiskered, has longer bill and different flight. Breeding plumage: black cap and loral stripe, white forehead extending over eye, pale grey upperparts, grey or pale grey rump, tail, and underparts. Pale grey upperwing with outer primaries blackish with white shafts, white underwing with dark grey on primaries. Yellow bill with black tip, yellow legs. Non-breeding plumage: dark eye-line, black bill sometimes with yellow base, dirty yellow legs. Juvenile: like non-breeding but has scaly grey and brown upperparts and a faint carpal bar on underwing. Urgent flight, often hovering before plunging onto prey or skimming the surface. Solitary or in small flocks.

Voice: *Tchik, tchik, tchik….*

Status and distribution: Resident. Common on coasts, mud-flats, and tank edges of dry zone. Occasionally in wet zone.

Nesting: Colonially in shallow scrape on open ground or in thin vegetation; May–August.

Range: Europe, Africa, Asia, Australia.

SAUNDERS'S TERN *Sterna saundersi* PLATE 29 (4)

(Black-shafted Little Tern)
(Saunders's Little Tern)

Identification: (23 cm) Very similar to Little but breeding adult lacks the white eyebrow, has a grey uppertail, more extensive black on outer primaries and the legs are a dirtier yellow. Flight similar to that of Little. Not normally found inland.

Voice: Unknown but probably similar to Little.

Status and distribution: Resident in coastal areas of dry zone, rarely in wet zone.

Nesting: In small colonies in shallow scrape above tide line on mud or sand; May–June.

Range: E Africa, Red Sea, W India.

GREAT CRESTED TERN *Thalasseus bergii velox* PLATE 27 (2)

(Large Crested Tern) (*Sterna bergii*)

Identification: (48 cm) Prominent crest, large slightly down-curved yellow-green bill and deeply forked tail. Larger and stockier than Lesser and much darker above with relatively longer wings. Breeding plumage: black cap and crest separated from bill by broad white band, grey upperparts and tail usually with paler rump; white below. Dark grey upperwing with white-tipped secondaries making pale trailing edge, pale underwing with dark tips to primaries. Non-breeding plumage: white on forehead extends onto fore crown. Some white streaks on crown. Juvenile: like non-breeding with brown streaks on grey upperparts, a faint carpal bar on upperwing and brown secondaries. Strong flight on long wings, plunging onto prey. Rests on rocks, quays, and buoys. Singly or in small flocks.

Note: *T. b. thalassinus,* with paler upperwing, is a winter vagrant to the W coast.

Voice: A grating *kirruk* and *kreee.*

Status and distribution: Resident. Common in most coastal areas.

Nesting: Colonially on bare sand; May–July.

Range: Seas of S and E Africa, Indian Ocean, SE Asia, Australia.

LESSER CRESTED TERN *Thalasseus bengalensis* PLATE 27 (3)
(Smaller Crested Tern) (*Sterna bengalensis*)

Identification: (42 cm) Smaller, more graceful and paler above than Great Crested (race *velox*), and with an orange bill and shorter wings. Non-breeding plumage: white forehead and crown with indistinct dark line through eye to nape and crest, pale grey upperparts and white below. Pale grey upperwing with paler primaries and dark tips to outer primaries, white underwing with grey tips to primaries. Breeding plumage: black cap from bill to crest. First year immature: like non-breeder with brown outer primaries. Graceful flight, plunging from some height to fish. In flocks, often rests on buoys, along with Great Crested.

Voice: A *kreeek* and *kee, kee, kee...*

Status and distribution: Common winter visitor in most coastal areas also a summer loiterer.

Range: Seas off N and E Africa, Indian Ocean, SE Asia, Australia, W Pacific.

SANDWICH TERN *Thalasseus sandvicensis* PLATE 27 (4)
(*Sterna sandvicensis*)

Identification: (44 cm) Looks slimmer than Gull-billed and has long, slender black bill with yellow tip, a slight crest, white rump and has a more deeply forked tail. Looks almost white from a distance. Non-breeding plumage: broad white forehead, white streaks on the black cap which extends from hind crown to crest, pale grey upperparts with white rump, white underparts with pink tinge. Pale grey upperwing with darker primaries, white underwing with dusky tips to primaries. Breeding plumage: full black cap. First year immature: like non-breeding but browner, has buff streaks on crown (paler winged than Lesser Crested and has dark tipped tail). Strong flight with fast wingbeats, diving from fair height. Gregarious.

Voice: A grating *kee-rek* and *kee-kee-kee.*

Status and distribution: Uncommon winter visitor to waters of W and NW coasts.

Range: Europe, W Africa, Middle East, NW India, E coast of C America.

BROWN NODDY *Anous stolidus* PLATE 26 (5)
(Common Noddy)
(Philippine Noddy)

Identification: (42 cm) Largest, thickest billed and most likely of the Noddies. Browny-grey inner underwing with dark edges. Adult: mainly sooty brown with clear edged white forehead and crown, shading through grey on nape into brown on back. First year immature: like adult with grey forehead, grey-brown head and pale edged upperparts. Fast flight low over sea, with long glides, often hovering before swooping down to pick from surface showing paler underwing. Settles on water. Gregarious. Oceanic.
Voice: Has a low *karrrk*.
Status and distribution: Occasional visitor to coastal waters, especially during rough weather.
Range: Tropical seas, world-wide.

LESSER NODDY *Anous tenuirostris* PLATE 26 (6)
(White-capped Noddy)

Identification: (32 cm) Smaller, slimmer, and somewhat paler than Brown and with thin needle-like bill. Adult: mainly sooty brown with a grey-white head, shading to grey-brown cheeks and neck. Brown wings with darker flight feathers. First year immature: like adult but paler brown. Faster and more erratic flight than Brown; feeds in similar way. Gregarious. Oceanic.
Voice: Has a rattling *kaarrk*.
Status and distribution: Vagrant to coastal waters.
Range: Indian Ocean.

BLACK NODDY *Anous minutus* PLATE 26 (7)
(White-capped Noddy)

Identification: (37 cm) Smaller than Brown, larger than Lesser, blacker than both and with longer, thin bill and forked tail. Adult: mainly dark sooty brown with white forehead shading into pale grey crown, then grey nape. Sooty brown wings with black flight feathers, appearing evenly dark in flight. First year immature: less white on clearly defined crown. Fast fluttering flight. Feeding similar to Brown. Gregarious. Oceanic.
Voice: Has a nasal *churrrr* and a *kik-kirrik*.
Status and distribution: Vagrant to coastal waters.
Range: Tropical areas of Pacific and Atlantic Oceans.

PIGEONS AND DOVES

Order: Columbiformes
Family: Columbidae

LARGE bodied, small headed, strong winged birds capable of fast and sustained flight with rapid wingbeats. The wings are pointed and the tail can be broadly fanned. The wings of the bigger pigeons commonly make a considerable noise when in full flight or when flushed. They are short legged but good walkers. Voices are mainly low and cooing. Food is mainly vegetable: seeds, fruit, buds, and leaves.

There is no clear distinction between pigeons and doves but 'pigeon' is usually used for the bigger and heavier birds, while the 'doves' tend to be slimmer and longer tailed.

ROCK PIGEON *Columba livia* PLATE 30 (1)

(Blue Rock Pigeon)
(Rock Dove)
(Feral Pigeon)

Identification: (33 cm) Two black bands across inner wing showing as two lines across closed wing, blue-grey rump (Feral often has white) and black band across tip of tail. Metallic sheen on neck and breast. Fast and direct flight. Wings clapped and then held at steep angle in display flight. Feeds on ground. Rarely perches on trees. Usually in flocks.

Note: The Feral or Street Pigeon is the domesticated descendent of the Rock Pigeon, occurring in many plumage forms. Inter-breeding with wild birds occurs.

Voice: *Koor- koo* and *koo-roo-oo.*

Status and distribution: Resident. The wild Rock Pigeon is scarce and restricted to rocky islets off E SE, and nearby coasts. The Feral Pigeon is common and widespread in towns and villages.

Nesting: Colonially, on a pad of sticks and grasses between rocks or on ledge. Sometimes in trees; February–June. The Feral Pigeon nests in or on buildings year round.

Range: Europe, N Africa, Middle East, S Asia. (Feral Pigeon occurs worldwide.)

SRI LANKA WOODPIGEON *Columba torringtoni* PLATE 30 (2)

Identification: (36 cm) Prominent black and white 'chess-board' on nape, white throat, dark grey wings with a green tinge, dark grey rump, dark vinous underparts and broad tail. Sexes alike. Juvenile: duller with only a hint of the 'chess-board'. Strong flight. Arboreal, feeding on fruits in deep forests, rarely coming to ground. In pairs or sometimes small groups. Shy.

Voice: Normally silent but has a deep, mournful, owl-like *hooo* courtship call.

Status and distribution: Endemic species. Dense forests, from 300 m up.

Nesting: On a scanty platform of twigs in canopy of forest tree; February–May and August–October.

Range: Sri Lanka.

PALE-CAPPED PIGEON *Columba punicea* PLATE 30 (3)
(Purple Woodpigeon)

Identification: (36 cm) Greyish-white cap extending below eye and onto nape (no 'chess-board'), vinous-chestnut upperparts with glossy metallic sheen, slate-grey rump, and dark brown tail, brown undertail. Female: slightly smaller and duller with more brown on cap. Juvenile: like female but with head almost chestnut. Slow flight for a pigeon, showing black flight feathers. Feeds on fruit in trees, also takes seeds on ground. Prefers forest edge. Shy.

Voice: A soft mew.

Status and distribution: Vagrant to lowlands.

Range: NE India, SE Asia.

ORIENTAL TURTLE DOVE *Streptopelia orientalis* PLATE 30 (4)
(Rufous Turtle Dove)

Identification: (33 cm) Much larger, stockier, and darker than Spotted. Grey crown and nape, grey and black lines on sides of hind neck, scaly rusty-brown scapulars, dark grey rump. In flight the grey rump and grey or white-tipped blackish tail contrast with the rusty scapulars. Sexes alike. Juvenile: more generally brown lacking the grey and black lines on neck. Feeds on seeds on ground, flying to trees when disturbed. Forms flocks.

Voice: A gentle *koo-koo-kakoor.*

Status and distribution: Winter vagrant, possible in stubble fields throughout.

Range: E and SE Asia.

EURASIAN COLLARED DOVE *Streptopelia decaocto* PLATE 30 (5)
(Indian Ring Dove)

Identification: (32 cm) Distinguish from Red Collared female by larger size and different tail pattern. Pale sandy grey with a lilac tinge on breast. Narrow white-fringed black half collar below the nape. Upper tail much paler than Oriental Turtle. Sexes alike. Juvenile: greyer, lacking the half collar. Fast, direct flight. Also has a wing clapping display, climbing steeply then gliding down with wings held low and tail fanned. Feeds on seeds in stubble and open areas in scrub, never in forest. In pairs or small groups. Shy.

Voice: A repeated *kuk-koooo-kuk* and a hoarse *krrreee* made when landing.
Status and distribution: Resident. Restricted to narrow coastal strip in north.
Nesting: On a thin platform of twigs in tree, thorn bush or mangrove. April–May.
Range: Europe, Asia.

RED COLLARED DOVE *Streptopelia tranquebarica* PLATE 30 (6)
(Indian Red Turtle Dove)

Identification: (23 cm) Very small and plump with a short, white-cornered tail. Male: generally warm pinky-brown with grey head, narrow black hind collar, grey lower back and rump, whitish vent and undertail. Female: resembles Eurasian Collared but is much smaller and shorter tailed with a different tail pattern. Juvenile: like female but has rusty fringes. Fast flight. Feeds on seeds in stubble and open ground. Gregarious. Shy.
Voice: A harsh repeated *groo-gurr-goo*.
Status and distribution: Vagrant to coastal areas of north.
Nesting: One record of nesting in last century. On flimsy platform of twigs high in tree.
Range: S and SE Asia.

SPOTTED DOVE *Streptopelia chinensis ceylonensis* PLATE 30 (7)
(Spotted-necked Dove)

Identification: (30 cm) Commonest of the local pigeons. Slender with a rather long wedge-shaped tail. Large 'chess-boards' on sides of neck, grey-brown mantle with pale spots. Sexes alike. Juvenile: browner, lacking the 'chess-boards' and barred not spotted. Strong and direct flight. Also displays with wing clapping, ascending to height, then parachuting down with wings and tail spread. Loud wing clapping also when flushed. Feeds on ground. In pairs or flocks.
Voice: A mournful repeated *ook-oo-oo-ow*, also *kookeroo* and *kookoo-krroo-kroo-kroo-kroo-kroo*.
Status and distribution: Endemic race. Common in cultivation, gardens and open forests of dry zone, less common in most other areas.
Nesting: On a few twigs concealed in tree or bush. Most of year but peaks in April and September.
Species range: E and SE Asia.

EMERALD DOVE *Chalcophaps indica robinsoni* PLATE 30 (8)
(Bronze-winged Pigeon)

Identification: (27 cm) Distinctive coral red bill, slate-grey crown and nape, white eyebrow. Back and wing coverts bronze-sheened golden green and distinctive pattern of black and white bars on back, and brown tail with grey outer feathers. Female: duller with wine flush on crown and a less obvious eyebrow. Flight is fast, silent and usually low showing chestnut underwing. Feeds mainly on ground, walking around with head jerking at each step. Solitary or in pairs. Normally wary but can become confident on jungle tracks.

Voice: A repeated, mournful *tk-hoon tk-hoon.*

Status and distribution: Endemic race. Common in forests, wooded country and jungle throughout apart from very dry areas, rarely in higher hills.

Nesting: On a twig platform not very high in small tree or bush. Possible all year but peaks in February–May and September.

Species range: S and SE Asia, New Guinea, Australia.

ORANGE-BREASTED GREEN PIGEON *Treron bicincta leggei*

PLATE 30 (9)

Identification: (29 cm) Male: grey nape and hind neck, grey uppertail. Distinguish from male Pompadour by green (not maroon) mantle, purple and orange breast band and cinnamon undertail coverts. Female: very similar to Pompadour female but has grey nape, paler mantle, almost plain buff vent and under tail, and slaty-grey on upper central tail feathers. Juvenile: like female but duller and darker. Fast flight with rapid wingbeats. Often waves tail when perched. Mainly arboreal, feeding on fruit and hiding in foliage when threatened. Very argumentative. Comes to ground to drink, walks rather clumsily with tail held high. In small flocks. More coastal than Pompadour.

Voice: A low, melodious soft whistle *chuk-cheeow* and a *kek kek kek* bickering call.

Status and distribution: Endemic race. Very common in scrub and wooded patches of dry zone, less so in lowlands of wet zone, occasionally in lower hills.

Nesting: On a concealed platform of twigs usually 3–5 m from ground in small tree at woodland edge or in open.

Species range: S and SE Asia.

POMPADOUR GREEN PIGEON *Treron pompadora pompadora*

(Grey-fronted Green Pigeon) PLATE 30 (10)

Identification: (27 cm) Ashy-blue rear crown and nape becoming green on hind neck. Male: maroon mantle, green central uppertail with pale-tipped dark outer feathers. Female has green mantle. Distinguish from very similar female Orange-breasted by the vent and under tail strongly marked dark green. Juvenile: like female but duller and greyer. Fast, direct flight with wing clapping when flushed. Mainly arboreal, feeds on fruit and hides in foliage when threatened. Argumentative. In small flocks.

Voice: A low mellow whistling *ooh, ooh-ooh, oo-aa* and an extraordinary unbirdlike 'song'.

Status and distribution: Endemic race. Common in woods and forest of lowlands and hills to 1000 m, tends to avoid coasts.

Nesting: On flat platform of twigs on small tree in scrub; December–June and August–September.

Species range: S and SE Asia.

YELLOW-FOOTED GREEN PIGEON *Treron phoenicoptera phillipsi*

(Yellow-legged Green Pigeon) PLATE 30 (11)
(Southern Green Pigeon)

Identification: (30 cm) Only local pigeon with chrome yellow legs and feet. Generally very pale with grey head, yellow-green collar, a lilac patch on the shoulder and a dark grey tail. Female: duller with less distinct shoulder patch. (Note: Vagrant *T. p. chlorigaster* is slightly larger, generally brighter and has bright yellow underparts.) Fast and direct flight, loud wing claps when flushed. Mainly arboreal and difficult to see in foliage, rarely comes to ground to drink or collect grit. In flocks especially on ripe fruit trees.

Voice: A low musical whistle.

Status and distribution: Endemic race. Scarce resident in eastern foothills and nearby lowlands. (*T. p. chlorigaster* is a vagrant to dry lowlands of the north.)

Nesting: On platform of twigs in tree; March–April.

Species range: S and SE Asia.

GREEN IMPERIAL PIGEON *Ducula aenea* PLATE 30 (12)

Identification: (42 cm) Largest local pigeon. Plain lilac-grey head, neck and underparts. Glossy green back, dark green tail, and chestnut undertail coverts. Sexes alike. Fast and direct flight with relatively slow wingbeats, often high. Loud wing claps when flushed. Arboreal, feeds on fruit early and late in day, rests between feeds in canopy but comes to ground to drink. In pairs or small flocks. Shy, avoiding settlements.

Voice: A deep, repeated *ah-a-ah-a-ah*, a *cheewuk*, and a *wuk-wooor*

Status and distribution: Resident in forests of lowlands and lower hills.

Nesting: On a thin saucer of twigs about 5 or 6 m up a forest tree.

Range: S and SE Asia.

PARAKEETS AND LORIKEET

Order: Psittaciformes
Family: Psittacidae

MAINLY green arboreal birds with short, strong, curved, hooked bills which feed largely on fruit and seeds, climbing about the branches to do so gripping with the bill as well as the feet. The feet have two toes forward and two to the rear. Their colouring is excellent camouflage in tree-top foliage. The flight is fast and direct with rapid beats of narrow pointed wings. They are sociable birds and form often noisy flocks. Parakeets have long, pointed tails, the much smaller lorikeet has a short, rather square tail.

SRI LANKA HANGING PARROT *Loriculus beryllinus* PLATE 31 (1)
(Ceylon Lorikeet)

Identification: (14 cm) Much smaller than the parakeets and with short tail. Mainly green with red crown shading to orange on nape, back and scapulars tinged orange, deep red rump and uppertail coverts and a faint blue patch on throat. Female: duller with only a trace of blue on throat. Juvenile: like female but with green head and no blue on throat. Flight more undulating than parakeet's with flaps alternating with nearly closed wings, usually with loud calling. Rests hanging upside down from branches, bat-like. Strictly arboreal.
Voice: A distinctive three syllable *Tweet-tweet-tweet, tweet-tweet-tweet.*
Status and distribution: Endemic species. Common in wooded areas in wet zone and hills up to 1500 m. Also in dry zone bordering hills, rare in north.
Nesting: In hole in tree; March–June and sometimes August–September.
Range: Sri Lanka.

ALEXANDRINE PARAKEET *Psittacula eupatria* PLATE 31 (2)
(Ceylon Large Parakeet)

Identification: (48 cm) Largest local parakeet. Distinguish from Rose-ringed by size, large deep all-red bill and large maroon shoulder patch. Mainly green with black line from bill below cheek to a pink hind-collar which shades to a blue-grey tinge on nape, greenish-blue upper tail with a yellow tip, yellowish under tail. Female and juvenile lack the black and pink collar. Very mobile, showing large head and long tail in flight, usually calling. Feeds in trees or on paddy. In small flocks.
Voice: A loud, raucous *kee-arr* squawk.
Status and distribution: Resident in forests of lowlands and hills to 1000 m. Common in dry zone.
Nesting: In hole in tree; November–May.
Range: S and SE Asia.

ROSE-RINGED PARAKEET *Psittacula krameri* PLATE 31 (3)
(Ring-necked Parakeet)

Identification: (40 cm but tail length variable) Much smaller bill than Alexandrine's with red upper and black lower mandible, and lacking the red shoulder patches. Male: mainly green with blue-grey tinge on nape and a collar, black in front and rose pink behind. Female and juvenile lack the collar and the blue tinge on nape. Flight is fast and noisy, often high when making long flights. In flocks, sometimes large. Can be destructive to crops.
Voice: A raucous and often repeated *kee-ak*.
Status and distribution: Resident. Common where there are trees throughout lowlands, less common in hills.
Nesting: In tree hole; November–June.
Range: NE Africa, Jordan, S Asia. (Naturalized in SE Britain.)

PLUM-HEADED PARAKEET *Psittacula cyanocephala* PLATE 31 (4)
(Blossom-headed Parakeet) (*Psittacula roseata*)

Identification: (34 cm) Small (has long slender tail) with a yellowish bill. Male: mainly green with plum-coloured head and a black and green collar, small dark maroon shoulder patch, blue tail with yellow outer and white tips to central feathers. Female: dull grey-blue head, yellow collar and almost lacks the maroon shoulder patches. Juvenile: generally green with shorter tail. Very fast twisting flight, calling as it goes. Usually in small flocks.
Voice: *Pwink, pwink, pwink*... flight call and various high-pitched squeaks.
Status and distribution: Resident in lowlands and hills to 1100 m. Less frequent in north.
Nesting: In tree hole; February–May.
Range: India.

LAYARD'S PARAKEET *Psittacula calthropae* PLATE 31 (5)
(Emerald-collared Parakeet)

Identification: (31 cm) Blue-grey head with a green forehead and eye-patch, pale blue-grey back and relatively short deep blue tail. Male: mainly green with a pale tipped coral red bill, a broad black and deep green collar, blue rump and tail with central tail feathers tipped yellow-green. Underparts green. Female: duller with a black bill and no black on collar. Juvenile: green with a darker head and blue lower back, rump and tail, the bill is dull orange soon turning black. Fast flight with constant calling. More arboreal than Plum-headed or Rose-ringed. In pairs or small flocks.
Voice: A loud scream *ak-ak-ak-ak-ak-ak*.
Status and distribution: Endemic species. Forests and wooded areas in hills to 1750 m and nearby lowlands.

Nesting: In tree hole; January–May and often July–September.
Range: Sri Lanka.

CUCKOOS, KOELS, MALKOHAS AND COUCALS
Order: Cuculiformes Family: Cuculidae

A VARIED family which falls into three groups, all mostly insectivorous with tapered, down-curved bills and two toes pointing forward and two backward.

The cuckoos have long, narrow, pointed wings and short rather weak legs, tails are fairly long and graduated. They are all mainly arboreal and are brood parasites, making no nest but laying their eggs in the nests of other birds. The calls are usually distinctive and repetitive. The females in several species occur in two morphs: grey and hepatic.

The malkohas have short, rounded wings and long graduated tails, with strong legs. They are mainly arboreal, not very vocal and are not brood parasites.

The coucals are mainly terrestrial birds with short, rounded wings and long broad tails. They have deep booming calls and are not parasitic.

CHESTNUT-WINGED CUCKOO *Clamator coromandus* PLATE 32 (1)
(Red-winged Crested Cuckoo)

Identification: (46 cm) Larger than Pied Cuckoo; and with white hind collar and chestnut on wings. Distinguish from coucals in flight by rufous-buff throat and white belly. Crest not usually erect in flight. White tips to tail feathers but these are often worn off the central feathers. Sexes alike. Juvenile: brown upperparts with rufous fringes, white underparts. Fast, direct flight. Solitary or very small groups. Strictly arboreal, often skulking in understorey.
Voice: Generally silent in Sri Lanka but has a raucous scream.
Status and distribution: Scarce winter visitor possible in any wooded area. Most likely in dry zone.
Range: India, SE Asia.

PIED CUCKOO *Oxylophus jacobinus* PLATE 32 (2)
(Pied Crested Cuckoo) (*Clamator jacobinus*)
(Black and White Cuckoo)

Identification: (32 cm) Slender with long tail. Black crest, white underparts. White patch on primaries. Sexes alike. Juvenile: browner above, buff below. Rather heavy but direct flight on black wings showing white tips to tail feathers. In pairs or small flocks often perching on tops of bushes seeking insect food. Prefers open country scrub, reed-beds and swamps, avoiding deep forest. Not shy.

Voice: A descending four or five note call *pee-pee, pew, pew, pew*. Noisy in breeding season.

Status and distribution: Resident in lowlands and hills to 1000 m. More common in dry zone.

Breeding: Parasitic mostly on babblers, mainly the Yellow-billed. Possible all year but peaks February–May.

Range: Africa, S Asia.

COMMON HAWK CUCKOO *Cuculus varius ciceliae* PLATE 32 (3)
(Ceylon Hawk Cuckoo) (*Hierococcyx varius ciceliae*)

Identification: (34 cm) Very similar plumage to Shikra (p. 52, Plate 10 (5)) but has pointed bill, short legs and four or five black and grey bars across tawny tipped tail. Sexes alike. Juvenile: no breast band, browner and barred above, streaks on breast. From juvenile Shikra in similar ways to adult but tail bars duller. Fast hawk-like flight with a few wing-beats alternating with glides. Mainly arboreal, feeding on insects and some fruit in canopy. Solitary or in pairs.

Voice: A repeated shrieking *too-trrroo-yer* rising in pitch and accelerating, suddenly stopping usually to begin again. Calls day and night when breeding, mainly silent out of season.

Status and distribution: Endemic race resident in hill country, preferring wetter areas and avoiding deep forest. Population is supplemented by winter visitors of the slightly darker *C. v. varius* but difficult to separate in field.

Breeding: Parasitic on babblers; January–April.

Species Range: India and Sri Lanka.

INDIAN CUCKOO *Cuculus micropterus* PLATE 32 (4)
(Short-winged Cuckoo)

Identification: (32 cm) Like the Common Cuckoo but has broad black sub-terminal band on paler grey tail, broader barring below, darker eye and has a distinctive call. Grey morph female has warmer brown on throat and breast than female Common. Hepatic morph female possible. Juvenile: broad white tips to head, mantle and wing feathers. Hawk-like flight. Mainly arboreal, feeds on insects in canopy. Wary and difficult to see but is often heard.

Voice: A monotonous, repeated *kuk-kuk-kee-oh*, heard day and night. Female has a bubbling call.

Status and distribution: Resident in forests of dry lowlands with winter visitors to forests throughout.

Breeding: Brood parasitic, possibly on orioles and drongos; thought to be January–May.
Range: India, SE Asia, Sumatra, Java.

COMMON CUCKOO *Cuculus canorus* PLATE 32 (5)
(Eurasian Cuckoo)

Identification: (33 cm) Hawk-like but has small pointed bill, graduated tail and short legs. Distinguish from Indian Cuckoo by dark grey tail contrasting with paler grey rump and pale yellowish iris. **Females** occur in two morphs: grey and hepatic (see plate). Hawk-like flight but faster with weaker wing-beats, wings held low. Does not glide in normal flight. Solitary.
Voice: Normally silent in Sri Lanka but has a repeated *cuck-oo* call, female a bubbling call.
Status and distribution: Winter vagrant, possible in all areas.
Range: Europe, Africa, Asia, Japan, New Guinea.

LESSER CUCKOO *Cuculus poliocephalus* PLATE 32 (6)
(Small Cuckoo)
(Little Cuckoo)

Identification: (25 cm) Small version of Common but has broader barring on the underparts and a blackish tail contrasting little with the dark rump. The female resembles the male but is slightly browner and there is a hepatic morph. Most records in Sri Lanka are of immatures which resemble hepatic females. Flight like that of scaled down Common. Prefers scrub and small trees. Very tame.
Voice: Normally silent in Sri Lanka but has a six syllable chattering call with the third stressed, likened to *that's your smoky paper*.
Status and distribution: Scarce and irregular winter visitor, possible in gardens and wooded areas of lowlands and lower hills.
Range: India, China, Japan.

BANDED BAY CUCKOO *Penthoceryx sonneratii waiti* PLATE 32 (7)
(Bay-banded Cuckoo) (*Cacomantis sonneratii*)

Identification: (25 cm) Distinguish from hepatic morph of Plaintive by white eyebrow and prominent dark ear coverts. Underparts off-white barred brown. Sexes alike. Juvenile: like adult but more rufous on upperparts. Often flies up from perch to take flying insects. Arboreal. Solitary or in pairs.
Voice: A loud and repeated *peu-peu-peupeu—peu-peu-peupeu* often from bare branch at top of tree heard most often in mornings and evenings, higher pitched than Indian Cuckoo's call. Also has a rising *peu-peu-peu-u-u, peu-u-u, peu-u-u*, ending abruptly.

Status and distribution: Endemic race resident in forest edge, cultivation and open scrub in lowlands and lower hills. In winter some move into hills up to 1300 m.

Breeding: Parasitises minivets, possibly also bulbuls and babblers. Young seen June, September and October.

Species Range: India, SE Asia, Philippines, Java.

PLAINTIVE CUCKOO *Cacomantis merulinus passerinus* PLATE 32 (8)

(Grey-bellied Cuckoo) (*Cacomantis passerinus maculatus*)

Identification: (23 cm) Small and slim. Dark grey above, paler below with white vent. Blackish tail with white tips. Sexes alike but female also occurs in hepatic morph with bright orange-rufous upperparts and longitudinal markings on tail, not bars. Hepatic morph female differs from Banded Bay by lack of white eyebrow. Juvenile: very similar to hepatic morph female. Fast hawk-like flight showing white patch on underwing. Feeds on insects by picking from foliage, taking during flycatcher-like flight, or picking from ground. Solitary or, rarely, in flocks. Not shy.

Voice: Normally silent in Sri Lanka but has ventriloquial *ka-veer* and *pee-pipee-pee, pipee-pee.*

Status and distribution: Common winter visitor to gardens, scrub, and open forest of lowlands and lower hills. Also some summer loiterers.

Range: India, SE Asia, Philippines, Sulawesi.

ASIAN EMERALD CUCKOO *Chalcites maculatus* PLATE 32 (10)

(*Chrysococcyx maculatus*)

Identification: (18 cm) Tiny. Male: green with black and white barred belly. Female: green mantle, barred rufous crown; brown and white barred below. Rapid and direct flight showing white patch on bases of underwing primaries. Very active in tops of trees, hawking after insects. Perches in crouched posture along branch. Solitary or in small groups.

Voice: Probably silent in Sri Lanka.

Status and distribution: Winter vagrant. Prefers forests.

Range: N India, SE Asia.

DRONGO CUCKOO *Surniculus lugubris* PLATE 32 (9)

Identification: (25 cm) Very similar to Black Drongo (p. 198, Plate 48(1)) but has white barring on bases of outer tail feathers and undertail coverts. Also has smaller, finer, curved bill and smaller head, and the tail is broader and less deeply forked. Generally glossy black with forked tail, white barring on bases of outer undertail feathers and coverts. Sometimes has variable white patch on nape. Sexes alike. Juvenile lacks the gloss and is spotted white.

Flight is direct and less energetic than the Drongo. Arboreal. Solitary or in small flocks. Not shy.

Voice: A repeated ascending scale of four–eight notes.

Status and distribution: Resident in open forest and trees of lowlands, visiting hills up to 1300 m in winter.

Breeding: Thought to parasitise Common Iora and smaller babblers. December–May.

Range: S and SE Asia, Philippines, Java.

ASIAN KOEL *Eudynamys scolopacea* PLATE 31 (8)

Identification: (42 cm) Slimmer than crows with longer tail and red eyes. Male: glossy black. Yellow-green bill. Female: brown, spotted above, barred below. Young birds have rufous tinge to spots and bars. Fast and direct flight with rapid wingbeats. Arboreal. Spends much time skulking in foliage, easily overlooked out of breeding season. Often harried by crows. In pairs.

Voice: A repeated, loud, ascending and accelerating *ko-el, ko-el, ko-el, ko-el*.... also a *ho-iy-o, ho-iy-o*..., and various other cackles and shrieks. The female has a *kik, kik, kik, kik*.

Status and distribution: Common resident in gardens, wooded areas, anywhere with trees and crows in lowlands and hills to 500 m.

Breeding: Parasitises crows; April–August.

Range: S and SE Asia, New Guinea.

BLUE-FACED MALKOHA *Rhopodytes viridirostris* PLATE 31 (7)
(Small Green-billed Malkoha) (*Phaenicophaeus viridirostris*)

Identification: (39 cm) Pale green bill, bare blue skin around eye, white-tipped feathers on long graduated tail showing as broad white bars across underside of tail. Green gloss especially on the wings and tail. Sexes alike. Slow and laboured flight showing the white-tipped tail feathers. Skulks in tree foliage feeding on insects and fruit, rarely descending to ground. Solitary or in pairs.

Voice: Normally silent but has *kraa* alarm.

Status and distribution: Resident in thorny scrub and secondary forest in lowlands and hills to 400 m, more common in dry zone.

Nesting: On leaf-lined flimsy, open platform of twigs in tree. Mainly March–May but possible anytime.

Range: S India.

SIRKEER MALKOHA *Taccocua leschenaultii* PLATE 31 (9)
(Southern Sirkeer) (*Phaenicophaeus leschenaultii*)
(Sirkeer Cuckoo)

Identification: (41 cm) Much paler than other malkohas and mostly terrestrial in habits. Cherry red bill and broad white-tipped outer feathers on the long, graduated tail. Sexes alike. Laboured and flapping flight, usually preferring to run from danger. Feeds by taking insects mainly on ground. Solitary or in pairs. Shy.

Voice: Normally silent but has a *kek, kek, kek* and a *kerek, kerek, kerek*.

Status and distribution: Scarce resident in open wooded areas of dry zone and nearby lower hills.

Nesting: On leaf-lined saucer of twigs low in fork of tree or shrub. February and June–July.

Range: India.

RED-FACED MALKOHA *Phaenicophaeus pyrrhocephalus* PLATE 31 (6)

Identification: (46 cm) Finely bristled crimson red face, strong pale green bill, white underparts with black breast. Long, graduated, white tipped tail showing as white edges above and broad white below. Green sheen on upperparts. Sexes alike apart from brown iris in male and white in female. Juvenile: small red eye-patch, grey streaked crown and shorter tail. Arboreal. Slow laboured direct flight, preferring to hop through vegetation if possible. Solitary or in small groups. Shy.

Voice: Normally silent but can give single whistles. Has a *kok* call and a low *kraa*.

Status and distribution: Probably an endemic species (see below). Scarce in forests of lowlands and hills.

Nesting: On loose shallow saucer of twigs and grass in high bush; January, April–May, possibly August–September.

Range: Sri Lanka. Has been recorded in S India but now thought to be extinct there.

GREEN-BILLED COUCAL *Centropus chlororhynchus* PLATE 31 (10)
(Ceylon Coucal)

Identification: (43 cm) Like the Greater Coucal but smaller with a pale yellowish-green or ivory bill (not black), purple sheen on head and neck, deep chestnut wings and a distinctive call. Sexes alike. Slow and cumbersome flight, rarely more than flapping from one tree to the next. Feeds mainly on ground in deep cover, more often heard than seen. Very shy.

Voice: A descending *poo-hoop* repeated usually three, sometimes four times and a coughed *chook*.

Status and distribution: Endemic species. Forests, preferrably with dwarf bamboo undergrowth, in wet lowlands and hills to 1000 m. Endangered.

Nesting: In lined, domed nest set in thorny bush a metre or two above ground; January–July.

Range: Sri Lanka.

GREATER COUCAL *Centropus sinensis* PLATE 31 (11)
(Common Coucal)

Identification: (48 cm) Distinguish from Green-billed by black bill, blue sheen on head and neck, and brighter chestnut wings. Long graduated tail. Sexes alike. Juvenile: upperparts barred brown and rufous with some streaking and black barred grey tail: underparts barred brown and white. Clumsy and reluctant flight, preferring to walk or run. Ground feeder, mainly on insects and other small animals in undergrowth or clambering in vegetation. Solitary or in pairs.

Voice: A deep, resonant and repeated *ooop, ooop, ooop*...sometimes heard at night and a *k-wisss* alarm.

Status and distribution: Common resident throughout.

Nesting: In a lined, domed nest concealed in deep cover, sometimes quite high up.

Range: India, SE Asia, Philippines, Java.

LESSER COUCAL *Centropus bengalensis* PLATE 31(12)

Identification: (37 cm) Breeding adult very similar to Greater but smaller with pale streaks on mantle. Non-breeding and juvenile distinguishable from Sirkeer Malkoha by brown bill not red. Flight and habits similar to those of Greater.

Voice: A repeated *whooot, whooo*... and a *kurook, kurook*....

Status and distribution: Doubtful vagrant to lowlands, preferring tall grass and scrub by forests, or reed beds by swamps.

Range: India, SE Asia, Philippines, Java.

BARN OWLS Order: Strigiformes Family: Tytonidae

MEDIUM to large owls with heart-shaped facial discs of erectile feathers and eyes with dark irises. Legs are long and slender with feathers on tarsi.

BARN OWL *Tyto alba* PLATE 34 (5)

Identification: (36 cm) Slender, long-legged, and long winged. Round head (no ear tufts), heart-shaped white facial disc. Sexes nearly alike, female slightly darker. Slow, flapping flight with glides, appearing very pale. Crepuscular and nocturnal, mobbed if emerges too early. Flies low often hovering over tussocky grass when feeding.

Voice: Various harsh screeches, shrieks, and hisses.

Status and distribution: Resident near cultivation and settlements in northern dry zone, also possible around Colombo and in SE at Yala. Scarce.
Nesting: In hole in building, ruin, cave, or tree; mainly February–March.
Range: Almost world-wide.

ORIENTAL BAY OWL *Phodilus badius assimilis* PLATE 34 (4)

Identification: (28 cm) Medium sized owl with short ear-tufts, flat-topped rather triangular vinous-brown facial disc with dark eyebrows, rich chestnut upperparts, pink-buff below. Short, rounded wings and short tail. Legs feathered to feet. Sexes alike. Strictly nocturnal and shy.
Voice: A series of long drawn out whistles.
Status and distribution: Rare endemic race. Forests of wet zone and hills to 1300 m. Endangered.
Nesting: In hole in tree.
Species Range: India, SE Asia, Java.

OWLS Order: Strigiformes Family: Strigidae

LARGE to small mostly nocturnal, carnivorous birds with large, forward facing eyes and rounded heads, some bearing erectile ear-tufts and some with obvious facial discs. They have strong hooked bills and strong feet, feathered to the toes in some species. Wings tend to be long and broad and are adapted to silent flight. Tails are generally short and rounded. Colours tend to be muted. They mostly live solitarily or in pairs.

ORIENTAL SCOPS OWL *Otus sunia leggei* PLATE 33 (1)
(Little Scops Owl)

Identification: (17 cm) Tiny, variably plumaged yellow-eyed owl with ear-tufts (not always erect). Distinguish from Collared Scops by whitish scapular stripe, well marked underparts, and lack of pale collar. Two morphs present, grey and rufous, intermediate forms also occur. Sexes alike. Nocturnal. Freeze with eyes half closed when disturbed. More often heard than seen.
Voice: A repeated liquid ***tuk, tok, torok***.
Status and distribution: Endemic race in lowland forests and hills to 1600 m. Most likely in eastern dry lowlands, scarce elsewhere.
Nesting: In hole in tree, February–April.
Species range: India, SE Asia.

COLLARED SCOPS OWL *Otus bakkamoena* PLATE 33 (2)
(Indian Scops Owl)

Identification: (23 cm) Larger than Oriental Scops, with dark brown eyes, buff collar on hind neck and poorly marked underparts. Ear-tufts usually erect. Plumage somewhat variable but less so than in Oriental Scops. Sexes alike. Rapid, silent flight with fast wingbeats, sometimes flies to buildings to take geckos off walls near lights.

Voice: A slowly repeated croaking *wha* and a descending *wa, wa, wa, wa* often followed by a shriek.

Status and distribution: Common resident in forest and town gardens in lowlands and hills to 1000 m.

Nesting: In tree hole or building crevice; February–May.

Range: Middle East, S and SE Asia.

SPOT-BELLIED EAGLE OWL *Bubo nipalensis blighi* PLATE 34 (1)
(Sri Lanka Forest Eagle Owl)

Identification: (61 cm) Largest of local owls. Strikingly spotted above: whitish below with bars, Vs, or heart-shaped spots. Prominent black and white ear-tufts, brown eyes (possibly paling with age) and strong, feathered legs. Flight feathers brown with grey bands. Sexes alike but female a little larger than male. Juvenile: buff with brown bars, darker on upperwings. Mainly nocturnal.

Voice: A long drawn out haunting *ooooo-oh* and various shrieks.

Status and distribution: Endemic race. Scarce in forests throughout but prefers lower hills.

Nesting: In tree hollow; April–May.

Species range: India, Myanmar.

BROWN FISH OWL *Bubo zeylonensis zeylonensis* PLATE 34 (2)
(Ceylon Fish Owl) (*Ketupa zeylonensis*)

Identification: (54 cm) Only large local owl with yellow eyes. Smaller than Spot-bellied Eagle Owl, with shorter ears and bare tarsi. Sandy brown upperparts with dark streaks, white mottling on scapulars and wing coverts, buff-brown underparts with fine dark streaks and some barring: flight feathers and tail dark brown with paler bars. Sexes alike. Takes fish but also reptiles and other small animals. Mainly nocturnal.

Voice: A deep *oomp-ooo-oo* rather like a distant Eurasian Bittern, reported to be a duet between a pair, the middle *ooo* being made by a different bird from the one that hoots the first and third syllables.

Status and distribution: Endemic race relatively common where forest borders water in lowlands but possible up to 2000 m.

Nesting: In tree hole, cave, or rock ledge near water; January–May.
Species range: Middle East, S and SE Asia.

BROWN WOOD OWL *Strix leptogrammica ochrogenys* PLATE 34 (3)

Identification: (46 cm) Large with dark rimmed pale chestnut facial disc, dark brown eyes and white eyebrows, finely barred upperparts with narrow white lines on mantle and finely barred off-white underparts. Sexes alike but female slightly larger. Juvenile: barred upperparts, off-white underparts. Nocturnal. Feeds mainly on small mammals, occasionally birds or reptiles.
Voice: A low *huhu-hooo* and various shrieks, also snaps bill.
Status and distribution: Endemic race. Relatively common in forests throughout.
Nesting: In tree hole; January–March.
Species range: S and SE Asia, Borneo, Java.

JUNGLE OWLET *Glaucidium radiatum* PLATE 33 (4)
(Barred Jungle Owlet)

Identification: (20 cm) Small. Distinguish from the Scops by lack of ear-tufts and barred dark brown and white back and underparts; from Chestnut-backed by barred dark brown and white above and below, the barring below continuing onto the rear flanks (Chestnut-backed has streaked flanks). White eyebrows, yellow eyes. Sexes alike. Fast, hawk-like flight. Diurnal but most active at dawn and dusk feeding mainly on insects, also takes small birds, reptiles, and mice.
Voice: Thought to be a *kaow* repeated, slowly accelerating to a repeated *kaow-whap*, stopping suddenly.
Status and distribution: Resident in dense forests of dry lowlands and eastern hills.
Nesting: Probably in tree holes; possibly March–May.
Range: India.

CHESTNUT-BACKED OWLET *Glaucidium castanonotum* PLATE 33 (5)
(Sri Lanka Cuckoo Owlet) (*Glaucidium cuculoides castanonotum*)

Identification: (20 cm) Similar to Jungle Owlet but has chestnut mantle finely and faintly barred black, also flanks are streaked, not barred. Yellow eyes, white eyebrows, and no ear-tufts. Arborial. Diurnal. Feeds on insects and occasionally small vertebrates. Shy.
Voice: A rising, trilling *cooo, cooo, cooo,...*
Status and distribution: Endemic species. Scarce in wet zone forests.
Nesting: In tree hole; March–May.
Range: Sri Lanka.

BROWN HAWK OWL *Ninox scutulata* PLATE 33 (3)

Identification: (30 cm) Slender and hawk-like. Medium sized, round-headed with yellow eyes but no obvious facial disc. Brown above, white heavily streaked brown below. Sexes alike. Fast hawk-like flight with glides on long wings taking insects on the wing. Upright posture when perched, often jumping up to take passing insect. Nocturnal.

Voice: A descending *koo-ook, koo-ook...*

Status and distribution: Resident in wooded areas in lowlands and hills to 1500 m. Prefers to be close to water.

Nesting: In tree hole; March–April and November.

Range: S, E, SE Asia, Philippines, Java.

SHORT-EARED OWL *Asio flammeus* PLATE 34 (6)

Identification: (38 cm) Dark-streaked buff facial disc with yellow eyes, short ear-tufts, and greyish head. Heavily spotted mantle: breast heavily streaked, less so on flanks, belly, and vent. Legs feathered to feet. Sexes alike. Slow, harrier-like flight on relatively long wings showing rich buff on upperwing primaries, white below with dark crescents on the primary coverts and dark bars on the tips of primaries. Active during day feeding on small invertebrates, often over marshes. Usually perches on ground or a fence post.

Voice: Normally silent in winter.

Status and distribution: Irregular winter visitor, sometimes in considerable numbers, to open scrub, swamps and marshes throughout.

Range: Europe, N Africa, N Asia, Americas and some Pacific islands.

FROGMOUTH Order: Caprimulgiformes Family: Podargidae

SIMILAR in many ways to nightjars with short, rather weak legs and feet but they have very wide, short, slightly hooked bills, short, rounded wings and long, graduated tails. They are strictly nocturnal, feeding mainly on insects.

SRI LANKA FROGMOUTH *Batrachostomus moniliger* PLATE 33 (6)

Identification: (23 cm) Very wide bill with a tuft of bristly feathers at the base and large yellow eyes with a broken fore collar of white spots. Long barred tail. Sexes similar but male greyer, female browner. Spends day perched across a branch (not along, like a nightjar) with bill up and facial plumes erect, looking rather like a broken branch.

Voice: A low, repeated *cheeow, cheeow...*, a *cheeowik, cheeowik...*, and a trilling, descending throb.

Status and distribution: Scarce resident in dense forests throughout.
Nesting: On a small pad set on a branch, camouflaged with lichen and bark; February–March and August–September.
Range: SW India.

NIGHTJARS

Order: Caprimulgiformes
Family: Caprimulgidae

NOCTURNAL or crepuscular, insectivorous birds with long wings and tails. The bill is small yet wide but not as wide as the Frogmouth, the eyes are large and the legs are short. Flight is normally a few rapid, jerky flaps of stiff wings followed by long glides with wings held in a V. Ground nesting and often also roosting on the ground during the day, being adapted to these habits by their cryptic colouring. Also sometimes roost by perching along a branch with bill held up looking like a broken branch. Usually sit tight when approached, exploding from beneath feet if in real danger. Calls are important aids to identification.

GREY NIGHTJAR *Caprimulgus indicus kelaarti* PLATE 33 (7)
(Highland Nightjar)
(Jungle Nightjar)

Identification: (27 cm) Darkest local nightjar. Male: white spots on primaries, small white patch on tips of outer tail feathers and usually shows two white spots on throat. Female lacks white except for moustachial stripe. Emerges at dusk, flying to a vantage point to call. Male display flight is with wings held high and tail fanned to expose the white tail spots.
Voice: A repeated *chuk-m, chuk-m, chuk-m*... often continuing for some time and a *hoo, hoo, hoo, hooteter, hooteter*... display flight call.
Status and distribution: Endemic race. Grassy slopes in hills, avoiding forest. Rare.
Nesting: On bare ground without nest; February–June.
Species range: S, E, and SE Asia, Japan, Java.

JERDON'S NIGHTJAR *Caprimulgus atripennis*
(Large-tailed Nightjar) (*Caprimulgus macrurus aequabilis*)
(Horsfield's Jungle Nightjar) PLATE 33 (9)
(Long-tailed Nightjar)

Identification: (28 cm) Large; more contrastingly marked and relatively longer tailed with larger white patches on wings and tail than other local nightjars.

Appears darker than Indian. Similar to Grey but paler, especially on crown and mantle, and with black spots on scapulars. Single large white patch on throat (Grey has two). Female has smaller and duller patches on throat, primaries, and tail than male. Sometimes seen perched in road, red eyes reflecting car headlights. Easy sailing flight with strong flaps and glides. Roosts on ground during day, sitting tight when approached.

Voice: A laboured *grog, groggrog*, a rich, trilled *cheeowow*, also a repeated *quoffrr, quoffrr....*

Status and distribution: Endemic race. Relatively common in scrub and wooded areas of dry lowlands and nearby hills to 1000 m.

Nesting: On ground without nest; February–May.

Species range: India, SE Asia, Philippines, New Guinea, N Australia.

INDIAN NIGHTJAR *Caprimulgus asiaticus eidos* PLATE 33 (8)

(Common Nightjar)

Identification: (23 cm) Smallest and palest of local nightjars. Similar to Jerdon's but paler sandy-buff with two white throat patches and smaller white patches on tail. Finely streaked black on back. White spots on primaries, broad white tips to outer tail feathers. Female: duller with smaller white patches. Usual nightjar flight and roosting habit.

Voice: A repeated and accelerating *chik, chik, chik, churrrrrick* likened to a marble dropped on concrete and a bubbling *bub, bub, bub, bubbubbub.*

Status and distribution: Endemic race. Relatively common in open country, dunes, scrub and thin woodland of dry lowlands and dry hills to 1300 m. Scarce in wet zone.

Nesting: On bare ground, often in open; February–July and September.

Species range: Madagascar, Aldabra, S and SE Asia.

SWIFTS Order: Apodiformes Family: Apodidae

AERIAL birds with long, crescent-shaped, narrow wings. They have short but very wide bills enabling them to trawl their insect prey on the wing. Their short legs are adapted for clinging rather than perching or walking. The flight is fast and dashing on rather stiff wings with much swooping and gliding. They are very mobile, often ranging widely to seek insects. They nest in holes, ledges in caves, or in buildings and at the nest site they shuffle rather than walk. Colouring is mainly black and brown with patches of white. The sexes are generally alike. Look for tail shapes.

INDIAN SWIFTLET *Aerodramus unicolor* PLATE 38 (6)
(Indian Edible-nest Swiftlet) (*Collocalia unicolor*)

Identification: (12 cm) Small with notched tail. Sturdier and broader, less pointed winged than Palm, smaller than Little and lacks the white rump. Upperparts glossy browny-black with rump slightly paler than mantle. In flocks, often feeds with Palm Swifts. Roosts colonially in caves.
Voice: Normally silent in flight but makes a clicking *chit, chit* call in caves.
Status and distribution: Common resident throughout but more so in hills.
Nesting: Colonially in shallow cups glued to wall with saliva in cave or tunnel; March–September.
Range: SW India.

BROWN-BACKED NEEDLETAIL *Hirundapus giganteus* PLATE 38 (4)
(Brown Needletail) (*Chaetura gigantea*)
(Brown Spinetailed Swift)
(Brown-throated Spinetail Swift)

Identification: (23 cm) Large, cigar-shaped body with very short square tail, normally appearing pointed. The 'needles' are only visible when turning in flight at extremely close range. White spot in front of eye. Distinguish from Alpine by white 'horseshoe' flank stripe joining white undertail coverts, dark throat and belly, square tail and broader wings. Sexes alike. Leisurely flight when hawking for insects with wings straight out from body and held slightly below horizontal with tail normally closed. Also has very fast flight with wings fluttered and raked back from the body making a whooshing noise. Feeds over forest or grassland. Drinks on the wing. In flocks, occasionally solitary.
Voice: A sharp *eek, eek, eek...*
Status and distribution: Scarce resident in hills, occasionally in lowlands.
Nesting: In small colony in hollow tree; February–April.
Range: India, SE Asia, Java.

ASIAN PALM SWIFT *Cypsiurus balasiensis* PLATE 38 (2)
(*Cypsiurus batasiensis*)
(*Cypsiurus parvus*)

Identification: (13 cm) Small and dark with sharply pointed wings and deeply forked tail (fork only apparent if tail fanned when turning). Distinguish from Indian Swiftlet by narrower and more pointed wings and forked tail. Sexes alike. Fluttering flight with much gliding on bow-shaped wings. Often feeds with Indian Swiftlet. Gregarious.
Voice: A shrill *tittyree* uttered in flight.

Status and distribution: Common resident around fan palms in lowlands and hills to 1000 m.
Nesting: In small cup of feathers and cotton glued with saliva under old palm frond; possible year round.
Range: India, SE Asia, Philippines, Java.

ALPINE SWIFT *Tachymarptis melba* PLATE 38 (3)
(White-bellied Swift) (*Apus melba*)

Identification: (22 cm) Large. Dark brown with long wings and forked tail. Distinguish from Needletail by white throat and belly with brown breast band, and no white on flanks or under tail. Sexes alike. Fast swooping flight, making loud swishing noise. In flocks.
Voice: Shrill *chee-chee* flight calls.
Status and distribution: Scarce resident in hills usually not far from cliffs but possible throughout.
Nesting: Thought to be in shallow cup glued to wall of crevice or cave on cliff; early in year.
Range: S Europe, Africa, Middle East, India.

FORK-TAILED SWIFT *Apus pacificus* Not illustrated
(Pacific Swift)

Identification: (18 cm) Larger than little Swift with longer more deeply forked tail and longer, narrower wings. Dusky black with broad white rump; pale throat, narrow white fringes on underparts giving scaly pattern (only visible when close). Erratic flight when feeding. Associates with other swifts.
Status and distribution: Winter vagrant. Two sight records to date, at Bundala in SE in 1996 and at Bentota in 1997.
Range: N India, China, Japan, SE Asia, Australia.

LITTLE SWIFT *Apus affinis* PLATE 38 (5)
(White-rumped Swift)
(House Swift)

Identification: (14 cm) Small and dark with white throat and rump, and square tail. Fast, graceful flight with much gliding between rapid shallow wing-beats. In flocks, often large, with other swifts and swallows.
Voice: A shrill, chattering *siksiksiksik, sik-sik, siksiksik*… flight call.
Status and distribution: Common resident in lowlands and lower hills, often near cliffs.
Nesting: Colonially in small cups of grass and feathers glued to roof of cave or building; April–September. Long established colonies at Sigiriya and over the entrance to Ratnapura Rest House.
Range: Africa, Middle East, S and SE Asia, Philippines, Java.

TREESWIFT Order: Apodiformes Family: Hemiprocnidae

INSECTIVOROUS birds superficially similar to swifts but are more colourful and have long forked tails. Like the swifts they take insects on the wing but unlike swifts they perch on tree branches or wires usually overlooking open areas or water and make brief flycatcher-like flights after insects. The sexes differ in plumage.

GREY-RUMPED TREESWIFT *Hemiprocne longipennis* PLATE 38 (1)
(Indian Crested Swift) (*Hemiprocne coronata*)
(Crested Treeswift)

Identification: (24 cm) Distinguish from the swifts by long tail extending beyond wings when perched, crest on forehead (usually erect only when perched), and perching habit; from Palm Swift in flight by larger size, paler belly, and long tail. Female: dark cheeks and fine white moustachial stripe, lacking the chestnut. Juvenile: brown and white edged feathers on upperparts and brown bars below. Graceful flight on slightly downward-held wings, showing forked tail when turning. Drinks on the wing. In small groups.

Voice: A loud, creaky chirping *keek-ko* often heard when in flight and perched.

Status and distribution: Common resident in lowlands and hills to 1000 m preferring open country with trees. More frequent in dry zone.

Nesting: In a small cup of bark and lichens glued to a branch; March–May and July–August.

Range: India, SE Asia, Java.

TROGON Order: Trogoniformes Family: Trogonidae

COLOURFUL arboreal birds with short, rounded wings and long, graduated tails. The strong bill is short and wide adapted for taking insects on the wing. Legs are short and weak, used mainly for perching. The plumage is soft and fluffy.

MALABAR TROGON *Harpactes fasciatus fasciatus* PLATE 35 (1)

Identification: (28 cm) Male: black head, white fore collar, and red underparts, fine black and white barring on wing, long square-ended tail. Female: brown head, buff fore collar, orange-brown underparts. Juvenile: like female but duller, the maturing male assuming the red in patches. Rapid flight, swooping from tree to tree with much flashing of white outer tail feathers taking insect prey on wing. Often feeds well into dusk. Normally rather inactive, perches upright with tail hanging down.

Voice: A whinnying *ihiiiii, ihiiiii* often made while fanning tail, also a *krrrr* and *piu, piu, piu,...* or *tchooog, tchooog, tchoog* and a *twang*.
Status and distribution: Endemic race. Deep forests throughout, more common in wet lowlands.
Nesting: In hole in tree; February–June.
Species range: W and S India.

KINGFISHERS Order: Coraciiformes Family: Alcedinidae

MEDIUM to small, mainly fish-eating birds with relatively large heads, long strong pointed bills, short legs, and short tails. Most are brightly coloured with blues predominating. Commonly perch over water, sometimes hovering, to plunge onto their prey but some feed on terrestrial prey well away from water. Flight is fast and direct. Calls are loud and raucous. Usually nest in burrows in waterside mud cliffs or sand banks. Live solitarily, in pairs, or small groups.

PIED KINGFISHER *Ceryle rudis* PLATE 35 (8)
(Lesser Pied Kingfisher)

Identification: (29 cm) Only local black and white kingfisher. Male has two black bands across upper breast, female only one, usually broken in the centre. Frequently hovers over water, head down, to plunge steeply onto prey.
Status and distribution: Resident on estuaries, lagoons, slow flowing rivers, and larger lowland tanks. Not in hills.
Voice: A raucous *chreek-chreek* and various chattering notes.
Nesting: In burrow or hole in bank near water; March–May.
Range: Africa, Middle East, S Asia.

COMMON KINGFISHER *Alcedo atthis* PLATE 35 (7)
(River Kingfisher)

Identification: (16 cm) Small with brilliant colouring. Distinguish from Blue-eared by orange ear-coverts, paler greener blue crown, scapulars and wings, and lighter orange below. Sexes alike but male has black bill, female has orange on lower bill. Fast flight with rapid wingbeats often only a little above the water's surface swooping up to settle on branch or post. Perches, often with head bobbing and tail flicking, to plunge onto fish or other aquatic animal prey, also sometimes hovers. Not very shy.
Voice: A sharp *peee, peep* flight call.

Status and distribution: Common resident alongside water or marshy places throughout. Avoids deep forest.
Nesting: In burrow not too far from water; February–June.
Range: Europe, N Africa, Middle East, S Asia, Philippines, New Guinea.

BLUE-EARED KINGFISHER *Alcedo meninting* PLATE 35 (6)

Identification: (16 cm) Similar to (and deep forest replacement of) Common but has deep royal blue upperparts, dark orange below and blue ear coverts not chestnut. Sexes alike but female has more orange on bill. Perches on branch over forest stream, bobbing before plunging into water. Shy.
Voice: Thought to be a sharp *peep-peep* and *chick*.
Status and distribution: Very rare resident in forests of lowlands and eastern foothills.
Nesting: In hole in waterside bank; season uncertain.
Range: India, SE Asia, Java.

ORIENTAL DWARF KINGFISHER *Ceyx erithacus* PLATE 35 (5)
(Black-backed Kingfisher)
(Three-toed Kingfisher)

Identification: (14 cm) Smallest Sri Lankan kingfisher. Vermilion bill, orange-purple glossed lilac head, neck, rump and tail; deep blue and white ear patch. Purple wings. Despite the alternative name has violet-blue back not black in Sri Lankan race. Sexes alike. Fast, direct flight showing rufous patch on pale underwing. Perches and plunges for prey. Shy.
Voice: A shrill piping *peepeep*.
Status and distribution: Scarce resident alongside streams in forests of lowlands and lower hills.
Nesting: In hole in streamside bank, hole smaller than those of other kingfishers; March–April.
Range: India, SE Asia, Sumatra, Philippines.

STORK-BILLED KINGFISHER *Halcyon capensis* (*Pelargopsis capensis*) PLATE 35 (2)

Identification: (39 cm) Largest local kingfisher. Large red bill. Brown head with buff collar. Sexes alike. Juvenile: dark edges on collar and breast feathers. Strong direct flight showing no white on wing. Perches on waterside branches and plunges after prey. Rather inactive, more often heard than seen. Solitary or in loose pairs.
Voice: A loud, laughing *piu, piu, piu, piu,* ... call.

Status and distribution: Resident by water in forests or mangroves of low country and hills to 600m. More common in dry zone.
Nesting: In well concealed hole in bank, larger diameter than for other kingfishers; January–May and August–September.
Range: India, SE Asia, Philippines, Java.

WHITE-THROATED KINGFISHER *Halcyon smyrnensis* PLATE 35 (3)
(White-breasted Kingfisher)

Identification: (28 cm) Distinctive red bill, dark chocolate brown head and underparts with white throat and bib; brilliant blue mantle. Sexes alike. Direct flight showing obvious white patch at base of primaries (beware of confusion with Black-capped). Commonly perches on roadside phone wires, often well away from water, to drop down onto lizards, frogs, insects, and other small animal prey.
Status and distribution: Common resident in open country, paddy, and gardens throughout.
Voice: A loud descending trill flight call and a *chik*. Very noisy in breeding season.
Nesting: In hole in bank not necessarily near water. Sometimes in a hole in a tree or building; December–June, peaking in March–April.
Range: Turkey, Middle East, S and SE Asia, Philippines.

BLACK-CAPPED KINGFISHER *Halcyon pileata* PLATE 35 (4)
(Black-capped Purple Kingfisher)

Identification: (31 cm) Smaller than Stork-billed with black cap and white collar. Sexes alike. Direct flight showing conspicuous white wing patches (as White-throated but that has no white collar). Sits on post or branch by water watching for small animal prey.
Voice: A shrill laughing call. Much quieter than White-throated.
Status and distribution: Rare winter visitor. Most likely in mangrove fringed estuaries, lagoons, or coastal rivers of SE dry zone.
Range: India, China, Philippines.

BEE-EATERS Order Coraciiformes Family: Meropidae

MEDIUM to small sized, slender and brightly coloured but predominantly green birds (in Asia) with long, thin, curved, tapering bills. Wings are pointed and the legs short. Some species have extended streamer central tail feathers. Fast swallow-like flight. Feed on insects (not only bees) on the wing either during long, hawking flights with much gliding or darting out from perch, flycatcher-like, returning to eat the catch. Roost socially. Dig burrows in earth or sand banks, or even in a slight hump, to nest.

LITTLE GREEN BEE-EATER *Merops orientalis ceylonicus* PLATE 35 (9)
(Green Bee-eater)

Identification: (25 cm including long tail streamers) Smallest of local bee-eaters and only one with pale green throat. Bronze rear crown, chestnut underwing. Sexes alike. Often perches in pairs or small groups on wires or branches, darting out to feed on passing insects. Form roosting flocks at dusk.
Voice: A high pitched *tree, tree, tree*... and *tit, tit, tit*....
Status and distribution: Endemic race. Common in open country and cultivation of dry zone up to 600 m preferring scrubby areas near coast. Occasionally in wet zone.
Nesting: In burrow; April–August.
Species range: N Africa, Middle East, S Asia.

BLUE-TAILED BEE-EATER *Merops philippinus* PLATE 35 (12)
(Blue-cheeked Bee-eater) (*Merops superciliosus philippinus*)

Identification: (30 cm including long tail streamers) Larger than Little Green with green crown, blue cheeks, yellow chin, chestnut throat and blue tail; deep chestnut underwing. Sexes alike. Easy flight, gliding often when hunting but in direct flight closes wings between bursts of wingbeats. Likes water and will plunge while on wing to bathe. Perches in small groups on tops of trees or bushes to fly out after insects.
Voice: A loud *chirrup*.
Status and distribution: Scarce resident in eastern dry lowlands, supplemented by winter visitors arriving in August becoming common over whole island only avoiding deep forest. Leaves by May.
Nesting: Colonially in burrows in banks; March–June.
Range: India, SE Asia, Philippines, Borneo, New Guinea.

EUROPEAN BEE-EATER *Merops apiaster* PLATE 35 (10)

Identification: (28 cm including short tail streamers). Larger than Chestnut-headed, and has white forehead, chestnut and yellow upperparts and short tail streamers; green-blue breast and belly. Pale grey brown underwing. Sexes alike. Juvenile: much greyer. Graceful flight with bursts of wingbeats then long glides, more robust than Chestnut-headed. Feeds in typical bee-eater manner. In pairs or small groups.

Voice: Frequent *crrooic* flight calls.
Status and distribution: Rare winter visitor to open country of dry zone. Recent sightings have been in SE up to 750 m.
Range: S Europe, Africa, Middle East, C Asia, Kashmir.

CHESTNUT-HEADED BEE-EATER *Merops leschenaulti* PLATE 35 (11)
(Bay-headed Bee-eater)

Identification: (21 cm) Distinguish from Little Green by yellow throat and no tail streamers. Chestnut crown, nape, and upper back. Blue tinge on rump. Square tail. Sexes alike. Typical bee-eater flight and habits. More associated with forest edge than others in the family. In small groups.
Voice: Various *tree, tree*... and *tetrew* calls. Noisy.
Status and distribution: Resident in scattered colonies in forests and open country with trees in lowlands and up to 1400 m in dry hills.
Nesting: In burrow; March–May.
Range: India, SE Asia, Java.

ROLLERS Order: Coraciiformes Family: Coraciidae

SOMEWHAT crow-like birds with relatively large heads and strong beaks. Their wings are fairly long and broad, the tails quite short. Mainly insectivorous but also take small vertebrate prey, they perch on vantage points to pounce on prey or fly out to take on the wing. The name comes from the aerobatic display flight.

INDIAN ROLLER *Coracias benghalensis* PLATE 35 (13)

Identification: (32 cm) Dull brown and blue when perched, brilliant lilac and pale blue in flight. Distinguish from kingfishers by much shorter bill. Sexes alike. Heavily flapping flight. Often perches on branch or wire, lifting tail up and down, looking for prey sometimes feeding well into dusk. Solitary or in pairs.
Voice: Various croaks, a chattering *quak, quak, quak*... and *kyow, kyow, kyow*... Noisy in courtship.
Status and distribution: Common resident in coconut plantations and open areas in low country dry zone, occasionally in lower hills and wet zone.
Nesting: In tree hole or rotten palm, occasionally in derelict wall; January–June.
Range: Saudi Arabia, S and SE Asia.

DOLLARBIRD *Eurystomus orientalis* PLATE 35 (14)
(Eastern Broad-billed Roller)

Identification: (30 cm) Dark green-blue with glossy green sheen on upperparts. Broad orange bill. Blue wings with darker flight feathers and a very pale blue 'dollar' on base of primaries. Orange legs. Sexes alike. Faster and more direct flight than Indian Roller, showing 'dollar' patches. Feeding habit similar to Roller. Solitary or in pairs.
Voice: A harsh *chak, chak* and a faster, repeated *chuk-chuk-chuk-chuk....*
Status and distribution: Rare resident in forests of wet lowlands, eastern dry zone and lower hills. Endangered.
Nesting: In hole high in tree; February–April.
Range: S, E, and SE Asia, New Guinea, Australia.

HOOPOE Order: Coraciiformes Family: Upupidae

THERE is only the one species in this family.

EURASIAN HOOPOE *Upupa epops* PLATE 35 (15)

Identification: (30 cm) Strikingly patterned in cinnamon, black, and white with large fan-shaped crest and thin, slightly down-curved black bill. Sexes alike. Undulating and flapping flight on broad wings. Feeds mainly on insects and other small animals taken on ground by turning over fallen leaves and other bits. In pairs. Not shy.
Voice: A soft but carrying *oop-oop-oop*.
Status and distribution: Resident in open country with some trees in dry lowlands and eastern hills to 1300 m. Occasionally in wet zone. Avoids deep forest. Possibly also a winter visitor.
Nesting: In hole in tree, bank or building; November–April and possibly again in June–July.
Range: Europe, Africa, S, E, and SE Asia.

HORNBILLS Order: Coraciiformes Family: Bucerotidae

LARGE birds with massive down-curved bills which, despite their rather clumsy-looking appearance, are quite graceful in their undulating flight, strong wing-beats alternating with glides, and neck extended. The wings are broad, short, and rounded, the tail long and graduated. The two species in Sri Lanka are raucous and noisy, even the wings in normal flight generate a low throbbing sound. They feed on fruit and small animals, usually in groups or pairs. The nest is in a hole in a tree, the entrance to which is partly walled up by the female from within, the male passes food through the remaining slot until the brood is fledging. The female then breaks out to wall in the chicks, both parents then feed the young until they are ready to emerge.

SRI LANKA GREY HORNBILL *Tockus gingalensis* PLATE 34 (7)
(Malabar Grey Hornbill) (*Tockus griseus gingalensis*)
(*Ocyceros gingalensis*)

Identification: (59 cm) Lacks the large casque of the Malabar Pied, is smaller and has white throat and fore neck. Outer tail feathers become whiter with age. Underparts also pale with age. Sexes alike but female has dark pattern on bill. Typical hornbill flight. Spends a lot of time feeding hidden in forest trees.
Voice: A loud *kaa…kaa…ka ka ka ka* and a rolling *kuk-kuk-kuk ko ko kokoko*.
Status and distribution: Endemic species. Lowland forests and hills to 1300 m, more frequent in dry zone.
Nesting: In tree hole usually at some height; April–August.
Range: Sri Lanka.

MALABAR PIED HORNBILL *Anthracoceros coronatus* PLATE 34 (8)
(Lesser Pied Hornbill)

Identification: (92 cm) Very large, black and white with huge casque on bill. Black neck. Male has black on rear of casque, blue facial skin and red iris, female has white facial skin and brown iris. Sexes otherwise alike. Typical hornbill flight showing white trailing edge. Less secretive than Sri Lanka Grey Hornbill. In small groups.
Voice: Noisy, making loud yelping and clanging contact calls.
Status and distribution: Resident in forests and riverside trees of dry zone.
Nesting: In tree hole; April–July.
Range: S India, SE Asia.

BARBETS Order: Piciformes Family: Capitonidae

SMALL to medium sized, arboreal birds of stocky build with heavy bills fringed by facial bristles. The wings are short and rounded and the tail is short. They are fruit eaters but take insects when feeding young. Nesting is in holes in trees. The Sri Lankan barbets have mainly green plumage. Look for head pattern and colouring, listen for distinctive but monotonously repetitive low-pitched calls made with bill closed.

BROWN-HEADED BARBET *Megalaima zeylanica* PLATE 36 (3)
(Oriental Green Barbet) (*Thereiceryx zeylanicus*)

Identification: (25 cm) Largest local barbet and only one with streaked brown head and breast. Bare orange-yellow eye-ring and facial skin extending to sturdy reddish bill. Yellow-brown legs and feet. Sexes alike. Dipping flight with brief glides. In pairs or in small groups. Not shy but sometimes difficult to see in foliage.

Voice: Low trill rising to a monotonous *kuk-errrrr-kuk, kuk-errrrr-kuk*... or *kuk-ra, kukra*... repeated up to forty times, very commonly heard in breeding season. Longer and more throbbing than Yellow-fronted.

Status and distribution: Common resident in gardens, open woods, and cultivated land with trees in lowlands and hills to 1000 m. Not in deep forest.

Nesting: In tree hole; February–September.

Range: India.

YELLOW-FRONTED BARBET *Megalaima flavifrons* PLATE 36 (4)
(*Cyanops flavifrons*)

Identification: (22 cm) Distinguish from Brown-headed by yellow and blue on the head and smaller greenish-horn coloured bill, lacks the red foreheads of Crimson-fronted and Coppersmith. Sexes alike. Dipping flight with glides. Feeds mainly on fruit sometimes doing damage to crops. Not shy.

Voice: Ascending trill *poppopopopop*... running into a monotonously repeated *kokeeoo, kokeeoo, kokeeoo*..., shorter and higher pitched than Brown-headed.

Status and distribution: Endemic species. Common in wet lowlands and hills to 2000 m, also in parts of the dry zone. Prefers, but not restricted to, deep forest.

Nesting: February–May and August–September but possible all year.

Range: Sri Lanka.

CRIMSON-FRONTED BARBET *Megalaima rubricapilla rubricapilla*
(Ceylon Small Barbet) (*Xantholaema rubricapilla*)
(Ceylon Coppersmith)
(Crimson-throated Barbet) PLATE 36 (2)

Identification: (16 cm) Smaller than the two previous species. Has red forehead, yellow face patches, and black bill. Distinguish from the Coppersmith by blue patch below cheek, small red spot on breast, unstreaked breast, and its faster call. Sexes similar. Direct flight with steady wingbeats (beware of confusion with Lorikeet). Sometimes sings from bare branch at top of tree. Solitary, in pairs or, out of breeding season, in flocks.

Voice: A brisk *pop-pop-pop-*... (faster than Coppersmith) in bursts of up to six, also a slower *wonk, wonk, wonk*.

Status and distribution: Endemic race (considered by some authorities as separate species). Common in open woods, cultivated land with trees and gardens in the wet zone up to 1000 m and parts of the dry zone.

Nesting: In tree hole; January–June.

Species range: India.

COPPERSMITH BARBET *Megalaima haemacephala* PLATE 36 (1)
(Crimson-breasted Barbet) (*Xantholaema haemacephala*)

Identification: (15 cm) Darker green than Crimson-fronted, lacks blue below cheeks, has larger red patch on upper breast and is streaked below. Sexes alike. Direct flight with steady wingbeats. Solitary, in pairs or small groups.

Voice: A slow *ponk, ponk, ponk*..., like a hammer on a copper pan, hence the name.

Status and distribution: Common resident in cultivation, open woodland, gardens of dry lowlands and hills up to 1200 m.

Nesting: In tree hole; November–May and July–September.

Range: India, SE Asia, Java.

WOODPECKERS Order: Piciformes Family: Picidae

COLOURFUL, mainly arboreal birds with long, strong bills, short, pointed wings and long, stiff tails. Most do not normally perch but cling to trees, always head up (nuthatches are sometimes head down) using their tails as props, feeding by chipping into the bark to uncover insects which are then taken with the long sticky tongue. A further adaptation to these habits is the arrangement of the toes, two forward and two back (*Dinopium benghalense* unusually has only three full toes, the fourth being only vestigial). Flight is undulating with a series of wingflaps followed by wings held closed. Some species 'drum' with their bills on hollow bark as a courtship or territorial call. The Wryneck is an exception to some of these general rules.

EURASIAN WRYNECK *Jynx torquilla* Not illustrated.

Identification: (19 cm) Short, sharp bill, relatively long tail, generally appearing grey with paler underparts. Mainly grey upperparts mottled brown with dark eye-stripe, fine barring on head with central dark stripe down nape onto back, dark bars across tail; off-white underparts finely barred brown. Sexes alike. Not very woodpecker-like in habits. Undulating flight but less so than other woodpeckers. Clings to trunk but also perches across branches. Does not chip into bark but picks food from it, also often feeds on ground, hopping with raised tail. When threatened has snake-like neck movements (hence the name) with slight crest raised. Solitary or in pairs.

Voice: Has a loud nasal falcon-like *keee-hee-hee...* call but normally silent in winter. Does not drum.

Status and distribution: Unconfirmed winter vagrant. Prefers open woodland, scrub, and cultivation with trees.

Range: Europe, N Africa, Asia.

BROWN-CAPPED WOODPECKER *Picoides moluccensis gymnophthalmus*

(Ceylon Pygmy Woodpecker) (*Dendrocopos nanus*) PLATE 36 (5)
(Brown-capped Pied Woodpecker) (*Dendrocopos moluccensis*)
(Brown-capped Pygmy Woodpecker) (*Picoides nanus*)
(*Dryobates hardwickii*)

Identification: (12 cm) Smallest local woodpecker. Black and white with dark brown cap. Male: has often hidden flash of red above the white eyebrow. Female: lacks red flash, has grey on forehead and crown, and is duller. Typical woodpecker flight. Prefers the thinner branches at tops of trees. In pairs, sometimes joining other insectivorous birds.

Voice: A tinkling trill contact call. Also drums.

Status and distribution: Endemic race. Estates, open wooded areas, and forest of lowlands and hills to 1500 m.

Nesting: In tree hole; May–July.

Species range: S and SE Asia.

YELLOW-CROWNED WOODPECKER *Picoides mahrattensis*

PLATE 36 (6)

(Yellow-fronted Woodpecker) (*Dryobates mahrattensis*)
(Yellow-fronted Pied Woodpecker) (*Dendrocopos mahrattensis*)

Identification: (18 cm) Larger than Brown-capped (but smaller than other local woodpeckers). Pale yellow-grey face gives pale appearance. Yellow forehead, red hind crown, bright red patch on belly. Female lacks red on crown otherwise sexes similar. Busy, normally in pairs or small groups which feed working their way up a tree stem then fly to next tree.

Voice: A sharp *chik* and a *chik-rrr* anxiety call. Also drum.

Status and distribution: Resident in open country, park land, and scrub but also in forests of dry lowlands and nearby hills to 1000 m.

Nesting: In tree hole; March–July.

Range: Pakistan, India, Myanmar.

RUFOUS WOODPECKER *Celeus brachyurus* (*Micropternus brachyurus*) PLATE 36 (9)

Identification: (24 cm) Rufous, with a crimson patch below eye in male (only visible in good light). Female is paler and lacks the red patch. Typical woodpecker flight, usually only from tree to tree with an audible rustling of the feathers. Sometimes perches across branch. Commonly feeds on tree ants, also feeds on ground. In pairs. Shy.

Voice: A *queemp-queep*, sometimes with a third syllable. Also drums.

Status and distribution: Scarce resident in open woodland and forests of lowlands and hills to 700 m.

Nesting: Often in old ant nest in tree, sometimes in tree hole; February–June.

Range: S, E, and SE Asia.

LESSER YELLOWNAPE *Picus chlorolophus wellsi* PLATE 36 (7)
(Yellow-naped Woodpecker)

Identification: (24 cm) Distinguish from Streak-throated by yellow nape and darker green underparts with faint white barring on throat, belly and flanks. Red on inner primaries and secondaries. Male: crimson crown and moustachial stripe. Female lacks the crimson moustachial stripe. Typical woodpecker flight. Usually in pairs. Tends to feed low in trees, also on ground taking ants.

Voice: A harsh *queeeer* and a *piu, piu-piu-piu-piu*, but not normally noisy. Also drums.

Status and distribution: Endemic race. Gardens, wooded areas, and forests of hills to 1800 m and in wet zone. Also spills over into nearby dry zone.

Nesting: In tree hole; February–May.

Species range: India, SE Asia.

STREAK-THROATED WOODPECKER *Picus xanthopygaeus* PLATE 36 (8)
(Small Scaly-bellied Green Woodpecker) (*Picus myrmecophoneus*)

Identification: (28 cm) Paler and greyer below than Yellownape lacking the yellow nape. Whitish eyebrow and moustachial stripe. Bright yellow rump. Dusky brown flight feathers with white bars and spots. Male: black-edged crimson crown and crest. Female: like male but has black crown and nape with brown streaks, lacking the red. Typical woodpecker flight showing the yellow rump. Sometimes perches on rocks. Solitary or in pairs.

Voice: A sharp *queeep* but generally silent. Also drums.

Status and distribution: Resident in tea plantations and open woodland in dry zone hills to 1500 m and nearby lowlands. Not in deep forests.

Nesting: In tree hole. May–September.

Range: S and SE Asia.

BLACK-RUMPED FLAMEBACK *Dinopium benghalense* PLATE 36 (10)
(Lesser Flameback) (*Brachypternus benghalensis*)

Note: There is debate on the taxonomy of this species. Here it is considered as a single species with two races and intermediate forms:

Golden-backed Woodpecker *D. b. jaffnense*

Identification: (28 cm) Slightly smaller than Greater Flameback with much shorter bill (no longer than head). Lacks the white triangle and black on back of White-naped. Red-brown eye, white eyebrow and moustache, white-speckled black throat and eye-stripe and black nape. Golden back and scapulars with white spots on shoulders. Creamy white belly with black streaks. Black rump and tail. Only three toes, the fourth being vestigial. Male: bright red forehead, crown, and crest with black streaks on forehead. Female: like male but has white-spotted forehead and fore-crown, not red. Typical woodpecker flight. Feeds off tree bark or on ground. Solitary or in pairs. Not very shy.

Red-backed Woodpecker *D. b. psarodes*

Similar to Golden-backed but has bright red upper back and scapulars, black with red tinge on lower back and rump.

Voice (both races): A loud, rattling scream; also drums.
Status and distribution: Endemic races. Trees and scrub, not in deep forest. *Red-backed*: common in wooded gardens, coconut plantations, and open scrub of lowlands and hills to 1300 m; *Golden-backed*: replaces Red-backed in coastal areas of north. Intermediates occur in fringe areas.
Nesting: In tree hole; March–September.
Species range: Pakistan, India.

GREATER FLAMEBACK *Chrysocolaptes lucidus stricklandi* PLATE 36 (11)
(Crimson-backed Woodpecker) (*Chrysocolaptes guttacristatus stricklandi*)

Identification: (29 cm) Slightly larger than Black-rumped with longer paler horny bill, (longer than head) with very pale tip. White throat and hind neck. Narrow double black lines from bill to neck. Deep crimson mantle. Four toes (Lesser has three). Female has white-spotted black crown and crest, not crimson as in male. Typical woodpecker flight. Mainly arboreal, feeding on invertebrates on and under tree bark. Solitary or in pairs. Shy.
Voice: A high pitched, tinny, laughing flight call; also drums.

Status and distribution: Endemic race. Forests throughout but more common in wet zone and hills.
Nesting: In tree hole; October–March.
Species range: S and SE Asia, Java, Philippines.

WHITE-NAPED WOODPECKER *Chrysocolaptes festivus tantus*
(Black-backed Yellow Woodpecker) PLATE 36 (12)
(Black-rumped Woodpecker)

Identification: (29 cm) Large. Distinguish from the Golden-backed by longer and darker bill, and white nape continuing into an obvious white triangle on mantle. Crimson crown and crest (yellow in female), white underparts with black streaks. Feeds off tree stems and on ground. Solitary or in pairs. Shy.
Voice: Thought to be a weak trill.
Status and distribution: Endemic race. Scarce and local, mainly in coconut plantations in dry lowlands.
Nesting: In tree hole, often a palm; January–March and August–September.
Species range: India.

PITTA Order: Passeriformes Family: Pittidae

THE first family in the large order, Passeriformes, the perching birds. The pittas are brightly coloured, round-winged, and short-tailed. They are mainly terrestrial birds.

INDIAN PITTA *Pitta brachyura* PLATE 42 (9)
(Blue-winged Pitta)

Identification: (17 cm) Bold yellow-brown, black and white head pattern, green mantle, bright blue rump and uppertail coverts, black tail tipped blue; white throat, fawn breast and upper belly, scarlet lower belly and vent. Sexes alike. Whirring flight showing green and black wings with a prominent white patch on primaries. Skulking. Feeds on forest floor, hopping around and often flicking wings to show white patches and slowly lifting tail up and down, with a habit of taking snails to a stone anvil to break the shell. Roosts in trees. Solitary and fiercely territorial. Not shy.
Voice: A loud whistling *wieet-tieu* likened to *quite clear* often heard at dawn and dusk, also a *hh-wit-wiyu*.
Status and distribution: Common winter visitor throughout where there are trees.
Range: Himalayas, India.

LARKS — Order: Passeriformes — Family: Alaudidae

SMALL brown birds of open country or scrub with longish legs. Distinguished from wagtails and pipits by sturdier build, heavier bills, broader wings, and shorter tails. Mainly terrestrial, the song in most larks is delivered on characteristic fluttering song flights but some species perch on fence poles or low stumps to sing. On the ground they have a crouching stance and run, not hop. When disturbed they often hide behind stones or other cover. Ground nesting. Identification can be difficult, note habits and songs.

RUFOUS-WINGED LARK *Mirafra assamica* — PLATE 37 (1)

(Rufous-winged Bushlark) (*Mirafra affinis*)
(Ceylon Bushlark)

Identification: (15 cm) Plumper, shorter-tailed, thicker-billed and more rufous brown than Skylark with rufous patch on wing. Sexes alike. Shows rufous wing patch in flight and no white on tail. Characteristic display flight rising to about 10m then 'parachuting' down, singing all the way. Perches on fence posts and, unusually for a lark, on trees often with tail up. In pairs or small groups.

Voice: A thin *tilee, tilee, tilee…* given in song flight or from post or tree branch.

Status and distribution: Common resident in open country of lowlands, more common in dry zone.

Nesting: In well concealed hollow at base of tussock; March–July.

Range: India, SE Asia.

ORIENTAL SKYLARK *Alauda gulgula* — PLATE 37 (2)

(Indian Skylark)

Identification: (16 cm) Somewhat greyer, thinner-billed and neater shaped than Rufous-winged with greyish neck contrasting with rufous ear coverts. Plumper and shorter-tailed than Paddyfield Pipit and has crouching gait. Small crest (normally down), rufous edges on primaries when newly moulted (less obvious than in Rufous-winged) and buff outer tail feathers. Sexes alike. Mainly terrestrial, walking in crouched stance, often 'freezing' in crouch when threatened. In display song-flight, ascends with fluttering wings, then dives with closed wings. In pairs or small groups.

Voice: A warbling song-flight, often continuing for several minutes.

Status and distribution: Common resident in open country throughout supplemented by winter visitors to all lowlands.

Nesting: In a hollow under a tussock; March–July.

Range: S and SE Asia.

ASHY-CROWNED SPARROW LARK *Eremopterix grisea* PLATE 37 (3)
(Ashy-crowned Finch Lark)
(Ceylon Finch Lark)

Identification: (13 cm) Rather like a small sparrow with dark underparts in male. Thick, conical bill, off-white and black face pattern, ashy brown upperparts and off-white outer tail feathers; browny-black underparts. Female: uniform pale sandy-brown (beware of confusion if seen away from male). Display song-flight of steep ascents and dives with wings closed. Terrestrial, 'freezing' in crouch when threatened. Does not perch in trees. In pairs or, in winter, flocks. Relatively tame.
Voice: A trilling *jingly-jingly-eeee* given on the descent of the song-flight.
Status and distribution: Common resident in open, coastal areas of dry zone. Also a visitor to wet zone.
Nesting: In small scrape lined with grass; March–July.
Range: Pakistan, India.

SWALLOWS AND MARTINS

Order: Passeriformes
Family: Hirundinidae

GRACEFUL, insectivorous birds with relatively long, pointed wings and, in most species, forked tails. The bill is short and wide, the legs are short and used mainly for perching. They feed on the wing but, unlike the swifts, perch readily on wires or thin bare branches. Most are very sociable often also with other members of the family. Graceful, dashing flight with 'open and shut' wing flaps, unlike the stiff-winged fluttering of the swifts, and much gliding. Sexes alike.

PALE MARTIN *Riparia diluta* PLATE 38 (7)
(Sand Martin) (*Riparia riparia*)
(Bank Swallow)

Note: *R. diluta* has only recently been accepted as a separate species. Early records were of *R. riparia* (race unspecified) but there was a probable sight record of *R. diluta* at Kalametiya on the south coast in February 1998.
Identification: (13 cm) Small. White underparts with variable dark band across upper breast; grey-brown upperparts, dark underwing, and shallow fork on tail. Feeds in scattered flocks often quite high.
Voice: A brittle twitter but normally quiet in winter.
Status and distribution: Rare winter visitor to open country of southern dry lowlands. Often near water.
Range: C, and S. Asia.

DUSKY CRAG MARTIN *Hirundo concolor* (*Ptyonoprogne concolor*) PLATE 38 (8)

Identification: (13 cm) All uniform dark brown apart from a row of white spots across square tail, obvious when turning in flight. Hawks for insects around crags or old buildings. In pairs or small flocks in normal range.
Voice: A *chit, chit...* flight call but fairly quiet in winter.
Status and distribution: Winter vagrant to wet lowlands.
Range: India, SE Asia.

BARN SWALLOW *Hirundo rustica* PLATE 38 (9)

Three races occur in Sri Lanka, the most likely of which is:

East Asian Swallow, *H. r. gutteralis*

Identification: (18 cm) Deeply forked tail. Brighter chestnut forehead and throat, and paler underparts than Hill Swallow. Blue-black chest band usually broken in centre, rest of underparts white with rufous tinge. In flocks.
Voice: A twitter but generally silent in winter.
Status and distribution: Common winter visitor throughout.

Eurasian Swallow, *H. r. rustica*, with a complete dark blue chest band occurs as a less common winter visitor.

Tytler's Swallow, *H. r. tytleri,* with chestnut underparts (replacing white of East Asian) is a rare winter visitor to lowlands.

Species range: Europe, Africa, Asia, Americas.

HILL SWALLOW *Hirundo tahitica domicola* PLATE 38 (10)
(Pacific Swallow) (*Hirundo javanica domicola*)
(Nilgiri House Swallow) (*Hirundo dumicola*)

Identification: (13 cm) Shallow forked tail without streamers with white spots on underside. Uniform dingy grey underparts. Smaller than Barn Swallow. Less dashing flight than Barn, often feeding only a metre or so above ground. Not shy, often lives close to man.
Voice: A twittering call and song.

Status and distribution: Common resident in plantations, gardens, and grassy areas in hills. Visitor to foothills of wet zone.

Nesting: In a mud and straw cup bracketed on a wall; February–May and September.

Range: S India, SE Asia, Philippines, Java, Australia, Pacific islands.

WIRE-TAILED SWALLOW *Hirundo smithii* PLATE 38 (11)

Identification: (14 cm with up to 15 cm of tail 'wires' in male) White underparts and the two outside tail feathers extended into long 'wires', shorter in female, with the inner feathers almost squared. Chestnut cap, glossy dark blue upperparts. Fast, swooping flight often low over water or over grazing. Roosts communally in reed beds with other swallows, wagtails, etc.

Voice: A twitter in winter.

Status and distribution: Winter vagrant to open areas and cultivation near water in lowlands.

Range: Africa, S Asia.

RED-RUMPED SWALLOW *Hirundo daurica* PLATE 38 (12)

Three races occur in Sri Lanka, the most likely of which is:

Sri Lanka Swallow, *H. d. hyperythra*

Identification: (19 cm) Deep chestnut underparts and rump, sturdy build, relatively slow flight and deeply forked tail diagnostic. Glossy blue-black upperparts with dark chestnut rump and uppertail coverts; chestnut underparts finely streaked with brown and 'dipped-in-ink' tail. Rather slow sailing flight often close to ground. In pairs or in small groups.

Voice: A loud musical call.

Status and distribution: Endemic race. Common resident in open pasture, paddy, and grassy hillsides of lowlands and hills to 1000 m.

Nesting: In a 'bottle' of plastered mud stuck on roof of cave or under a bridge; April–July.

Nepal Red-rumped Swallow, *H. d. nipalensis*, with a paler chestnut rump and coarser streaks on underparts is a possible irregular winter visitor to lowlands and low hills.

Indian Red-rumped Swallow, *H. d. erythropygia*, with a chestnut hind collar and buff-white underparts finely streaked with brown is a possible winter vagrant throughout.

Species range: S Europe, Africa, Asia.

STREAK-THROATED SWALLOW *Hirundo fluvicola* PLATE 38 (13)
(Indian Cliff Swallow)

Identification: (12 cm) Small with almost square tail. Chestnut cap, buff-brown rump; buff-white underparts with brown streaks on chin, throat and breast, fading out on belly. Weaker flight than most swallows with less gliding. Gregarious.
Voice: A flight call *trrr, trrr...*
Status and distribution: Winter vagrant preferring open country and cultivation near to water.
Range: Afghanistan, Himalayas.

WAGTAILS AND PIPITS

Order: Passeriformes
Family: Motacillidae

RATHER small, slender, mainly terrestrial birds with long tails, long legs, and slender bills. Insectivorous, they walk or run on the ground seeking food. The flight is undulating, showing the white outer tail feathers. The sexes are mostly alike.

Wagtails tend to be brightly coloured or boldly patterned. They are slimmer than pipits with a habit of wagging their tails up and down (side to side in the Forest Wagtail) when on the ground. They roost communally, often with other wagtail species, in trees or reed beds.

Pipits are mainly brown with dark streaks and have shorter tails than wagtails. There is possible confusion with the larks but the pipits have longer tails, are more slender and stand more upright. In display there is a characteristic 'parachute' song-flight. There is little plumage variation in the pipits making identification difficult, look for behaviour and listen for calls.

FOREST WAGTAIL *Dendronanthus indicus* PLATE 37 (4)
(*Motacilla indica*)

Identification: (16 cm) Bold breast pattern and two creamy bars across the wing coverts. Sexes alike. Spends much time foraging on forest floor, flying

up to tree branch when threatened. Also feeds in trees. Wags tail and hind part of body deliberately from side to side. Much more sedate walk than other wagtails. Solitary, in pairs or small, loose flocks. Not shy.
Voice: A metallic *pink, pink*... call.
Status and distribution: Winter visitor to wooded areas throughout.
Range: India, E Asia, Java.

YELLOW WAGTAIL *Motacilla flava* PLATE 37 (5)

Several races occur in Sri Lanka, the most likely of which is:

Grey-headed Wagtail, *M. f. thunbergi*

Identification: (17 cm) From Grey by olive brown back, two whitish wing bars and shorter tail. Breeding plumage with slate grey head is often assumed in Sri Lanka before migrating. Feeds in scattered flocks on pasture often with cattle. Roosts communally in reed bed or swamp scrub.
Four other races are possible (see Plate 37 (5)):-

Sykes' Yellow Wagtail, *M. f. beema*, Greyer head with clear white eyebrow and greener back.

Yellow-headed Wagtail, *M. f. lutea*, Plain yellow head, green back.

Siberian Yellow Wagtail, *M. f. simillima*, Slate grey head with clear eyebrow.

White-chinned Wagtail, *M. f. melanogrisea*, Slate grey head, shorter bill than thunbergi.

Voice: A *twzeeep* flight call.
Status and distribution: *M. f. thunbergi*: common winter visitor to damp meadows and pasture throughout; *beema, lutea, simillima*: rare winter visitors; *melanogrisea*: vagrant.
Species range: Europe, Africa, Asia, Philippines, Java.

CITRINE WAGTAIL *Motacilla citreola* PLATE 37 (6)
(Yellow-headed Wagtail)
(Yellow-hooded Wagtail)

Identification: (17 cm) Grey backed, yellow breast shading on belly to white under tail. Longer tail and heavier build than Yellow. Broad eyebrow in non-breeding plumage. Two broad white wing bars (in fresh plumage). Juvenile and first winter: mainly grey with broad eyebrow and the two white wing bars. Typical wagtail in flight and habits. Gregarious.
Voice: A piercing *tsreeeep*, harsher than Grey-headed, also a high but less harsh *pseeoow*.
Status and distribution: Winter vagrant. Prefers wet and marshy areas.
Range: Asia.

GREY WAGTAIL *Motacilla cinerea* PLATE 37 (7)

Identification: (18 cm) Long tail, dark grey back, and greenish-yellow rump. In breeding plumage (often in April–May) the male has a black patch on throat. Typical bounding wagtail flight. Feeds by picking from rocks in stream bed with much tail wagging and wing flicking or by flying up to take insects. Solitary or in loose pairs. Communal roosting in tree or scrub.
Voice: A *chittik* flight call, sharper and more metallic than White.
Status and distribution: Common winter visitor to rivers and streams throughout.
Range: Europe, Africa, Asia, Japan, Philippines.

WHITE WAGTAIL *Motacilla alba* PLATE 37 (8)
(Pied Wagtail)

Identification: (19 cm) Black and white, no yellow. Distinguish from White-browed by white forehead and fore crown, and pale grey back. Bounding flight showing black, white, and grey pattern on wings. Runs on ground with tail wagging, picking up insect food, sometimes briefly flying up to take airborne prey. Perches on roofs. Solitary or in small groups but roosts communally.
Voice: A *chissick* flight call.
Status and distribution: Scarce winter visitor to open country and cultivation in lowlands.
Range: Europe, N and E Africa, Asia, Japan, Philippines.

WHITE-BROWED WAGTAIL *Motacilla maderaspatensis* PLATE 37 (9)
(Large Pied Wagtail)

Identification: (22 cm) Largest of local wagtails. Distinguish from White by all black upperparts with long, bold white eyebrow. Black throat and breast, pale grey flanks, rest of underparts white. Female: similar but duller. **First winter**: browner. Bounding flight showing bold black and white pattern. Often feeds by water in typical wagtail fashion. In pairs.

Voice: *Chip-chip-seeooo* and variations. Also a loud *chizzit*.

Status and distribution: Rare winter visitor to northern coastal areas and lower hills.

Range: Pakistan and India.

RICHARD'S PIPIT *Anthus richardi* PLATE 37 (10)

(*Anthus novaeseelandiae richardi*)

Identification: (18 cm) Largest local pipit. Larger than Paddyfield with long, heavy bill, longer legs and very long hind claw, browny-buff underparts (paler when worn) with darker streaks on breast (less so than on Olive-backed) and contrasting warmer buff rear flanks. Rapid, undulating flight. Runs, then stops and stands tall, looking for insect prey. Does not normally perch in trees.

Note: Listen for calls to help identify the pipits.

Voice: A loud, harsh *schree-eep* flight call.

Status and distribution: Common winter visitor to grassland and open country of lowlands and lower hills, more frequent in dry zone and near coasts.

Range: Asia, Sumatra.

PADDYFIELD PIPIT *Anthus rufulus* PLATE 37 (11)

(Indian Pipit) (*Anthus novaeseelandiae rufulus*)

Identification: (16 cm) Similar to but smaller than Richard's with a shorter hind claw. Fast undulating flight. Runs and stands tall looking for insect prey. Sometimes perches in shrubs or trees. In pairs or in small flocks. Not shy.

Voice: An explosive *twit, twit-tit* flight call.

Status and distribution: Very common resident in grassland and low scrub throughout, less common in high hills.

Nesting: In cup of grass on ground beneath tussock; mainly March–July but possible anytime.

Range: S and SE Asia, Philippines, Java.

BLYTH'S PIPIT *Anthus godlewskii* PLATE 37 (12)

Identification: (16 cm) Very similar to Richard's but is slightly smaller and more compact, has slightly shorter and more pointed bill, paler lores, the ear coverts have a warmer tinge contrasting with greyer upperparts. It is more evenly warm buff below, has different median covert pattern, and shorter hind claw (difficult to see in field). Flight and behaviour are also similar but has a more horizontal stance.

Voice: A harsher song than other pipits. A high pitched *psheeoo* flight call, often made when flushed and a repeated *chep*.

Status and distribution: Rare winter visitor throughout.

Range: E and S Asia.

OLIVE-BACKED PIPIT *Anthus hodgsoni* PLATE 37 (13)
(Indian Tree Pipit)

Identification: (15 cm) Smaller than other local pipits. Distinctive ear covert pattern, olive-green back (fades to grey when worn) with variable brown streaking, strong streaking on breast and flanks. White bar on wings. Fast, undulating flight. Feeds on ground wagging tail like a wagtail but perches in trees when flushed. Stays close to trees or bushes avoiding open country. In pairs or small flocks.

Voice: A hoarse *keeeze* flight call.

Status and distribution: Winter vagrant to dry lowlands and hills.

Range: Asia, Japan, Borneo.

CUCKOOSHRIKES AND MINIVETS

Order: Passeriformes
Family: Campephagidae

RATHER shrike-like arboreal birds with strong bills, slightly hooked at the tip, fairly long wings and short legs with strong feet. They are mainly insectivorous, feeding among the foliage in crowns of trees. The cuckooshrikes are mainly grey, black, and white with rounded tails. The minivets are very brightly coloured with graduated tails and marked sexual dimorphism.

LARGE CUCKOOSHRIKE *Coracina macei layardi* PLATE 39 (2)
(Black-faced Cuckooshrike) (*Coracina novaehollandiae*)

Identification: (26 cm) Largest of the family locally. Mainly dark grey with a black bill, black mask, and brown-red eye. Female and juvenile: barred underparts. Undulating flight with short glides showing pale grey rump and white outer tail feathers. Very active in canopy with a habit of flicking wings alternately but also often perches upright on bare branches at top of tree. Rarely comes to ground. Solitary or in small flocks.

Voice: A frequent loud, harsh *kur-eech.*
Status and distribution: Endemic race. Scarce in forests of dry lowlands and nearby hills to 600 m.
Nesting: In a shallow cup in fork of tree; May–June.
Species range: S and SE Asia.

BLACK-HEADED CUCKOOSHRIKE *Coracina melanoptera* (*Coracina sykesi*) PLATE 39 (6)

Identification: (19 cm) Male: black head, white belly and vent. Female: pale grey barred brown on breast and flanks. Juvenile: barred above and below. Both sexes in flight show white patches on mainly black wings and conspicuous white tips to outer tail feathers. Actively feeds in canopy, occasionally comes to ground where it hops. Solitary or in small groups.
Voice: Loud whistles *wheep-wheep-wheep* also a *cheer* call.
Status and distribution: Resident in open woods and scrub of lowlands and hills.
Nesting: In shallow saucer in fork of tree; March–May.
Range: India.

SMALL MINIVET *Pericrocotus cinnamomeus* PLATE 39 (4)
(Little Minivet) (*Pericrocotus peregrinus*)

Identification: (15 cm) Smaller than Flame. Male: dark ashy grey head, nape and back, scarlet rump, uppertail coverts, and outer tail feathers; scarlet breast and flanks, paling on belly to off-white on vent and under tail. Female: distinctive grey above and scarlet rump. Arboreal, feeding actively in small fluttering flocks in tree canopy, then flying to next tree in 'follow-my-leader' procession showing orange patch on wing (less pronounced in female). In pairs during breeding season.
Voice: A thin, drawn out *wee-wee-wee*... often heard contact call.
Status and distribution: Common resident in trees of lowlands, also in hills to 1700 m.
Nesting: In a small cup on branch or fork of tree; February–May.
Range: S and SE Asia, Philippines, Java.

FLAME MINIVET *Pericrocotus flammeus* PLATE 39 (5)
(Scarlet Minivet)
(Orange Minivet)

Identification: (20 cm) Considerably larger than Small. Male: black above with bright orange-red rump, uppertail coverts, and outer tail feathers; black throat, rest of underparts bright orange-red. Female: distinctive grey and yellow. Juvenile: like female. Direct flight shows the bright colours in the wing and tail, orange in male, yellow in female. Feeding behaviour similar to Small.

Voice: A *twee-twee-tweetywee-tweetyweetywee* often heard contact call, louder and more piercing than Small.

Status and distribution: Resident in forests and wooded areas throughout, more common in hills.

Nesting: In small cup in canopy, well camouflaged with lichens; mainly in February–May and August–September.

Range: India, SE Asia, Java, Philippines.

BAR-WINGED FLYCATCHER-SHRIKE *Hemipus picatus leggei*

(Ceylon Pied Shrike) PLATE 39 (3)

Identification: (14 cm) Very small black, grey, and white, rather flycatcher-like, showing a white bar on closed wing, and white rump. Sexes alike in this race. Arboreal, feeding in canopy showing bold black and white wing pattern when flying flycatcher-like after insects. Often in mixed species flocks.

Voice: A *tirity-tirity-tirity*... often made contact call.

Status and distribution: Endemic race. Forests and wooded areas throughout, more common in hills to 1800 m.

Nesting: In shallow cup on branch high in canopy; March–May.

Species range: India, SE Asia, Sumatra.

COMMON WOODSHRIKE *Tephrodornis pondicerianus affinis* PLATE 39 (1)

(Ceylon Woodshrike)

Identification: (16 cm) Dull grey, shrike-like bird with dark mask through eye, off-white eyebrow, and a distinctive call. Narrow off-white band on rump, dark tail with white outer tail feathers. Sexes alike but female has paler mask. Arboreal and inconspicuous. Feeds on insects in canopy in similar way to the minivets. In pairs or small groups.

Voice: A descending *tweee-twee-twee-twee*....

Status and distribution: Endemic race, common in gardens and wooded areas of lowlands and hills to 1000 m but avoids deep forest. More common in dry zone.

Nesting: In a well camouflaged shallow saucer in fork or on branch of tree; February–June.

Species range: Pakistan, India, SE Asia.

BULBULS Order: Passeriformes Family: Pycnonotidae

SMALL to medium sized, arboreal, soft plumaged birds with short, rounded wings and short legs. Normally in pairs when breeding but they also form small mixed flocks. Mainly fruit-eating, they also take insects, sometimes hawking ants, etc. in short flycatcher-like flights. They are quite vocal. The sexes are alike and the juveniles are usually a duller form of the adults.

BLACK-HEADED YELLOW BULBUL *Pycnonotus melanicterus m.*

(Black-crested Bulbul) PLATE 40 (1)
(Black-capped Bulbul)

Identification: (17 cm) Distinguish from Yellow-browed by black hood. Olive green upperparts, brown tail with broad white tips to outer feathers; yellow throat and underparts with olive tinge on breast and flanks. Brown flight feathers, yellow underwing. Sexes alike apart from eye colour, male has red iris, female brown. Rather shy. Often in small groups with White-browed.

Voice: A rising *yor yer yee* and *wer wer wee wee.*

Status and distribution: Endemic race (considered by some authorities as separate species). Open forest and woodland of lowlands and hills to 1300 m.

Nesting: In small cup hidden in small tree or bush: mainly March–April and August–September.

Species range: India, SE Asia, Java.

RED-VENTED BULBUL *Pycnonotus cafer cafer* PLATE 40 (2)

(*Molpastes cafer cafer*)

Identification: (20 cm) Black head with tufted crest, brown upperparts with scaly white fringes, white (occasionally cinnamon) rump and tip of tail; brown breast with pale margins shading to white belly and to scarlet vent and undertail coverts. The white rump is very obvious in flight. Not shy, often lives close to houses.

Voice: Quiet songs likened to *ginger beer* and *sweet potatoes.* Also a harsh alarm shriek.

Status and distribution: Endemic race. Very common in gardens and cultivation throughout, less so away from settlements. Avoids deep forest.

Nesting: In small cup set in bush or hedge, even on buildings; mainly March–May and August–September.

Species range: Pakistan, India, Myanmar.

YELLOW-EARED BULBUL *Pycnonotus penicillatus* PLATE 40 (3)
(Yellow-tufted Bulbul) (*Kelaartia penicillata*)

Identification: (19 cm) Distinctive black and white head pattern and yellow 'ear' tufts. Olive-green upperparts, brown upperwings and tail; yellow underparts with olive tinge on breast and flanks, yellow underwing. Typical bulbul feeding habit. Not shy.

Voice: A loud whistling *wheet wit wit*, a chittering call when feeding, and a *krr krr*... anxiety call.

Status and distribution: Endemic species. Forest edges, woods, and wooded gardens in hills above 1000 m, common above 1300 m.

Nesting: In a deep cup in fork of low tree or bush; February–May and August–October.

Range: Sri Lanka.

WHITE-BROWED BULBUL *Pycnonotus luteolus insulae* PLATE 40 (4)

Identification: (20 cm) Only local bulbul with white eyebrow. Brown crown, obvious white eyebrow, olive-green upperparts, brown wings and tail; off-white underparts with brown tinge on breast shading to yellow on vent and undertail coverts. Upperwing brown, pale yellow below. Skulks in cover, more often heard than seen. Very shy.

Voice: A loud, rich, fluty whistling, also a churring *chrr chrr*... anxiety call.

Status and distribution: Endemic race. Scrub, forest understorey and shrubby gardens of lowlands and hills to 1000 m. Common in dry zone.

Nesting: In cup low in bush or scrub. Possible anytime but mainly February–March and December.

Species range: India.

YELLOW-BROWED BULBUL *Hypsipetes indicus* PLATE 40 (5)
(Golden-browed Bulbul) (*Iole icterica*)

Identification: (20 cm) Only local bulbul with yellow face. Yellow-green tinged bronze upperparts; yellow underparts. Typical bulbul behaviour.

Note: Occurs locally in two races very difficult to separate in field: *H. i. indicus* as described and *H. i. guglielmi* which is slightly smaller and greener on upperparts without the bronze tinge and yellow with green tinge below.

Voice: Rich conversational phrases, *to-roo, diddle diddle doo* and a *wheep-wheep-*... call.

Status and distribution: *H. i. indicus*: Common resident in trees and wooded areas of dry zone and nearby hills to 1500 m. *H. i. guglielmi*: Endemic race, common in forests of wet zone lowlands.

Nesting: In a cup in fork of low tree or suspended at end of inaccessible twig; March–April and August–September.
Species range: W and SW India.

BLACK BULBUL *Hypsipetes leucocephalus humii* PLATE 40 (6)
(*Microscelis psaroides humii*)
(*Hypsipetes madagascariensis humii*)

Identification: (24 cm) Largest of the local bulbuls. Dark with red bill and legs, and a slightly forked tail. Glossy black head with tufted crest, red-brown eye. Tends to feed actively in canopy in small chattering flocks.
Voice: Noisy with a range of squeaks and chattering calls *squeedlee-ee*, *whee-cheeek*, *creeeorer*, and a mewing scold note.
Status and distribution: Endemic race. Trees and forest edges of wet lowlands and hills to 1800 m. Also visitor to dry zone and high hills.
Nesting: In small cup in tree fork usually 3–7 m above ground; March–May and July–September.
Species range: India, China, Taiwan, SE Asia.

LEAFBIRDS AND IORA Order: Passeriformes Family: Irenidae

A DISPARATE family of active, arboreal birds which feed in the foliage of trees in small groups, often calling as they feed. The Iora and the leafbirds have longish slender, pointed, down-curved bills, rounded wings, and shortish tails. The Fairy Bluebird has a stout, slightly down-curved bill, pointed wings, and short legs.

COMMON IORA *Aegithina tiphia* PLATE 40 (7)
(Ceylon Iora)

Identification: (14 cm) Yellow underparts with two white bars across wings. Breeding male plumage: black upperparts paling to green on rump. Non-breeding plumage: dull black head and wings, rest of upperparts green with duller yellow on underparts. Female: green upperparts, darker on tail and wings. Direct fluttering flight usually only from tree to tree and a spiralling display flight. Feeds unobtrusively in canopy.
Voice: Drowsy short phrases, *wheeeee-too*, or *weet-we-too* and *whip-wee-bird-ee*, often uttered.
Status and distribution: Resident in gardens, scrub and forest edges in lowlands and hills to 1000 m. Possible as visitor to 1600 m. More common in dry zone.

Nesting: In cup on branch often low down in cover; January–August, mainly April–June.
Range: Pakistan, India, SE Asia, Java.

JERDON'S LEAFBIRD *Chloropsis cochinchinensis* PLATE 40 (8)
(Blue-winged Leafbird) (*Chloropsis jerdoni*)
(Jerdon's Chloropsis)

Identification: (19 cm) Distinguish from Golden-fronted by lack of orange forehead and smaller dark throat patch extending to eye, not beyond. Male plumage: black cheeks and throat with blue moustache, yellow-green forehead, eye-stripe and fringe around the black area; turquoise lesser wing coverts, rest of plumage grass green, darker above. Female: has cheek and throat patch greeny-blue with blue moustache. Juvenile: all green. Feeds hopping about in foliage. More often heard than seen.
Voice: Many and varied whistles, often mimicking other birds. Also harsh calls.
Status and distribution: Common resident in trees in gardens, scrub and open wooded areas of dry lowlands, less so in wet zone and hills to 1100 m.
Nesting: In small hammock hidden in foliage, often high in tree; November–May.
Range: S India, SE Asia, Java.

GOLDEN-FRONTED LEAFBIRD *Chloropsis aurifrons* PLATE 40 (9)
(Gold-fronted Chloropsis)

Identification: (19 cm) From Jerdon's by orange forehead and larger face and throat patch which extends behind eye. Black cheeks and throat with blue moustache, turquoise lesser wing coverts, some brown on flight feathers, rest of plumage grass green, darker above. Female is very similar but has smaller face and throat patch. Juvenile: all green. Direct flight, usually only from one tree to another. Feeds in foliage. Difficult to see.
Voice: Short bursts of whistling *twitter, chirp, twit, twitter, twitter, tip, weety weety* and much mimicry of other species.
Status and distribution: Resident in woods and open country with trees in lowlands, more common in hills to 1000 m.
Nesting: In shallow cup suspended and hidden at end of branch; early in year.
Range: India, SE Asia, Sumatra.

ASIAN FAIRY BLUEBIRD *Irena puella* PLATE 40 (10)
(Blue-backed Fairy Bluebird)

Identification: (27cm) Male: brilliant glossy blue upperparts with black greater wing coverts, flight feathers and tail; black face, throat, and underparts with bright blue undertail coverts. Female and juvenile: mainly dull turquoise blue with dark greater wing coverts, flight feathers and tail. Very active, feeding in foliage, calling frequently with a flick of the tail.

Voice: A loud *pee pit.*

Status and distribution: Uncertain. Possibly former resident in forests of wet lowlands and lower hills, now extinct or very rare visitor.

Range: India, SE Asia, Java.

SHRIKES Order: Passeriformes Family: Laniidae

SMALL to medium birds with relatively large heads and stout bills hooked at the tips. The Sri Lankan representatives each have a dark mask through the eye. They are mainly insectivorous, although the larger members of the family also take small vertebrates, perching upright on a branch or other vantage point to pounce on their prey which, if not eaten immediately, is sometimes stored impaled on a thorn. The flight is fast, direct, and usually close to ground. They are solitary and prefer open country.

BROWN SHRIKE *Lanius cristatus cristatus* PLATE 39 (7)

Identification: (19 cm). Brown upperparts with a white forehead and eyebrow, and black face mask. Sexes alike. Immature has some darker scaling on breast and flanks, and paler mask. Typical shrike feeding behaviour, often hunts well into dusk.

Voice: A loud, harsh chatter *chak-chak-chak-chak...*, alarm call.

Status and distribution: Common winter visitor to open country with trees and gardens throughout.

Note: The **Philippine Shrike,** *L. c. lucionensis*, also occurs as a scarce winter visitor throughout. It is similar to the Brown but is much greyer, especially on the head with a pale grey crown.

Species range: S and E Asia, Japan, Philippines.

RUFOUS-BACKED SHRIKE *Lanius schach* PLATE 39 (8)
(Rufous-rumped Shrike)
(Long-tailed Shrike)

Identification: (24 cm) Black forehead and mask, pale grey upperparts becoming rufous on rump; white underparts becoming rufous on flanks, hind belly, and vent. Black wings with white patch at base of inner primaries. Sexes alike. Direct flight, usually low. Often sits on exposed branch on bush or post to drop onto prey. Solitary or in loose pairs.

Voice: A quiet song including mimicry of songs of other birds. Also a harsh alarm.
Status and distribution: Resident in dry coastal areas of N and NW but strays widely.
Nesting: In cup set in untidy mass of stems usually on top of Acacia bush; February–June.
Range: C Asia, India, SE Asia, Philippines, New Guinea.

SOUTHERN GREY SHRIKE *Lanius meridionalis lahtora* PLATE 39 (9)
(Great Grey Shrike) *Lanius excubitor*

Identification: (25 cm) Largest of the local shrikes, with a sturdy bill. Distinguish from Rufous-backed by lack of rufous and more white in the wing. Grey upperparts with black mask, white edged black graduated tail. Black wings with large white patch, obvious in flight. Sexes alike. Often sits on exposed branch. Very wary.
Voice: A harsh *chack* or *kirrick.*
Status and distribution: Rare winter visitor throughout, more likely in open scrub of northern lowlands.
Range: SW Europe, N Africa, C and S Asia.

THRUSHES AND CHATS

Order: Passeriformes
Family: Turdidae

MEDIUM to small birds with relatively long legs, slender bills, and an upright perching posture. Mainly insectivorous, feeding mainly on the ground, but they also take berries and other vegetable food from trees and shrubs. The flight is strong and some species migrate considerable distances occurring as winter visitors or vagrants in Sri Lanka.

INDIAN BLUE ROBIN *Erithacus brunneus* PLATE 41 (3)
(Indian Blue Chat) (*Luscinia brunnea*)

Identification: (14 cm) Distinguish male from male Tickell's Blue Flycatcher by white eyebrow. Female from female Kashmir Flycatcher by lack of white on the tail, longer legs and behaviour. Male plumage: dull blue upperparts, black cheeks; bright orange-rufous below shading to white on belly and vent. Female plumage: olive brown above; off-white underparts with chestnut on breast and flanks. Hops around in undergrowth flicking tail while turning leaves for insects. In pairs.

Voice: A fast *cheek cheek teedleedleedlee*, variations on *wee-wee-chat-chat*, and a *chuk* alarm.
Status and distribution: Winter visitor to forests and ravines throughout. More common in wet zone and hills.
Range: Pakistan, India, Myanmar.

BLUETHROAT *Luscinia svecicus* (*Erithacus svecicus*) (*Cyanosylvia svecica*) PLATE 41 (2)

Identification: (15 cm) Male plumage: blue and rufous (and sometimes white) throat patch (bright and bold in breeding season), off-white eyebrow and rufous patch on sides of base of dark tipped tail. Female plumage: duller colours on throat, often lacking blue. First year birds have brown streaking on breast. Skulks in cover picking insects from ground, head down with tail up and spread showing the rufous patches (also conspicuous in flight). Also feeds robin-like in open. Solitary.
Voice: *Trak*, *churr*, and *weet* calls.
Status and distribution: Winter vagrant to grassy areas, cultivation, and gardens, often near water in wet lowlands and hills.
Range: Europe, N Africa, Asia.

ORIENTAL MAGPIE ROBIN *Copsychus saularis* PLATE 41 (5)
(Southern Magpie Robin)

Identification: (20 cm) Glossy blue-black with white patch on wings, white outer tail feathers; white belly, flanks, and undertail coverts, white underwing. **Female plumage**: duller with dark slaty grey throat and breast, off-white belly. Juvenile has dark areas mottled brown. Undulating flight showing black and white. Runs actively on ground seeking food, often cocks tail and spreads wings. Feeds well into dusk. Solitary or in pairs. Fierce in defence of breeding territory. Not shy.
Voice: A clear whistling song, a four note ascending call and a *chrrr* anxiety call.
Status and distribution: Common resident in gardens, cultivation, scrub, and open forest throughout. Not in deep forest.
Nesting: Untidy mass of stems in cavity in tree or building; March–September.
Range: Pakistan, India, SE Asia, Philippines, Java.

WHITE-RUMPED SHAMA *Copsychus malabaricus leggei* (*Kittacincla malabarica leggei*) PLATE 41 (4)
(Ceylon Shama)

Identification: (26 cm) Long tail with white on outer feathers. Black with white rump; chestnut belly, flanks, and vent; white under tail with black tip. Female plumage: ashy-brown not black. Juvenile: like female with rufous

spots on upperparts and brown mottling on throat and breast. Shows white rump and outer tail feathers in flight. Sometimes claps wings in flight. Feeds in undergrowth. More commonly heard than seen.
Voice: A beautiful, rich song often heard at dawn and dusk, a *chir chur* call and a harsh alarm.
Status and distribution: Endemic race. Common in forests of dry zone lowlands and hills to 1000 m, less so in wet zone.
Nesting: On pad of fibres in hole in tree; March–May.
Species range: India, SE Asia, Java.

RUFOUS-TAILED SCRUB ROBIN *Cercotrichas galactotes* PLATE 41 (1)
(Greyish Scrub Robin) *Erythropygia galactotes*
(Rufous Scrub Robin)
(Rufous Chat)
(Rufous Bush Robin)

Identification: (16 cm) White eyebrow, dark eye-stripe. Rufous tail, often cocked showing dark sub-terminal band with white tips to all but inner tail feathers. Brown above, creamy below. Sexes alike. Runs on ground hopping onto stones and perching on low scrub cocking and fanning tail, wings drooping. Solitary. Not shy.
Voice: A *tek tek* call.
Status and distribution: Winter vagrant. Prefers arid scrub and open country.
Range: Mediterranean, N and E Africa, Middle East, NW India.

PIED BUSHCHAT *Saxicola caprata atrata* PLATE 41 (6)
(Pied Stonechat)

Identification: (14 cm) Male plumage: all black with white on rump and vent, and broad white band on wing coverts. Female plumage: brown upperparts with rufous rump, upper- and undertail coverts; sand-brown underparts with dark streaks on throat and breast. Often perches on low bush or stump pouncing on passing insects. In pairs.
Voice: *Chepee cheeweechu* song, a *chep chepee* call, and a *chuh* alarm.
Status and distribution: Endemic race. Common in grassy areas of hills above 1100 m.
Nesting: In grass cup set in hole hidden under vegetation often near top of bank; February–May.
Species range: Iran, S and SE Asia, Philippines, Java, New Guinea.

PIED WHEATEAR *Oenanthe pleschanka* PLATE 41 (8)
(*Oenanthe leucomela*)

Identification: (14 cm) White rump extending onto tail to form black inverted T. Darker on scapulars and mantle than in Desert and Isabelline.

Non-breeding male plumage: crown, mantle, and scapulars browny-grey with pale fringes; cheeks and throat black with pale fringes. Female plumage: mantle and scapulars browny-grey with pale fringes; brown-grey head and breast, off-white belly. Breeding male plumage: white crown and nape, black upperparts; black cheeks and throat. (Note: The plumage can wear, changing the colours and markings. Look for tail patterns. See plate.) Often makes flycatcher-like sallies from perch to catch flies.

Voice: A harsh *zep zep*...call.

Status and distribution: Rare winter vagrant to lowlands. Prefers open country and sparse scrub.

Range: E Europe, E Africa, W Asia.

DESERT WHEATEAR *Oenanthe deserti* PLATE 41 (10)

Identification: (15 cm) From other wheatears by white rump without an inverted T on black tail. Paler buff back and scapulars than Pied, darker wing coverts than Isabelline. Non-breeding male plumage: black throat with pale fringes, pale eyebrow. Breeding male plumage: all black cheeks, throat, and wings. Often perches on rock or low bush to pounce onto insect prey, also takes prey in flight.

Voice: A *chit tit tit*... alarm.

Status and distribution: Winter vagrant. Prefers arid open country.

Range: N Africa, Middle East, W and C Asia.

ISABELLINE WHEATEAR *Oenanthe isabellina* PLATE 41 (9)

Identification: (16 cm) Very pale and plain. White rump with short stemmed broad topped inverted black T on tail. Paler wings than in other wheatears. Generally sand-brown with pale eyebrow. Sexes alike. Runs on ground to take insects. Upright posture with bobbing habit.

Voice: A *cheeep* call.

Status and distribution: Winter vagrant to lowlands. Prefers arid open country.

Range: E Europe, N and C Africa, C and S Asia.

BLACK-BACKED ROBIN *Saxicoloides fulicata leucoptera* PLATE 41 (7)

(Ceylon Black Robin)
(Indian Robin)

Identification: (16 cm) Chestnut undertail coverts. Male plumage: glossy blue-black with white lesser wing coverts (often hidden by mantle feathers). Female plumage: dark grey-brown lacking the white wing patch. Feeds actively on ground running after insects, often cocking tail nearly to touch the back of head and displaying the chestnut patch.

Voice: An often heard *cheery weee* and a harsh *cheee* anxiety call.
Status and distribution: Endemic race. Very common in gardens, cultivation and open scrub of lowlands and hills to 1600 m. Less frequent in wet zone.
Nesting: On mass of grass and stems in hole in tree, bank, or building; March–September.
Species range: Pakistan, India.

BLUE ROCK THRUSH *Monticola solitarius* PLATE 42 (1)

Identification: (22 cm) Non-breeding male plumage: dark blue body with pale fringes, dark brown wings and tail. Female plumage: grey-brown with dark fringes on breast, barred belly. From female Pied Thrush by faint pale eyebrow. Breeding male plumage: glossy bright blue body. Perches upright on boulders to fly down onto insect prey. Often bows and flicks tail. Solitary in winter. Not shy.
Voice: Mainly silent in winter.
Status and distribution: Scarce winter visitor mainly to open boulder strewn slopes of dry lowlands and dry hills.
Range: S Europe, N and C Africa, Middle East, S and SE Asia, Japan, Philippines.

SRI LANKA WHISTLING THRUSH *Myophonus blighi* PLATE 42 (2)
(Ceylon Arrenga) (*Arrenga blighi*)

Identification: (21 cm) Male plumage: slaty blue-black. Distinguish from Blackbird by black bill and shorter tail, blue tinge on back, scapulars and breast, and a bright blue patch on lesser wing coverts, often hidden on closed wing but visible in flight. Female plumage: brown, also with blue wing patch. Generally keeps in cover during day but active at dawn and late into dusk, often running on streamside rocks twitching tail frequently. In pairs. Shy.
Voice: A shrill whistle *sreee ree* and a thin *siiii*.
Status and distribution: Endemic species. Scarce resident often near streams in ravines and forests in hills between 1000 m and 2000 m. Endangered.
Nesting: On moss and twigs set on rocky ledge or in tree fork at forest edge usually near a stream; January–May.
Range: Sri Lanka.

PIED THRUSH *Zoothera wardii* PLATE 42 (3)
(Pied Ground Thrush) (*Geokichla wardii*)

Identification: (22 cm) Female from juvenile Spot-winged and female Blue Rock by long buff eyebrow and buff spots on wing. Male plumage: black and white with long white eyebrow extending from nape to yellow bill, white crescent on rump, white tip to tail and white on outer tail feathers. Female plumage: olive brown upperparts with long buff eyebrow, buff spots on wing coverts and flight feathers, white underparts with brown fringes on upper breast, dark brown crescents on lower breast and flanks. Feeds on ground beneath undergrowth, also forms small flocks to eat fruit in trees. Shy.

Voice: Mainly silent in winter.

Status and distribution: Winter visitor to forests, ravines and wooded gardens in hills between 800 m and 1600 m.

Range: India.

ORANGE-HEADED THRUSH *Zoothera citrina* PLATE 42 (6)
(Orange-headed Ground Thrush) (*Geokichla citrina*)

Identification: (22 cm) Orange head and neck, rest of upperparts blue-grey with a white bar on wing coverts; orange underparts with white vent and undertail coverts. Female is duller with brown tinge on grey upperparts. Generally feeds on ground, turning over leaves. Shy.

Voice: A high pitched *kreeee* alarm. Has a long-phrased, twittering song which can be heard in April before migrating.

Status and distribution: Rare winter visitor to forests of dry lowlands, also occasionally to wet lowlands.

Range: Pakistan, India, SE and E Asia, Java.

SPOT-WINGED THRUSH *Zoothera spiloptera* PLATE 42 (4)
(*Oreocincla spiloptera*)

Identification: (21 cm) Two rows of white spots on wing coverts. Rich olive brown upperparts. Bold black and white facial pattern, no eyebrow. White underparts with fan shaped black spots on throat, breast and upper belly. Sexes alike. Juvenile: similar to female Pied Thrush but has the facial pattern of the adult and no eyebrow. Feeds mainly on ground skulking in the undergrowth turning over leaves but also takes berries. Solitary or in pairs. Shy.

Voice: Song, a melancholic human-like whistle *pee, pee-poo, pee, pip-pee, pee, pee-poo* and a high *seep* call.

Status and distribution: Endemic species. Forests and well wooded country in wet lowlands and hills to 1900 m also in nearby dry zone.

Nesting: In an untidy mass of twigs, moss, and grass set low in fork or in roots of tree; March–April and August–November.

Range: Sri Lanka.

SCALY THRUSH *Zoothera dauma imbricata* PLATE 42 (5)
(White's Thrush) (*Oreocincla dauma*)
(Ceylon Mountain Thrush)

Identification: (24 cm) Olive brown upperparts with dark fringes; rufous-buff below, paler on throat and belly, also with dark scales. Sexes alike. Skulks in undergrowth turning over leaves on ground. Solitary or in pairs. Shy.
Voice: A loud clear song of short phrases with pauses between.
Status and distribution: Endemic race. Scarce in forests in hills between 600 m and 1700 m. Endangered.
Nesting: In mossy cup set in cover 4–7 m above ground; March–April and August–September.
Species range: N, E, and SE Asia, Japan, Java.

EURASIAN BLACKBIRD *Turdus merula kinnisii* PLATE 42 (8)
(Ceylon Blackbird) (*Turdus simillimus kinnisii*)

Identification: (25 cm) Slaty black with bright orange bill, orange eye-ring, orange-yellow legs, and longish tail. Sexes almost alike in this race. Juvenile has brownish head and neck, and brown underparts with buff streaks. Feeds on ground turning over leaves in undergrowth, also takes berries.
Voice: Long, melodious song usually from top branch of tree or tall post, often early and late in day. Also a *chuk, chuk, chuk*... anxiety call.
Status and distribution: Endemic race. Common in wooded gardens, cultivation with trees and forest edge in hills above 1000 m.
Nesting: In deep cup of moss and fibres hidden in fork of tree or shrub; March–April and August–September.
Species range: Europe, NW Africa, Middle East, S Asia.

EYEBROWED THRUSH *Turdus obscurus* PLATE 42 (7)
(Dark Thrush)

Identification: (23 cm) Grey head, neck, and throat with distinctive black and white markings around eye and whitish eyebrow. Olive brown upperparts; rufous breast and flanks, white belly and undertail coverts. **Female** and first year males have brown cap and nape, and paler throat. Feeds on ground or takes berries.
Voice: A *chuk, chuk* anxiety call.
Status and distribution: Winter vagrant. Most likely in forests and wooded areas in hills.
Range: E Asia, Indonesia.

BABBLERS Order: Passeriformes Family: Timaliidae

RATHER dull coloured, medium to small mainly ground-feeding birds with soft plumage. The wings are short and rounded, and the flight weak, fluttering, and generally brief. Usually found in forest and scrub, some species in small parties. The name 'babbler' comes from their vocal habits although many of their calls are harsh and chattering rather than babbling.

BROWN-CAPPED BABBLER *Pellorneum fuscocapillum* PLATE 43 (1)
(Brown-capped Jungle Babbler)

Identification: (16 cm) Dark brown crown and nape, brown upperparts; cinnamon eyebrow, face, and underparts. Sexes alike. Skulks in undergrowth turning over leaves on ground seeking insects. More often heard than seen. In pairs. Shy.

Voice: A whistling song up and down the scale. Also a whistling *prit-tee-dear*, *wee-too*, *wee-too* and *whe-he-weeoo* calls, a *chr chrr chrr*, and a fast *quit-it-it* alarm.

Status and distribution: Endemic species, in forest throughout.

Nesting: In untidy dome of leaves set at base of tree in forest; November–March and September.

Note: Three races occur in Sri Lanka: *P. f. babaulti* in the dry zone; *fuscocapillum* in the hills; and *scortillum* in the wet zone but the differences are very subtle and difficult to separate in the field.

Range: Sri Lanka.

INDIAN SCIMITAR-BABBLER *Pomatorhinus horsfieldii melanurus*
(Ceylon Scimitar Babbler) PLATE 43 (2)

Identification: (22 cm) Long yellow down-curved bill, long white eyebrow extending onto nape and black eye-stripe. Dark brown crown, rich rusty brown upperparts; white underparts with brown flanks, vent, and undertail coverts. Sexes alike. Feeds on ground turning over leaves or picking in mossy bark on branches. In pairs or small groups. Shy.

Note: In the dry zone and nearby hills the upperparts are olive brown (some authorities consider this a separate race, *P. h. holdsworthi*).

Voice: Very vocal, *oop-oop-oop-oop-...* and a duetted *pawp-a-pawp*, answered by *kaa-kree, kaa-kree*. Also a descending *do do do do*, a *pop pop-prrr*, a deep *woch wohorro*, and various other calls.

Status and distribution: Endemic race. Common in forests, scrub, and wooded gardens throughout.

Nesting: In a deep, rough dome in vegetation near ground or in hole in tree. December–May and August.
Species range: India.

TAWNY-BELLIED BABBLER *Dumetia hyperythra phillipsi* PLATE 43 (4)
(Rufous-bellied Babbler)
(White-throated Babbler)

Identification: (14 cm) Pale bill and face; white chin, throat, and centre of breast contrasting with rufous-buff underparts. Rufous forehead and crown, rest of upperparts olive brown. Sexes alike. In small flocks usually skulking in undergrowth or long grass, disappearing into cover when threatened.
Voice: A chattering *weech weech* contact call and a *tak tak*... alarm.
Status and distribution: Endemic race. In scrub and rough grass throughout.
Nesting: In a ball of grass stems set in bush or tussock; mainly March–June and August–September.
Species range: Nepal, India.

DARK-FRONTED BABBLER *Rhopocichla atriceps* PLATE 43 (3)
(Black-fronted Babbler) (*Alcippe atriceps*)
(Black-headed Babbler)

Identification: (13 cm) Brown cap, black forehead and ear coverts giving dark hooded appearance, yellow eye; white chin, throat, breast, and upper belly. Brown upperparts, rufous-olive flanks, vent and under tail. Sexes alike. Feeds by picking insects from undergrowth. In small groups. Shy.
Note: Two races are present: *R. a. siccata* as described and *nigrifrons* which is a warmer brown above but the differences are subtle.
Voice: *Chak chak*...,*chip,chip*,...,and *churrr* calls. Also a low rattling alarm.
Status and distribution: Both are endemic races preferring forest with dense undergrowth: *siccata* in dry lowlands and hills; *nigrifrons* in wet lowlands and nearby hills.
Nesting: In ball of leaves in fork of tree; February–May and October–November.
Species range: C and SW India.

YELLOW-EYED BABBLER *Chrysomma sinense nasale* PLATE 43 (5)

Identification: (17 cm) Black bill, yellow eye with obvious bright orange eye-ring, white eyebrow, lores, and underparts; pale brown upperparts. Sexes alike. Usually skulks in dense undergrowth but often emerges briefly at dusk to call from exposed branch. In pairs or small groups.

Voice: A fast *cutty-kra weerko wiwiwiwiwi* song, also *peer peer* and *peerpee kowhihihihi* calls and a *krrrr krrrr...* alarm.
Status and distribution: Endemic race. In rough grass and scrub throughout.
Nesting: In deep grass cup in scrub; mainly February–May.
Species range: Pakistan, India, SE Asia.

ORANGE-BILLED BABBLER *Turdoides rufescens* PLATE 43 (6)
(Ceylon Rufous Babbler)
(Ceylon Jungle Babbler)

Identification: (25 cm) Orange bill and rufous plumage. Yellow legs and feet Sexes alike. Feeds in small groups restlessly working their way through the lower foliage of trees and understorey, often with a squirrel nearby.
Voice: A high pitched whistling song and a continuous chattering, agitated *kraa-kraa-kraa-kraa...* contact call.
Status and distribution: Endemic species. Fairly common in forests of wet zone lowlands and nearby hills.
Nesting: Little information. Probably in grass cup well hidden in creepers or bush; March–May.
Range: Sri Lanka.

YELLOW-BILLED BABBLER *Turdoides affinis taprobanus* PLATE 43 (6)
(Common Babbler) (*Turdoides striatus*)
(White-headed Babbler)

Identification: (24 cm) Horny yellow bill, pale eye, and face. Generally drab grey with brown-grey on wings and tail. Sexes alike. Feeds in small parties, usually 6–12, moving slowly through the undergrowth. Weak flight usually little more than a fluttering glide between trees as the party moves on. Often prefers to hop.
Voice: A continual noisy chatter of urgent squeaks, trills, and whistles.
Status and distribution: Endemic race. Common in open scrub, cultivation, well vegetated gardens throughout up to 1700 m. Avoids forests.
Nesting: In a deep cup hidden in dense bush or tree; mainly March–May and August–November.
Species range: S India.

ASHY-HEADED LAUGHINGTHRUSH *Garrulax cinereifrons*
(Ashy-headed Babbler) (*Turdoides cinereifrons*)
PLATE 43 (8)

Identification: (24 cm) Black bill, pale eye, grey head with faint blue tinge shading on nape into deep rufous on rest of upperparts; whitish-buff chin shading into tawny-rufous on underparts. Dark legs. Sexes alike. Feeds in small chattering groups working their way through undergrowth in forest.

Voice: A constant chatter of squeaks and whistles.
Status and distribution: Endemic species. Rare in forests of wet zone lowlands and nearby hills.
Nesting: Thought to be in cup set in bush; probably March–July.
Range: Sri Lanka.

Old world warblers

Order: Passeriformes
Family: Sylviidae

Small to very small birds with thin, straight bills. Normally they are solitary or in pairs and very active, usually keeping to vegetation where they seek their mainly insect prey and are rarely seen on the ground. The name 'warbler' is somewhat inappropriate in Sri Lanka because the resident warblers do not have rich songs and the migrants do not usually sing away from their breeding areas.

SRI LANKA BUSH-WARBLER *Bradypterus palliseri* Plate 43 (9)
(Ceylon Warbler)
(Palliser's Warbler)

Identification: (15 cm) Generally dark with rusty-buff throat, dark grey breast, and rounded tail. Faint pale eyebrow and pale ring around eye. Olive-brown upperparts with a rusty tinge on rump; olive-grey belly with rufous tinge on flanks and under tail. Sexes alike but male has red eye and female pale buff. Very skulking. Feeds low, actively hopping from stem to stem picking insects from damp undergrowth in forests. In pairs. Flight usually only a brief flutter to the next clump of undergrowth.
Voice: A squeaky song from an exposed stem and a hard, metallic *chink* call.
Status and distribution: Endemic species. Scarce in forest with dense undergrowth in hills above 1000 m or occasionally in nearby tea plantations.
Nesting: In large, deep cup hidden near to ground in bush; February–May and September.
Range: Sri Lanka.

BROAD-TAILED GRASSBIRD *Schoenicola platyura* Not illustrated
(Broad-tailed Warbler)
(Broad-tailed Grass Warbler)

Identification: (18 cm) Ruddy-brown upperparts with a faint buff eyebrow and a very broad, rounded brown tail; chin, throat, and centre of belly white, rest of underparts tawny brown. Skulks in rough vegetation, retreating into cover when threatened. Solitary or in scattered pairs. Brief, heavy flight showing broad, rounded tail, usually to get to next patch of cover.

Voice: Emerges from cover early and late in day to call *pink pink pink...* from exposed stem.
Status and distribution: Unconfirmed vagrant. Prefers damp lowlands and low grassy hill slopes.
Range: SW India.

LANCEOLATED WARBLER *Locustella lanceolata* PLATE 43 (12)

Identification: (12 cm) Slightly smaller than very similar Pallas's Grasshopper with shorter plain brown tail and dark streaking on breast, upper belly and flanks (beware, juvenile in autumn can have only a few fine streaks); a less obvious eyebrow and more grey-brown upperparts when in worn plumage. Tertials have dark centres with well defined pale fringes. Undertail coverts usually spotted, rarely plain; never with pointed marks and pale tips as in Common Grasshopper. Sexes alike. Skulks in dense vegetation usually moving actively from stem to stem and running along ground, only taking to wing when closely threatened, returning to cover immediately.
Voice: A repeated, hard *pit, pit...*, also *tak*, and a harsh *cheek-cheek-cheek...*
Status and distribution: Rare winter vagrant possible in dense grass, paddy stubble, and low vegetation in wet lowlands.
Range: C, E, and SE Asia.

COMMON GRASSHOPPER WARBLER *Locustella naevia*
PLATE 43 (11)

Identification: (13 cm) Very similar to Pallas's Grasshopper but has more olive brown upperparts, a browner crown with narrower streaking, less obvious narrow eyebrow, less heavy streaking on mantle and scapulars, and a plain brown tail; few streaks on breast, streaked undertail coverts (but streaking variable). Tertials have not-so dark centres and poorly defined fringes, the undertail coverts are streaked with pointed dark centres. Sexes alike. Skulks in dense vegetation. Flight very brief, usually to nearest cover. Solitary.
Voice: A *chik chik* and a rarely heard *chrrr chrrr.*
Status and distribution: Winter vagrant possible in damp, dense vegetation, reed beds, and paddy stubble of wet lowlands.
Range: Europe, N Africa, N and C Asia.

PALLAS'S GRASSHOPPER WARBLER *Locustella certhiola*
(Pallas's Warbler) PLATE 43 (10)
(Rusty-rumped Warbler)

Identification: (13 cm) Grey-brown crown with more dark streaks than on Common Grasshopper, conspicuous buff eyebrow and generally more rufous-brown. Dark streaks on mantle, rusty unstreaked rump contrasting with streaks on back, rounded brown tail shading to dark sub-terminal band and off-white tips to all but central pair of feathers (best seen from below or when tail spread); off-white to buff underparts tinged rufous on sides of breast and flanks, plain unstreaked undertail coverts. Tertials have small pale spot at tips of inner webs. Sexes alike. Juvenile: usually some spotting on breast. Skulks in grass or reeds. Flight usually very brief to nearest cover. Solitary and territorial in winter.

Voice: A rolling *cheevee-cheevee-cheevee-...*and *chi-chi-chi-chi-...* songs and various calls; *chik-chik*, *tink-tink*, *chee*, *pitt*, *tchrrr*, and a descending *trrrrrr*.

Status and distribution: Winter visitor to wet marshy areas.

Range: C, E, and SE Asia.

BLYTH'S REED WARBLER *Acrocephalus dumetorum* PLATE 43 (13)

Identification: (13 cm) Smaller and greyer than Clamorous Reed with a short, faint, buff eyebrow, off-white throat and slightly rounded shortish tail. Plain olive-brown upperparts (grey-brown when worn); off-white belly with pale buff on breast and flanks, and longish undertail coverts. Sexes alike. Hops actively through bushes and scrub seeking insects. Solitary.

Voice: *Chuk*, *chreep*, and *crrrr* anxiety calls. The *...chek chek chwee chwee chek chek...* song can be heard at the end of their stay.

Status and distribution: Common winter visitor in gardens, reed beds, plantations, and scrub throughout up to 2000 m.

Range: C Europe, W, C, and S Asia

CLAMOROUS REED WARBLER *Acrocephalus stentoreus meridionalis* (Great Reed Warbler) PLATE 43 (14)

Identification: (18 cm) Considerably larger, browner, and with proportionally longer bill and tail than in Blyth's Reed but otherwise very similar. Warm brown upperparts with a longish faint buff eyebrow; pale buff throat and buff belly. Sexes alike. Skulks low in dense, damp vegetation seeking insects. Emerges to sing from exposed stems in breeding season.

Voice: A very loud and relentless *...kark kark karra karra tsee tsee tsee kirrik kirrik...* and a *tk* alarm.

Status and distribution: Endemic race. Reed beds and dense waterside vegetation in lowlands, more common in dry zone.

Note: *A. s. brunnescens* possibly occurs as a rare winter visitor. It is somewhat paler and slightly larger than *meridionalis.*

Nesting: A deep cup of reed stems in reed bed; March–August.

Species range: Egypt, Middle East, C, S, and SE Asia, Philippines, Java, Australia.

BOOTED WARBLER *Hippolais caligata* PLATE 44 (7)

(Booted Tree Warbler)

Note: Two races recorded in Sri Lanka. There is debate as to whether they should be considered as separate species.

Sykes's Warbler, *H. c. rama*

Identification: (12 cm) Resembles Blyth's Reed but is slightly smaller and paler, has a squarer tail with white outer tail feathers. Grey-brown upperparts with a short buff eyebrow (bolder than in Blyth's Reed); pale buff below becoming off-white on throat and mid-belly. Sexes alike. Flits about lower branches of trees and in bushes seeking insects. Sometimes makes flycatcher-like flights to take flies on the wing. Solitary or in small groups.

Booted Warbler, *H. c. caligata*

Identification: Similar to *rama* but darker, more tawny upperparts, finer bill, and shorter tail.

Voice: *Tsek-tsek-tsek* flight call, also a *chrrr* call. A soft jingling song is possible at end of winter stay.

Status and distribution: *H. c. rama*: Winter visitor mainly to acacias and other scrub in north, rarely elsewhere; *H. c. caligata*: probably a winter vagrant to dry lowlands.

Species range: Iran, C, E, and S Asia.

ZITTING CISTICOLA *Cisticola juncidis* PLATE 44 (1)

(Fantail Warbler)
(Streaked Fantail Warbler)

Identification: (10 cm) Very small with short, white-tipped, fan-shaped tail. Rufous-tawny upperparts with buff eyebrow, dark streaks on head, mantle and scapulars; off-white below, tinged pale buff on flanks and undertail coverts. Undulating song flight with a call uttered at each bounce as tail is fanned showing white-tips. Skulks in grass and other low vegetation catching insects.

Voice: A sharp ...*zit, zit, zit*...made in song flight and a *zit zit* anxiety call.

Status and distribution: Resident in open grassland, paddy, and tank edges throughout.

Note: Two races occur which are difficult to separate in the field: *C. j. omalura* is an endemic race in the wet zone and hills; *C. j. cursitans* is slightly smaller and paler, resident in the dry lowlands.
Nesting: A deep cup hidden in tussock; mainly March–April and July–September.
Range: S Europe, Africa, Middle East, C, S, and SE Asia, Australia.

GREY-BREASTED PRINIA *Prinia hodgsonii leggei* PLATE 44 (2)
(Franklin's Prinia)
(Franklin's Wren Warbler)

Identification: (11 cm) Small with typical Prinia long, graduated tail and grey band across breast (incomplete in female). Ash-grey upperparts with white cheeks, white tips on tail; black and white barring under tail. Pink-yellow legs. Juvenile: olive-brown upperparts and a tawny tinge on underparts, no breast band. Weak flight. Flits through low trees and scrub flicking tail up and down in typical Prinia habit. In pairs or small groups.
Voice: *Cheeoo, cheeoo,...* and a rapid chatter *chchchchch* quieter than the similar calls of Ashy.
Status and distribution: Endemic race. Scrub and small trees in dry lowlands and nearby hills to 1000 m in E and SE. Rarely in wet lowlands.
Nesting: In pouch of sewn leaves low in vegetation; March–June, possibly later.
Species range: India, SE Asia.

JUNGLE PRINIA *Prinia sylvatica valida* PLATE 44 (5)
(Ceylon Large Prinia) (*Prinia polychroa valida*)

Identification: (15 cm) Larger and darker than Plain and the faint eyebrow barely extends beyond the eye. Strong bill. Dusky brown upperparts with off-white tips to long graduated tail; brown cheeks shading to buff underparts, paler on belly, black and white barring under tail. Sexes alike. Flits through scrub and low vegetation flicking tail. In pairs or small groups.
Voice: Noisy, often sings from exposed twig *...titreer...titreer...titreer...* or *...thirlip...thirlip...*
Status and distribution: Endemic race. Scrub and rough grassland of lowlands and hills to 1800 m.
Nesting: In ball of grass and stems low in tussock or bush; mainly February–May.
Species range: India, Nepal, Bangladesh.

ASHY PRINIA *Prinia socialis brevicauda* PLATE 44 (4)

Identification: (12 cm) Distinguish from Grey-breasted by lack of grey breast band. Bluish-grey upperparts and long graduated tail with off-white tips; buff below paling on throat and centre of breast, black and white barring under tail. Sexes alike apart from a faint white line above lores on female. Weak, fluttering flight often fanning tail. Actively feeds in low vegetation, hopping from stem to stem and flicking tail. Solitary or in pairs.

Voice: Chirruping song, often from grass stem, *thrrip, thrrip, thrrip*...,also *cher, cher*... and *mee, mee* calls.

Status and distribution: Endemic race. In grass, low scrub, paddy, and cultivation throughout.

Nesting: In half dome of woven grass in tussock; mainly February–June and August–October.

Species range: Pakistan, Himalayas, India.

PLAIN PRINIA *Prinia subflava insularis* PLATE 44 (3)

(Tawny-flanked Prinia) (*Prinia inornata insularis*)
(Ceylon White-browed Prinia)

Identification: (13 cm) Smaller and paler than Jungle with dark eye-stripe and white eyebrow. Dull brown upperparts with white tips on long graduated tail; pale buff below with black and white bars under tail. Sexes alike. Weak, jerky flight with typical Prinia tail fanning. Feeds hopping actively in low vegetation. Solitary or in small groups often with other Prinias.

Voice: A rapid jingling ...tliktliktliktlik... song and a call like a finger-nail drawn across a comb.

Status and distribution: Endemic race. Common in long grass, paddy, and swamps throughout up to 1800 m.

Nesting: In deep cup of woven grass in tussock or low bush. Possible all year.

Species range: Africa, S and SE Asia.

COMMON TAILORBIRD *Orthotomus sutorius sutorius* PLATE 44 (6)

(Ceylon Long-tailed Tailorbird)

Identification: (12 cm; breeding male 14 cm) Long tail usually held erect. Rufous crown, yellow-green upperparts; off-white below. Sexes alike but breeding males have extended central tail feathers. Rarely flies any distance. Feeds actively in foliage constantly wagging tail, often quite tame. In pairs.

Note: *O. s. fernandonis* replaces *sutorius* in the higher hills, it is darker green above, has grey throat patch and grey on flanks.

Voice: A constant *teewit, teewit, teewit*...

Status and distribution: Both are common endemic races, *sutorius* in gardens, scrub, and almost anywhere with dense cover in lowlands and hills to 1500 m, *fernandonis* in higher hills.

Nesting: In pocket of leaves sewn together usually set in low bush or tree; mainly February–May.

Species range: S and SE Asia, Java.

GREENISH WARBLER *Phylloscopus trochiloides viridanus* PLATE 44 (10)
(Greenish Tree Warbler)

Note: There is debate as to whether this and the Bright Green Warbler are both races of *P. trochiloides*.
Identification: (10 cm) Duller generally than Bright-green. Dull olive-green upperparts with long pale yellow eyebrow and usually only one faint pale wing bar; greyish white below (never yellow). Sexes alike. Feeds actively in canopy, sometimes in undergrowth, also makes flycatcher-like flights to take insects. Solitary or in mixed flocks.
Voice: A high pitched *si-si-si-chiwee* and variations. Also loud *chee-weep* and *tsee-lee* calls.
Status and distribution: Scarce winter visitor to wet lowlands and hills.
Note: *P. t. trochiloides* also occurs as a winter vagrant to southern lowlands. It has a darker head, deeper olive upperparts and is greyer below.
Species range: NE Europe, W, C, S, and SE Asia.

BRIGHT-GREEN WARBLER *Phylloscopus nitidus* PLATE 44 (9)
(Green Tree Warbler) (*Phylloscopus trochiloides nitidus*)
(Green Leaf Warbler)

Note: See note for previous species.
Identification: (11 cm) Bright yellow-green upperparts with long yellow eyebrow, brown tail and wings usually showing a second wing bar; yellow below (but become very dull in late winter when plumage is worn). Feeds actively in canopy sometimes making flycatcher-like flights to take insects, occasionally in undergrowth. Solitary.
Voice: A constant *chee-weet* call, more tri-syllabic than Greenish.
Status and distribution: Common winter visitor in trees throughout.
Range: W Asia, India.

LARGE-BILLED LEAF WARBLER *Phylloscopus magnirostris*
(Large-billed Tree Warbler) PLATE 44 (11)

Identification: (13 cm) Stouter and darker than Bright-green with darker crown, obvious yellowish eyebrow, dark eyestripe, longer and thicker bill with paler lower mandible, and distinctive call. Dark olive-green upperparts, brown wings usually with two yellowish wing bars; pale greyish underparts with whitish outer tail feathers obvious from below. Sexes alike. Feeds in canopy of high trees. Solitary.
Voice: An ascending *yaw, wee, wee* call and *wee-chee*.
Status and distribution: Winter visitor to forests throughout.
Range: Himalayas, Tibet, W China, India.

LESSER WHITETHROAT *Sylvia curruca* PLATE 44 (8)

Note: Three races are recorded in Sri Lanka. There is debate as to whether they should be treated as separate species.

Hume's Whitethroat, *S. c. althaea*

Identification: (13 cm) Dusky-grey hood and white throat. Grey-brown upperparts with white on outer tail feathers; white below with faint warm tinge on breast and belly. Sexes alike. Hops quietly through foliage of trees and scrub. Shy.

Lesser Whitethroat, *S. c. blythi*

Identification: Similar to *althaea* but paler grey hood and warmer brown tinge on upperparts. Smaller bill.

Desert Lesser Whitethroat, *S. c. minula*

Identification: Smaller and paler than previous races with uniformly grey hood and white throat (no black on face).
Voice: A *tuk, tuk...* call.
Status and distribution: Hume's: Winter visitor to scrub of NW coastal areas; Lesser Whitethroat: Winter vagrant to dry lowlands.
Species range: Europe, N and C Africa, Asia.

OLD WORLD FLYCATCHERS

Order: Passeriformes
Family: Muscicapidae

SMALL, insectivorous, mainly arboreal birds with flattened, pointed bills and strong bristles fringing the base of the upper mandible. The wings are longish and pointed, the feet rather small and weak. Some have a characteristic 'flycatcher' hunting pattern of perching upright on a branch waiting for insects to fly by then making a brief flight to catch the prey, often with a loud click of the bill, returning to the original perch to eat the catch.

ASIAN BROWN FLYCATCHER *Muscicapa dauurica* (*Muscicapa latirostris*) PLATE 45 (8)

Identification: (13 cm) Slightly smaller than Brown-breasted with dark-tipped pale lower mandible and grey-brown legs. Grey-brown upperparts with large eye, off-white lores and eye-ring; obvious white patch on throat, off-white below with grey tinge on breast and flanks. Sexes alike. First winter birds show pale tips on greater coverts and have well marked tertials. 'Flycatches', often flicking wings and depressing tail while waiting. Feeds well into dusk. Solitary. Not shy.

Voice: Normally silent but has a faint *tse-te-te-te-te*. Also a *chik chik rr* call made while quivering tail.

Status and distribution: Common winter visitor to gardens, open forest, and plantations of lowlands and hills to 1300 m.

Range: E and SE Asia, Japan, Philippines, Borneo.

BROWN-BREASTED FLYCATCHER *Muscicapa muttui* PLATE 45 (7)
(Layard's Flycatcher)

Identification: (13 cm) Darker and slightly larger than Asian Brown with all pale lower mandible, a brown-grey tinge on breast and flesh coloured legs. White throat with a dark cheek stripe joining ear covert patch. Off-white eye ring and lores. Sexes alike. First year birds have buff wing bar and buff fringes on tertials. 'Flycatches', often from quite a low branch and well into dusk. Easily overlooked.

Voice: Generally silent in winter.

Status and distribution: Winter visitor to forests, especially near streams in lowlands and hills to 1700 m.

Range: India.

DULL-BLUE FLYCATCHER *Eumyias sordida* PLATE 45 (6)
(Sri Lanka Dusky Blue Flycatcher) (*Muscicapa sordida*)

Identification: (15 cm) Generally dull blue-grey with brighter blue forehead, dark lores; white belly and undertail coverts; brown flight feathers and tail. Sexes alike. Juvenile: brown with pale buff spots on head, back, wing coverts, and breast. Usually perches on low branches or stumps to 'flycatch'. Also eats berries.

Voice: A sweet rather loud song of five or six notes sung from a tree.

Status and distribution: Endemic species. Forests, ravines, and well wooded gardens of hills over 600 m.

Nesting: In mossy cup in hole in roadside bank or tree hole; March–September.

Range: Sri Lanka.

KASHMIR FLYCATCHER *Ficedula subrubra* PLATE 45 (5)
(Kashmir Red-breasted Flycatcher) (*Muscicapa subrubra*)
(*Siphia hyperythra*)

Identification: (12 cm) White eye-ring. Male plumage: dark ashy-brown upperparts with black tail and white panels at base of outer feathers;

dark-edged rich rufous breast and flanks, white belly. Female plumage: duller with pale throat and buff breast. Juvenile: as adult male but duller. 'Flycatches' from low perch, also feeds on ground hopping around flicking wings and tail showing the white tail panels.

Voice: A rattling call and a *chip chip chip* song followed by the rattle.

Status and distribution: Common winter visitor to forest edge, gardens, and tea plantations in hills.

Range: India.

BLUE-THROATED FLYCATCHER *Niltava rubeculoides* PLATE 45 (10)

(Blue-throated Niltava) (*Muscicapa rubeculoides*)
(*Cyornis rubeculoides*)

Identification: (14 cm) Male from male Tickell's Blue by blue throat and brighter blue. Male plumage: blue upperparts and throat; rufous breast shading to buff tinged white on belly. Female plumage: brownish-olive upperparts; buff throat, rufous breast paling to buff on flanks, white belly. Pale eye-ring. Moves restlessly through undergrowth and lower branches flicking tail. Sometimes takes food from ground.

Voice: A churring alarm and a winter song *cissy cissy cissy cissy see.*

Status and distribution: Rare winter visitor to forests of lowlands and lower hills.

Range: Himalayas, India, SE Asia.

TICKELL'S BLUE FLYCATCHER *Niltava tickelliae jerdoni*

(Tickell's Niltava) (*Cyornis tickelliae*) PLATE 45 (9)
(Ceylon Orange-breasted Blue Flycatcher) (*Muscicapa tickelliae*)

Identification: (15 cm) Male lacks the blue throat of male Blue-throated. Dull blue upperparts, bright rufous throat paling on breast, white belly and undertail coverts: Female is generally paler with off-white throat. Juvenile: brown with tawny streaks. Flits about in undergrowth and lower branches, very active towards dusk. Not shy.

Voice: A rapid six or seven note jingling song *whee-oo-ou-er-oo-ee* and variations; also a *tik, tik* call.

Status and distribution: Endemic race. Forest, wooded gardens, cultivation with trees in lowlands and hills to 1300 m. Has preference for stream banks.

Nesting: In cup of leaves, moss, etc. in cavity usually near ground.

Species range: India, SE Asia.

GREY-HEADED CANARY FLYCATCHER *Culicicapa ceylonensis*
(Grey-headed Flycatcher) PLATE 45 (4)

Identification: (11 cm) Grey head, neck, and sides of breast with a slight peaked crest and white eye-ring; greenish-yellow upperparts becoming yellow on rump; brown wings and tail; yellow belly. Sexes alike. Active when perched often flicking tail, 'flycatches' in typical way. In pairs. Tame.
Voice: Short and rapid *tit titu whee* or *see-si-si-see* song, often uttered and a *chip, chipchipchip, chip, chip* call.
Status and distribution: Common resident in forest, wooded ravines, and gardens in hills above 800 m in wet zone
Nesting: In mossy cup against tree stump or boulder, or in mossy bank; February–May.
Range: India, SE Asia, Java.

MONARCHS AND FANTAIL

Order: Passeriformes
Family: Monarchidae

LARGE headed, mainly arboreal birds with broad bills fringed by bristles. Insectivorous, the three species present are more active than the true flycatchers mostly taking their prey on the wing, rarely perching patiently.

BLACK-NAPED MONARCH *Hypothymis azurea ceylonensis*
(Black-naped Blue Monarch) (*Monarcha azurea*) PLATE 45 (1)
(Ceylon Azure Flycatcher)

Identification: (16 cm) Azure blue with black patch on nape (can be erected as small crest), relatively long, slightly notched tail and whitish belly. Female and juvenile are duller and greyer. Actively flits about foliage flicking wings and fanning tail taking insects on the wing. Keeps more to canopy than others in family. Solitary or in pairs.
Voice: A constantly uttered *tchreet.*
Status and distribution: Endemic race. Forests of lowlands and hills to 1700 m.
Nesting: In a deep cup set low in tree fork, sometimes in canopy; March–May and September.
Species range: India, SE Asia, Taiwan, Philippines, Java.

ASIAN PARADISE-FLYCATCHER *Terpsiphone paradisi* PLATE 45 (2)
(*Tchitrea paradisi*)

Note: Two distinct races occur in Sri Lanka:

Sri Lanka Paradise Flycatcher, *T. p. ceylonensis*

Identification: (20 cm with up to 30 cm of tail streamers in adult male) Glossy blue-black hood, crest and neck, chestnut upperparts and tail; ashy-grey breast shading into white on belly. Female and Juvenile: like male but lack the streamers (not full until after second moult), have more dusky breast and shorter crest. Fast dipping flight. Very active taking insects on the wing usually from higher branches; often flashing tail. Sometimes feeds on ground. Plunge dives to bathe. Solitary or in pairs. Not shy.

Indian Paradise Flycatcher, *T. p. paradisi*

Identification: Male plumage: similar to Sri Lanka race with blue-black hood but rest of plumage, including tail streamers, silvery-white with black and white wings. Female and Juvenile: blue-black hood, grey-brown collar shading to chestnut upperparts; grey breast shading to white below.

Voice: A descending then rising *peety-too-whit* song and a harsh *chreech* call.

Status and distribution: *T. p. ceylonensis*: endemic race. Forests, gardens, anywhere with trees in dry lowlands and eastern foothills. *T. p. paradisi*: winter visitor to trees throughout to 1700 m. More frequent in lowlands.

Nesting: *T.p. ceylonensis*: In cup set in fork of tree or climber; April–July.

Species range: S, E, and SE Asia, Java.

WHITE-BROWED FANTAIL *Rhipidura aureola* PLATE 45 (3)
(White-browed Fantail Flycatcher) (*Leucocirca aureola*)

Identification: (17 cm) Unmistakable habit of fanning black and white tail and flicking wings. Dull black with long, broad white eyebrow, a row of white spots across throat, two rows on wing coverts, white tips to outer tail feathers; white breast and belly. Sexes alike. Slow, direct flight. Restless, flitting through foliage flirting the wings and fantail, showing the black and white tail pattern. Takes insects on the wing. In pairs. Quite tame.

Voice: A human-sounding whistling song of seven or eight notes and a *ch-wch* alarm.

Status and distribution: Common resident in forests, wooded gardens, and tall scrub throughout.

Nesting: In small cup on branch, often not concealed; January–July.

Range: India, SE Asia.

TIT — Order: Passeriformes Family: Paridae

SMALL, plump birds with short, conical bills. They are very acrobatic, often hanging upside-down while working their way through tree foliage and along rough bark seeking invertebrate prey, also taking some seeds.

GREAT TIT *Parus major* PLATE 46 (1)
(Grey Tit)

Identification: (13 cm) Glossy black head with bold white cheek patch, bluish grey upperparts, white edged black tail; black throat and upper breast extending into broad black line centrally down belly, whitish sides to belly shading to grey on flanks. Sexes alike but female has less glossy cap and a narrower, less dense black stripe down front. Shows white wing bar in flight. Very active and acrobatic. In pairs or small flocks often with other insectivorous birds. Quite tame in hills, less so in lowlands.

Voice: Various repetitive songs: *cheewit cheewit...*, *waheechi waheechi...*, *tisswee tisswee...*, and a chattering anxiety call.

Status and distribution: Resident in forests, gardens, anywhere with trees throughout. Common in hills.

Nesting: In cavity in tree or building; mainly March–April and September–November.

Range: Europe, Morocco, Asia, Japan, Java.

NUTHATCH — Order: Passeriformes Family: Sittidae

SMALL arboreal birds with longish, straight, pointed bills; short legs but large, powerful feet. They behave in a woodpecker-like way clinging to tree bark searching for small invertebrates but, unlike woodpeckers, they work in any direction—head up or down. The tail is short and square and is not used as a prop.

VELVET-FRONTED NUTHATCH *Sitta frontalis* PLATE 46 (2)
(Velvet-fronted Blue Nuthatch)

Identification: (11 cm) Distinctive bright red bill, velvet black forehead and thin black eye-stripe continuing to nape, lavender blue upperparts; whitish chin and throat, rest of underparts pinkish-buff. Female lacks the black eyebrow and has blue tinge on lores. Very active, moving jerkily up and down tree bark seeking food. In pairs.

Voice: A *chik chik* and a chittering call.
Status and distribution: Resident in forests and trees in hills, infrequent in lowlands.
Nesting: In hole in tree; January–May.
Range: India, SE Asia, Philippines, Java.

FLOWERPECKERS Order: Passeriformes Family: Dicaeidae

VERY small, strictly arboreal birds with short bills, short tails, and weak legs and feet, not unlike sunbirds in appearance and habit but the flowerpeckers' much shorter bills are distinctive. They are restless, feeding on fruits, nectar and small invertebrates in foliage, calling constantly as they forage.

THICK-BILLED FLOWERPECKER *Dicaeum agile zeylonicum*

PLATE 46 (4)

Identification: (10 cm) A little larger than Pale-billed with a shorter, stubby bill, brown streak on sides of throat and white-tipped tail feathers. Olive-brown upperparts; reddish-brown eye, white chin and throat, pale buff below with faint brown streaks. Sexes alike. Moves continuously through upper branches feeding, often jerking tail sideways. Solitary or in pairs.
Voice: A repeated *tchik, tchik...* similar but harder than that of the Pale-billed Flowerpecker.
Status and distribution: Endemic race. Forest and woods of low country and hills up to 1300 m. Scarce in wet zone.
Nesting: In pocket of fibres hung from twig, high in tree; March–July.
Species range: India, SE Asia, Philippines, Java.

WHITE-THROATED FLOWERPECKER *Dicaeum vincens*

(Legge's Flowerpecker) PLATE 46 (5)

Identification: (10 cm) Distinguish from rather similar Purple-rumped Sunbird by short, stout bill. Male plumage: dark blue-grey upperparts with white tips on outer tail feathers (smaller and less obvious in female); white throat and upper breast, rest of underparts yellow paling to white on undertail coverts. Female plumage: generally paler with grey-olive upperparts. Keeps to tops of trees. Likes red cotton tree nectar and wild figs. Solitary or in pairs.
Voice: *Chip, chip, chwee, see, see* and *wheep-wheep-wheep* calls.
Status and distribution: Endemic species. Tops of trees in forests of wet zone and nearby hills to 1000 m.
Nesting: In small, felted pocket slung high in tree; January–August.

Range: Sri Lanka.

PALE-BILLED FLOWERPECKER *Dicaeum erythrorhynchos ceylonense*
(Tickell's Flowerpecker) PLATE 46 (3)
(Small Flowerpecker)

Identification: (8 cm) Smallest Sri Lankan bird. Distinguish from White-throated female by longer, finer, more pointed and slightly down-curved bill and no yellow on belly. From Thick-billed by fine bill and no streaks on breast. Olive-brown upperparts; very pale grey underparts darkening on flanks and with buff tinge on belly. Sexes alike. Dipping flight. Feeds actively flitting from branch to branch, usually high in trees. Attracted to the berries of the parasitic Loranthus. Solitary or in pairs.
Voice: A constantly repeated *chip-chip-chip-*... and a *chak, chak, chak,*...
Status and distribution: Endemic race. Common everywhere with tall trees.
Nesting: In small bag of fibres slung from a twig high in a tree; mainly January–August.
Species range: Himalayas, India, Bangladesh, Myanmar.

SUNBIRDS Order: Passeriformes. Family: Nectariniidae.

SMALL, strictly arboreal birds with long, thin, sharply pointed, down-curved bills, short legs, and weak feet. They feed mainly on nectar, probing into flowers with their long bills, but also take small invertebrates. The sexes differ in plumage, the males being brightly coloured with metallic sheens, the females somewhat drabber. There is a brief period in summer when the males of some species adopt an eclipse plumage rather similar to that of the female. Very active birds, usually in pairs (which helps in the identification of the females). Sunbirds are the Old World equivalent of the hummingbirds although they are not closely related.

PURPLE-RUMPED SUNBIRD *Nectarinia zeylonica zeylonica*
(*Cinnyris zeylonica zeylonica*)
PLATE 46 (6)

Identification: (10 cm) Female has paler ashy-grey face, warmer brown wings and clearer yellow underparts than female Purple. Male plumage: glossy green crown and shoulder patch, purple rump, rest of upperparts, face and throat dark with metallic sheen, tail has faint white tips to outer feathers; yellow breast and belly. Female and Juvenile: grey-brown upperparts with faint pale eyebrow and green tinge on back, warm brown upperwings with rufous edges; whitish underparts with yellow belly. Feeds continuously and noisily hopping and flitting through foliage with much flicking of wings and tail. Aggressively territorial. In pairs.

Voice: *Sweety-swee, sweety-sweety-swee.*

Status and distribution: Endemic race. Very common in trees in gardens, cultivation and open forest in all areas except high mountains.

Nesting: In fibrous pear-shaped bag hanging from a twig; February–June and August–September.

Species range: India, Bangladesh.

CRIMSON-BACKED SUNBIRD *Nectarinia minima* Not illustrated
(Small Sunbird) (*Cinnyris minima*)

Identification: (8 cm) Tiny. Smaller than rather similar Purple-rumped and male is more richly coloured crimson-brown on back and scapulars, lacks the green shoulder patch and the purple on the throat extends to the breast. Female resembles female Purple-rumped but has dull red rump. Habits similar to those of Purple-rumped.

Voice: A *see-see-wee-see-see-siwee*, *cheep-cheep-cheep-...* (higher than Purple's) and a *chik*.

Status and distribution: Unconfirmed vagrant. Prefers evergreen trees.

Range: S and W India.

LONG-BILLED SUNBIRD *Nectarinia lotenia lotenia* Plate 46 (7)
(Loten's Sunbird) (*Cinnyris lotenia lotenia*)

Identification: (14 cm) Largest local sunbird. Much longer down-curved bill than in other sunbirds. Female has buff-edged black tail. Male plumage: glossy black upperparts with green sheen; purple throat and breast separated from dark brown belly by band of maroon. In eclipse the male resembles the female but has a dark ragged line down throat and breast. Female plumage: olive-brown upperparts; dull yellow underparts. Typical sunbird habits with a preference for hibiscus blossom, jerking head backwards and forwards as it feeds. Displays by erecting normally hidden orange pectoral tufts and standing tall. Also has a looping display flight.

Status and distribution: Endemic race. Common in open areas with trees in the low country and lower hills, avoiding deep forest. Less frequent in high hills to 2000 m.

Voice: A sharp *tchit* and a cheery song *titti-titti-weechi-weechi-weechi*.

Nesting: In fibrous bag suspended from a twig in the wet zone. In dry zone, in down-lined hole pressed in dense mass of spiders' webs; February–May.

Species range: S India.

PURPLE SUNBIRD *Nectarinia asiatica* (*Cinnyris asiatica*) PLATE 46 (8)

Identification: (11 cm) Shorter bill than in Long-billed. Male distinguishable from Long-billed male by bill and blue-black belly; female from Long-billed female by faint pale eyebrow and lack of buff edge to tail. Male plumage: appears black but is dark blue-purple with narrow maroon band across top of belly and yellow pectoral tufts which are only obvious during courtship display. In eclipse the male resembles the female but has a dark ragged line down throat and breast. Female plumage: olive brown upperparts with faint pale eyebrow and deep bluish tail with white tips to outer feathers; dull yellow underparts. Active feeder similar in habit to other sunbirds.

Voice: *Chip*, *cheep-cheep-cheep-*... (deeper than Crimson-backed), *chweeet*, and a cheery song.

Status and distribution: Resident. Common in trees of low country dry zone. Visitor to wet zone and hills.

Nesting: In neat suspended fibrous bag or in hole in dense spiders' web; February–May.

Range: Iran, S and SE Asia.

WHITE-EYES Order: Passeriformes Family: Zosteropidae

SMALL, mainly green birds with a ring of fine white feathers around the eye; pointed, slightly down-curved bills and short, square tails. They are arboreal and active, working their way often in small, sometimes mixed species, flocks through the foliage of trees and shrubs but they do descend to bathe. The sexes and juveniles are alike. Can be quite tame.

ORIENTAL WHITE-EYE *Zosterops palpebrosa* PLATE 46 (9)
(Small White-eye)

Identification: (10 cm) Smaller and yellower than Sri Lanka White-eye. Mainly greenish-yellow, white eye-ring only narrowly broken to front; greyish-white lower breast, belly, and flanks. Active and acrobatic when feeding making contact calls, following one another through tree foliage seeking invertebrates and nectar.

Voice: A constant *tseer tseer* contact call.

Status and distribution: Common resident in forests, gardens, almost anywhere with trees in lowlands and hills to 1300 m in wet zone and up to 2000 m in drier eastern hills.

Nesting: In small cup slung between thin branches; mainly April–May and September.
Range: India, Nepal, China, Bangladesh, SE Asia, Java.

SRI LANKA WHITE-EYE *Zosterops ceylonensis* PLATE 46 (10)
(Ceylon Hill White-eye)
(Large Sri Lanka White-eye)

Identification: (11 cm) Larger and darker green above than Oriental and with a heavier bill. Mainly yellow-green with white eye-ring more widely broken at front than Oriental; lower breast, belly, and flanks greyish-white. Similar feeding habits to Oriental but will also feed in lower vegetation and is more sociable, often forming quite large scattered flocks.
Voice: A constant *cheep*, deeper than the Oriental's contact call, and a jingling song.
Status and distribution: Endemic species. Common in forests, gardens, and trees generally in higher hills, less frequent in wet zone foothills.
Nesting: A cup slung between branches, often low in foliage. Mainly March–May and August–September.
Range: Sri Lanka.

MUNIAS AND ALLIES

Order: Passeriformes
Family: Estrildidae

SMALL, gregarious birds with large, conical bills and mostly with relatively long, pointed tails. Seed-eaters, they mainly forage on grasslands and rice, often in large flocks.

WHITE-THROATED SILVERBILL *Lonchura malabarica* PLATE 47 (1)
(Indian Silverbill) (*Uroloncha malabarica*)
(White-throated Munia)

Identification: (10 cm) Appears rather pale. Dull brown upperparts with white rump and dark brown pointed tail; off-white below with light rufous barring on flanks. Despite the name the greyish bill is little help in identification. Sexes alike. Flight undulating showing white rump. Feeds on seeds in small to large flocks in open areas.
Voice: Various *chip* and *chirp* calls.
Status and distribution: Resident in paddy and pasture of dry lowlands especially in NE and SE coastal areas.

Nesting: In grassy dome set in tree, often a screw-pine; December–March.
Range: Middle East, S Asia.

WHITE-RUMPED MUNIA *Lonchura striata* PLATE 47 (2)
(White-backed Munia) (*Uroloncha striata*)

Identification: (10 cm) Much darker and more boldly marked than Silverbill and with blackish throat and breast. Blackish upperparts with some pale streaking and white rump, dark brown pointed tail; white belly and flanks, dark brown vent. Sexes alike. Juvenile is brown where adult is black. Undulating flight showing white rump. Feeds on grass and other seeds in small, tight flocks.
Voice: Twittering and chirping contact calls.
Status and distribution: Common resident in gardens, scrub and cultivation up to 1700 m.
Nesting: In untidy dome of grass in densely leafed tree; mainly February–May but possible all year.
Range: S and SE Asia, Taiwan.

SCALY-BREASTED MUNIA *Lonchura punctulata* PLATE 47 (3)
(Spotted Munia) (*Uroloncha punctulata*)
(Nutmeg Mannikin)

Identification: (11 cm) Paler and lacks the black face of the Black-throated. Tawny brown upperparts with yellowish brown rump and pointed tail; rich chestnut face and throat, white with brown scales on breast, upper belly, and flanks. Sexes alike. Juvenile: all brown with buff head keeping in flock with parents. Undulating flight in tight flocks. Feeds on grass seeds and in paddy. Roosts communally in low trees and scrub.
Voice: *Kitty kitty kitty*... and various reedy chirps.
Status and distribution: Common resident in gardens and cultivation throughout.
Nesting: In football-sized grass dome in low trees or shrubs; mainly October–May.
Range: China, S, SE Asia, Philippines, Java.

BLACK-THROATED MUNIA *Lonchura kelaarti kelaarti* PLATE 47 (4)
(Rufous-bellied Mannikin) (*Uroloncha kelaarti kelaarti*)
(Ceylon Hill Munia)

Identification: (10 cm) Look for black face and throat, pinky-fawn patch on sides of neck. Brown upperparts with pale streaks and black rump with white spots; white below chequered dark brown. Sexes alike. Juvenile: dull brown upperparts; throat finely barred dark brown and white, barred buff breast and belly. Fast undulating flight often higher than other Munias. Feeds on seeds even picking through dung. Less gregarious than other munias keeping in pairs or small groups. Roosts communally.

Voice: A reedy *chirp* and a quiet five note song.

Status and distribution: Endemic race (considered by some authorities as separate species). Gardens, tea plantations, scrub, and forest in hills above 250 m.

Nesting: In grass dome set in creepers, often near habitation; mainly April–September.

Species range: India.

BLACK-HEADED MUNIA *Lonchura malacca* PLATE 47 (5)

(Chestnut Mannikin) (*Munia malacca*)

Identification: (10 cm) Large silver-blue bill. Black hood with brown eye, chestnut upperparts; white flank and belly patch, rest of underparts black. Sexes alike. Juvenile: rufous brown upperparts, buff below. From juvenile Scaly-breasted by darker lores, wings, and tail. Undulating flight. Feeds in long grass and on paddy in flocks.

Voice: A triple *chirp* and a plaintive *ink*.

Status and distribution: Resident in marshes, long grass, and paddy throughout. More frequent in eastern hills.

Nesting: In grassy ball in low vegetation; March–August.

Range: India, Nepal, SE Asia, Taiwan, Philippines, Java.

JAVA SPARROW *Padda oryzivora* PLATE 47 (6)

(*Lonchura oryzivora*)
(*Munia oryzivora*)

Identification: (Note: Not a sparrow but in Munia family.) (15 cm) Distinctive large red bill, black head with white cheek patch. Grey upperparts, black tail; black throat, grey breast, wine belly shading to white on undertail coverts. Sexes alike. Juvenile: grey upperparts; buff below with grey on breast. Feeds in flocks on paddy, roosting in nearby scrub. Gregarious.

Voice: Constant *chirrup*'s.

Status and distribution: Escaped cage birds occasionally breed around Colombo.

Nesting: In cavity, often under eaves of house.

Range: Sulawesi, Java. Introduced to parts of SE Asia.

SPARROWS AND WEAVERS

Order: Passeriformes
Family: Ploceidae

SMALL, sturdy birds with short, strong, conical bills adapted for seed eating. The sexes have different plumages and the juveniles resemble the females. They are gregarious, some forming large flocks. The name 'weaver' comes from their colonial nesting habit of weaving elaborate nests suspended from trees. The sparrows build domed nests in cavities in trees or buildings.

HOUSE SPARROW *Passer domesticus* PLATE 47 (7)

(Indian Sparrow)

Identification: (15 cm) Male plumage: grey crown and black bib. Newly moulted birds have grey or buff fringes making the black bib appear grey. These soon wear off and later the plumage can get very worn. Female plumage: dull brown upperparts with darker streaks and a pale eyebrow; dirty white below. Feeds in flocks on seeds, insects, or food waste around settlements and on cultivation, even comes into houses. Roosts communally.

Voice: A repeated *chirrrip* and various *chirps* and *cheeps*.

Status and distribution: Common resident around habitation and cultivation throughout.

Nesting: In cavity in building; all year.

Range: Has followed humans world-wide.

CHESTNUT-SHOULDERED PETRONIA *Petronia xanthosterna* PLATE 47 (8)

(Yellow-throated Sparrow) (*Gymnorhis xanthocollis*)
(Yellow-spotted Rock Sparrow) (*Petronia xanthocollis*)

Identification: (14 cm) Appears generally grey. Unstreaked above with chestnut shoulder patch, yellow throat patch (not easy to see), and a whitish wing bar. Sexes almost alike but female is paler and duller with smaller, paler yellow throat patch. Likely to join flocks of others in the family. Ground feeding.

Voice: Sparrow-like *chirp*'s and a *chilp chalp*.

Status and distribution: Winter vagrant to dry lowlands of NW. Possible in gardens and open areas with trees.

Range: N Africa, Middle East, S Asia.

STREAKED WEAVER *Ploceus manyar* PLATE 47 (9)

(Striated Weaver)

Identification: (15 cm) Darker than Baya and with dark streaks on breast. Breeding male plumage: yellow crown, rest of upperparts dark brown with tawny margins; dark brown face and throat, tawny breast and flanks with dark streaks, whitish belly, vent, and undertail coverts. Female and non-breeding male plumage: dark brown head with tawny margins and obvious pale eyebrow; pale throat. Forms noisy flocks feeding on seeds and insects in paddy and swamps.

Voice: A constant chattering and whistling.

Status and distribution: Resident locally in swamps and tank edges of dry lowlands, mainly in coastal areas.

Nesting: In scattered colonies in globular nests of woven reeds with much shorter entrances than Baya; February–October.

Range: S and SE Asia, Java.

BAYA WEAVER *Ploceus philippinus* PLATE 47 (10)

Identification: (15 cm) Breeding male plumage: bright yellow cap (more extensive than in Streaked), unstreaked breast, dark brown face paling on throat, dark brown upperparts with yellow margins on back and scapulars; buff belly and undertail coverts. Female, non-breeding male, and juvenile plumage: dark brown upperparts with tawny margins, tawny eyebrow; pale tawny below shading to off-white on belly. Strong, fast flight. Feeds in noisy flocks on seeds and insects, often on paddy.

Voice: A constant chattering and whistling.

Status and distribution: Resident on edges of open country and scrub in lowlands and hills to 500 m. More common in dry zone.

Nesting: Colonially in woven chamber with long entrance tube hanging below, suspended in tree; most of year.

Range: S and SE Asia.

STARLINGS AND MYNAS

Order: Passeriformes
Family: Sturnidae

SMALL to medium sized birds with strong, slightly down-curved bills, strong legs and feet, and short tails. They are active, gregarious, and some are argumentative. The mynas have yellow wattles on the head.

WHITE-FACED STARLING *Sturnus senex* PLATE 48 (9)

(White-headed Starling)

Identification: (22 cm) Slender. Off-white face, forehead, eyes, and throat, grey-green bill, dark slaty grey upperparts with pale streaks on nape, neck, and back; lavender-grey below with pale streaks on breast, belly, and flanks. Sexes alike. Juvenile: brown tinge above, darker below and broader streaks on breast and belly. Strictly arboreal feeding on fruit, nectar, and insects high in trees, usually in small groups.

Voice: Is reported to have a *chirp* but normally quiet.

Status and distribution: Endemic species. Rare in tall forests in hills of wet zone.

Nesting: In hole in tree; April but little known.

Range: SW Sri Lanka.

CHESTNUT-TAILED STARLING *Sturnus malabaricus* PLATE 48 (8)

(Ashy-headed Starling)
(Grey-headed Myna)

Identification: (21 cm) Paler than White-faced with rufous belly and undertail coverts. Silver-grey streaked head and neck, grey upperparts becoming darker to rear with chestnut tinge on tail; black and grey wings; lilac-grey throat and breast becoming rufous on belly but variable on underside. Sexes alike. Fast flight, few strokes then glides. Hops through foliage acrobatically in noisy groups, often with other starlings. Occasionally on ground.

Voice: A sharp two syllable metallic call and a whistle.

Status and distribution: Rare and irregular visitor, possible in open wooded areas and scrub in lowlands mainly in north.

Range: India, SE Asia.

BRAHMINY STARLING *Sturnus pagodarum* PLATE 48 (6)

(Brahminy Myna) (*Temenuchus pagodarum*)
(Black-headed Starling)

Identification: (22 cm). Glossy black crown and nape crest, reddish-buff neck, rest of upperparts grey, brown tail with white edges and tips to outer feathers; reddish-buff underparts shading to off-white vent and undertail coverts. Sexes alike but female has shorter crest. Juvenile: duller and lacks crest. Fast flight with strong regular wing-beats showing white edges on tail. Takes invertebrates, fruit, and nectar. Often feeds on ground. In small flocks, roosting communally. Shy.

Voice: Various chattering and whistling calls. Has a rambling song delivered with crest raised.

Status and distribution: Unconfirmed reports of breeding in nineteenth century. Now thought to be winter visitor, mainly to open or scrubby areas and cultivation of dry lowlands in north, west and south. More frequent near coasts.

Nesting: In hole in tree; July–August.

Range: Afghanistan, India.

ROSY STARLING *Sturnus roseus* PLATE 48 (7)
(Rosy Pastor) (*Pastor roseus*)
(Rose-coloured Starling)

Identification: (23 cm) Most likely seen in winter or immature plumage. Winter: dull black head and neck with buff fringes, yellow tinge to base of lower mandible, pinky-brown body, slate-grey wings and tail. Male has long crest, female has shorter. Immature: grey-brown with poorly developed crest, darker wings and tail. Breeding adult is distinctive: rosy-pink with glossy black head, wings, and tail. Gregarious, roosts communally. Feeds mainly on ground often with cattle but also take seeds, fruit, and nectar.

Voice: Noisy chattering and warbling.

Status and distribution: Irregular winter visitor, sometimes in large numbers, to open country and cultivation of dry lowlands usually near coast, more frequent in north.

Range: E Europe, W, C, and S Asia.

COMMON MYNA *Acridotheres tristis melanosturnus* PLATE 48 (12)

Identification: (24 cm) Glossy black head, neck, and breast with yellow bill and bare skin below and behind eye; dark brown elsewhere apart from white lower belly to vent, white tips on tail and white wing patches. Yellow legs. Sexes alike. Juvenile: generally duller. Fast direct flight showing white on wings and tail. Feeds mainly on ground, often with cattle, but also takes fruit. In pairs or flocks. Roosts communally. Not shy.

Voice: Various chatterings, squeaks, and whistles. Noisy.

Status and distribution: Endemic race. Very common in gardens, cultivation, and pasture throughout up to 1700 m. Not in dense forest.

Nesting: On mass of sticks in hole in tree or building; mainly March–September.

Species range: S and SE Asia. Also introduced to S Africa, Australia, and elsewhere.

SRI LANKA MYNA *Gracula ptilogenys* PLATE 48 (10)
(Ceylon Grackle) (*Eulabes ptilogenys*)

Identification: (26 cm) Slightly larger than Hill Myna and with only one pair of wattles. All glossy black with a pair of yellow wattles on the nape and a white wing patch. Very pale grey eye, black-based orange-red bill. Sexes alike. Juvenile: duller with smaller wattles. Feeds high in trees on fruits, etc. In pairs or small groups.

Voice: Loud, deep, whistled *tcheeyu*, *oooeee* contact calls and various croaks.

Status and distribution: Endemic species. Forests and wooded areas of wet zone to 2000 m.

Nesting: In hole in tree, often high; February–May.
Range: SW Sri Lanka.

HILL MYNA *Gracula religiosa* PLATE 48 (11)
(Common Grackle) (*Eulabes religiosa*)
(Southern Grackle)

Identification: (25 cm) More elaborate wattles than Sri Lanka Myna and has no black at base of orange-yellow bill. All glossy black with yellow wattles on crown, nape and below brown eye, broad white wing patch. Sexes alike. Juvenile: duller with much smaller wattles. Direct, strong flight with rapid wing-beats making obvious hum. Feeds high in trees mainly on fruit. In pairs or small groups.
Voice: A rich *peeoo-peeoo-peeoo* and rising and falling whistles similar to Ceylon Myna but higher pitched.
Status and distribution: Resident in forest edges and wooded areas of southern lowlands and nearby lower hills in wet and dry zones.
Nesting: In hole in tree; May–August.
Range: India, SE Asia, Java.

ORIOLES Order: Passeriformes Family: Oriolidae

MEDIUM sized birds with long, pointed wings and short tails. They are strictly arboreal, feeding mainly on fruits but also take some insects. The flight is strong and direct. They are solitary, or in pairs when nesting, and the songs are rich. Look for head patterns.

EURASIAN GOLDEN ORIOLE *Oriolus oriolus kundoo* PLATE 40 (13)

Identification: (25 cm) Dark stripe through eye. Male plumage: bright yellow with black eye-stripe, black wings, and black tail with yellow on outer feathers. Female plumage: green upperparts with brown eye-stripe, darker green cheeks, off-white below streaked brown. Juvenile: like female but only faintly streaked on underside. Active and mobile.
Note: *O. o. oriolus* with the eye-stripe ending at the eye and less yellow on the wing occurs as a vagrant to southern dry lowlands.
Voice: A harsh call. Also has a rich fluted *hoo-hoo-heee-oo* song, unlikely in Sri Lanka.
Status and distribution: *O. o. kundoo*: Scarce winter visitor to wooded areas of lowlands and lower hills.
Species range: Europe, Africa, S Asia.

BLACK-NAPED ORIOLE *Oriolus chinensis* PLATE 40 (12)

Identification: (25 cm) Black eye-stripe extends to form band across nape. Less black in the wing than in Eurasian Golden. Bright yellow with black on wing and black tail with yellow edges. Female is a dull yellow-green. Feeds solitarily in canopy. Shy.
Voice: A harsh *chak* call.
Status and distribution: Vagrant to forests of wet lowlands.
Range: India, Nepal, SE Asia, Philippines, Java.

BLACK-HOODED ORIOLE *Oriolus xanthornus ceylonensis* PLATE 40 (11)
(Black-headed Oriole)

Identification: (24 cm) Black hood. Bright yellow with black on wings and black tail with yellow edges. Female plumage: like male but duller and greener yellow. Juvenile: like female with white streaks on throat and some yellow on forehead.
Voice: A loud, fluty *hyaw haw wheeyo* song, a *cheeeoreep*, and a harsh *kuwak* call.
Status and distribution: Endemic race. Common in forest, gardens, anywhere with trees in lowlands and hills to 2000 m.
Nesting: In hammock of stems and leaves hung in foliage; October–May.
Species range: India, SE Asia.

DRONGOS Order: Passeriformes Family: Dicruridae

MEDIUM sized, predominantly black or dark grey birds with long, forked tails (shed during moult); long, pointed wings and short legs. The stout bill is covered at the base by a fringe of short bristly feathers. They feed on insects, commonly taking much of their prey on the wing by perching upright, often flicking tail, to make short 'flycatcher' flights or by pouncing on grasshoppers. The flight is buoyant and agile. They normally live in pairs and are noisy birds, often mimicking other species. Frequently mob owls and woodpeckers. Full adult plumage is not achieved until the second year.

BLACK DRONGO *Dicrurus macrocercus minor* PLATE 48 (1)
(*Dicrurus adsimilis minor*)

Identification: (26 cm) All black (primaries appear grey-brown in flight). Pale spot at base of bill. From Drongo Cuckoo (p. 121, Plate 32) by lack of white barring under tail. Sexes alike. Juvenile and first year: shorter tail, duller with

white fringes on belly. Perches in trees, on posts, or even on cattle to 'flycatch'.
Voice: Loud and varied ringing calls.
Status and distribution: Endemic race, in open country with trees in dry coastal areas of N and NW. Occasionally inland and in S.
Nesting: In cup often not well hidden in fork of tree; March–May.
Species range: Middle East, S and SE Asia, Taiwan, Java.

GREY DRONGO *Dicrurus leucophaeus longicaudatus* PLATE 48 (2)
(Ashy Drongo) (*Dicrurus longicaudatus*)

Identification: (30 cm) Palest of local drongos. Crimson eyes. Glossy, slate-grey upperparts; dull grey below. Sexes alike. Juvenile and first year: shorter tail, duller and browner. Mainly arboreal. Feeds late into dusk. May form small flocks.
Voice: Various harsh *chak*'s and whistling calls, including *cheece-cheece-chichuk* and *kil-kil-kil.*
Status and distribution: Winter visitor to forest edges and open woodlands in lowlands, more frequent in E.
Range: S, E, and SE Asia, Sumatra, Java.

WHITE-BELLIED DRONGO *Dicrurus caerulescens* PLATE 48 (4)
(Common Drongo)

Note: Two races are present:

White-bellied Drongo, *D. c. insularis*

White-vented Drongo, *D. c. leucopygialis*

Identification: (24 cm) Only local drongo with white on ventral area (beware of confusion with juvenile Black Drongo with white fringes on belly). Long forked tail.
White-bellied Drongo: very dark grey with dusky upper-belly, white lower-belly, vent, and undertail coverts.
White-vented Drongo: glossy blue-black with white vent and undertail coverts.
Both races: Sexes alike. Juveniles dull black. Commonly perch on pole or wire to catch insects.
Voice: *Reep-cheeow* and various whistles.
Status and distribution: Endemic races. *White-bellied*: common in wooded areas and gardens of dry lowlands and drier hills, avoiding forests. *White-vented*: common in trees of wet lowlands and nearby hills avoiding forests.

Nesting: In shallow cup on fork in tree; February–May.
Species range: India.

GREATER RACKET-TAILED DRONGO *Dicrurus paradiseus* PLATE 48 (3)
(*Dissemurus paradiseus*)

Note: Two races are present with intermediate forms at edges of ranges:

Racket-tailed Drongo, *D. p. ceylonicus*

Crested Drongo, *D. p. lophorhinus*

Identification (both races): All glossy black with tufted crest on forehead. Juvenile and first year: small crest, shorter tail, duller black with white fringes on belly.
Racket-tailed Drongo: (60 cm approximately including rackets) Outer tail feathers extended into long, bare-shafted rackets. Large crest. Rackets make humming noise in flight.
Crested Drongo: (35 cm) Long, deeply forked tail. Small crest.
Both races: Sexes alike. Juvenile: duller black, shorter crest and tail. Very active, 'flycatching' with much tail flicking.
Voice: Loud, fruity, often bell-like whistles and ratchet-like *chacks*. Noisy.
Status and distribution: Both are endemic races. *Racket-tailed*: forests of dry zone and eastern hills to 700 m. *Crested*: wet zone forests and nearby hills to 1700 m.
Nesting: High in forest tree; March–May.
Species range: India, SE Asia, Java.

WOODSWALLOW Order: Passeriformes Family: Artamidae

WOODSWALLOWS, or Swallow-shrikes, are small insectivorous birds with relatively large heads and strong, conical bills. The wings are long and pointed and the tail short and square. They feed entirely on the wing soaring high in loose flocks.

ASHY WOODSWALLOW *Artamus fuscus* PLATE 39 (10)
(Ashy Swallow-shrike)

Identification: (19 cm) Sturdier than swallows with blue conical bill and short, square tail. Grey head, grey-brown back, scapulars, and rump, off-white uppertail coverts, black tail with white tip; slate wings with white tips to flight feathers; grey underparts becoming paler on undertail coverts. Sexes alike. Juvenile: like adult but brown-grey with pale fringes on mantle and wings. Rapid flight with long periods of soaring. Often perches in rows on a bare branch, wire, or stone in open country slowly bobbing tail.

Voice: A wheezy *chee chee chee.*

Status and distribution: Resident in open country with trees, especially palms, forest edge in lowlands, and hills to 1000 m.

Nesting: In untidy cup in tree, often in palm; February–June.

Range: India, northern part of SE Asia.

MAGPIE AND CROWS Order: Passeriformes Family: Corvidae

MEDIUM to large, omnivorous birds with strong, sturdy bills and strong legs and feet.

SRI LANKA MAGPIE *Urocissa ornata* PLATE 48 (5)
(Ceylon Blue Magpie) (*Cissa ornata*)
(*Kitta ornata*)

Identification: (47 cm). Mainly bright blue with red bill and eye-ring, chestnut head and neck; long graduated blue tail with black and then white tip. Sexes alike. Juvenile: generally paler and shorter tail. Rather weak and usually brief flight. Hops through foliage acrobatically seeking food, also feeds on ground. Solitary or in small groups.

Voice: A loud *chreep-chreep*, a loud *whee whee*, rasping *krakrakrakrak*; *chak, chak-chak*, and other calls.

Status and distribution: Endemic species. Primary forests in wet zone and hills.

Nesting: High in forest tree; January–March.

Range: Sri Lanka.

HOUSE CROW *Corvus splendens* PLATE 34 (9)
(Grey-necked Crow)

Identification: (42 cm) Smaller than Large-billed and with smaller bill. Mainly glossy black with dark brown nape and neck, shading to black on breast. Sexes alike. Juvenile: duller. Steady powerful flight. Scavenges on anything edible visiting rubbish dumps. Gregarious. Roost in noisy flocks. Very confident.

Voice: A raucous *caw*. Very vocal.

Status and distribution: Resident in towns and villages in coastal areas. Expanding inland.
Nesting: On mass of twigs in tree; May–September.
Range: S and SE Asia.

LARGE-BILLED CROW *Corvus macrorhynchos* PLATE 34 (10)

(Jungle Crow)
(Black Crow)

Identification: (47 cm) Larger than House Crow and all black. Sexes alike. Strong, direct flight, often high. Scavenges but less dependent on human settlement than House Crow. In pairs, occasionally in small groups.
Voice: A deep *caw*, less raucous than House Crow.
Status and distribution: Common resident in towns, villages, and country throughout.
Nesting: On heap of twigs in tree; April–September.
Range: S and E Asia, Japan, Philippines.

Bibliography

Henry, G. (1971). *A guide to the birds of Ceylon.* Second edition. K. V. G. de Sylva & sons.

Henry, G. (revised by T. Hoffmann, D. Warakagoda, and U. Ekanayake) (1998). *A guide to the birds of Ceylon.* Oxford University Press, New Delhi.

Howard, R. and Moore, A. *A complete checklist of the birds of the World.* Academic Press.

Sibley, C. G. and Monroe, B. L., Jnr. (1990). *Distribution and taxonomy of the birds of the World.* Yale University Press.

Supplement to above. 1993.

Inskipp, T. Lindsey, N. and Duckworth, W. (1996). *An annotated checklist of the birds of the Oriental Region.* Oriental Bird Club.

Legge, W. V. (1880.) *A history of the birds of Ceylon.*

Wijesinghe, D. P. (1991). *Checklist of the birds of Sri Lanka.* CBC.

Phillips, W. W. A. (1978). *An annotated checklist of the birds of Ceylon*

Salim Ali and Dillon Ripley, S. (1987). *A compact handbook of the birds of India and Pakistan, together with those of Bangladesh, Nepal, Bhutan, and Sri Lanka.* Second edition, Oxford University Press.

Harris, A., Shirihai, H., and Christie, D. (1996). *Macmillan birders guide to European and Middle Eastern birds*

Harrison, P. (1985). *Seabirds, an identification guide*, Revised Edition. Helm.

Hayman, P., Marchant, J., Prater, A. (1986). *Shorebirds.* Helm.

Hoffmann, T. W. (1998). *Threatened birds of Sri Lanka.* National Red List, Ceylon Bird Club.

Olsen, K. M. and Larsson, H. *Skuas and Jaegers: a guide to the Skuas and Jaegers of the World.* Pica Press Identification Guides.

King, B., Woodcock, M., and Dickinson, E. C. (1975). *Field guide to the birds of South-east Asia.* Collins.

de Zylva, T. S. U. (1984). *Birds of Sri Lanka*, Trumpet Publications.

Phillips, W. W. A. (1949). *Birds of Ceylon.* Ceylon Daily News Press, Colombo.

Notes of the Ceylon Bird Club.

Index

Bold type indicates the preferred vernacular name. Plate numbers are shown in italics. *N* = not illustrated.